VIETNAM

★

About the author

MARTIN GAINSBOROUGH is a recognized international expert on Vietnam and its politics. He is a Reader in Development Politics at the University of Bristol. He is also director of the Bristol–Mekong Project, and consults widely on aspects of Vietnam's politics and business, notably for the United Nations Development Programme, the UK's Department for International Development, and the World Bank. He teaches on development studies, Vietnamese and Asian politics, and state theory. He is the author of *Changing Political Economy of Vietnam: The Case of Ho Chi Minh City* (2003) and editor of *On the Borders of State Power: Frontiers in the Greater Mekong Sub-region* (2009).

VIETNAM

Rethinking the State

★

MARTIN GAINSBOROUGH

ZED BOOKS
London & New York

SILKWORM BOOKS
Chiang Mai, Thailand

Vietnam: Rethinking the State was first published in 2010

Published in Thailand, Burma, Laos, Cambodia and Vietnam by
Silkworm Books, 6 Sukkasem Road, T. Suthep, Chiang Mai 50200, Thailand
www.silkwormbooks.com

Published in the rest of the world by
Zed Books Ltd, 7 Cynthia Street, London N1 9JF, UK
and Room 400, 175 Fifth Avenue, New York, NY 10010, USA
www.zedbooks.co.uk

Typeset in Monotype Bulmer by illuminati, Grosmont
Cover designed by Lucy Morton @ illuminati
Cover image by Lucas Jans
Printed and bound in Great Britain by
CPI Antony Rowe, Chippenham and Eastbourne

FSC
www.fsc.org
MIX
Paper from
responsible sources
FSC® C013604

Distributed in the USA exclusively by Palgrave Macmillan, a division of
St Martin's Press, LLC, 175 Fifth Avenue, New York, NY 10010, USA

A catalogue record for this book is available from the British Library
Library of Congress Cataloging in Publication Data available

ISBN 978 1 84813 565 9 Hb
ISBN 978 1 84813 310 5 Pb
ISBN 978 1 84813 311 2 Eb
ISBN 978 616 215 002 9 (Silkworm Books)

CONTENTS

PREFACE

I first visited Vietnam in September 1990. I remember it well: my first view of the waterways of the Mekong River delta as we flew into Ho Chi Minh City (formerly Saigon), the clapped-out Citroën car that passed for a taxi which drove us into city, and above all the quiet streets around the famous Givral Restaurant and the Continental Hotel. There was no *Lonely Planet* guidebook then, only a few photocopied sheets from the travellers who had been before us via a travel agent in Bangkok that had started issuing tourist visas. In those days, to travel outside of the main cities, you needed travel permits. When we could not get them, we took off anyway, only to have our passports confiscated by the police in Danang, in central Vietnam, who appeared to have been tipped off as they were there to meet us almost as we got off the bus. After much haggling, we were eventually forced to hire a guide for a vehicle trip to the old imperial city of Hue. Following a rather tense tour of the citadel, we soon broke free again, finally reaching the capital, Hanoi, and our plane out after an adventure of epic proportions, culminating in my very first bowl of *pho* (noodle soup) on a street near Hoan Kiem lake.

A year later I was back to begin the slow journey which was learning Vietnamese, taking lessons at the Hanoi Polytechnic University.

Again, Vietnam continued to test as I bumped against the authorities and cultural practices I did not really understand. However, my dominant memory was of the darkness of those days (and the size of the rats in the yard of my state-owned guest house!). Power cuts, low-wattage light bulbs even when the electricity was running, and the old state store on Trang Tri street before its glitzy refit ('nothing much to buy and seemingly sultry and disinterested shop assistants') – it was everything I had imagined as a child of the Cold War. For some reason, I kept coming back.

In 1996, my association with Vietnam stepped up a gear as I started a new life in Saigon, embarking on fieldwork for my doctoral dissertation. Learning Vietnamese began again in earnest with new determination now as I knew that mastery of the language would give my research its edge, and as I was shamed on a daily basis by how little I knew. Three years later, I returned to England to write up my doctorate following what was one of the richest if challenging experiences of my life. As is often the case, going away helps you define where you have come from, and that was certainly the case for me. I remember on one occasion being asked what my father did and replying in Vietnamese 'Ba toi la can bo nha nuoc, lam viec o Bo quoc phong o Luan Don' (My father is a civil servant, working for the Ministry of Defence in London). Hearing myself utter those words in Vietnamese and sensing the reaction ('Ah, good family, well-connected, military background...') was one of those penny-dropping moments when I became more aware than ever before of the privileged social class background from which I came. A member of the elite of one country studying the elite of another? Interesting, but what methodological problems does that throw up? But, equally, during those years in Saigon, given the kind of research I was doing, I learnt for the first time what it was like to be on the wrong side of the state and hence to fear it. I value that experience deeply as helping me comment authentically on politics.

The years 1996–99 were when I really cut my teeth as a researcher in Vietnam. I will never forget that feeling of arriving in Saigon as a doctoral student and realizing I had a blank sheet of paper to fill. Progress was slow but I had read Adam Fforde and Stefan de Vylder's newly published book, *From Plan to Market*, the summer before I had arrived in Saigon and I had a sense that 'the informal' was important in Vietnam. I also had heard that Ho Chi Minh City was a reformist city so I thought I would see if I could track the reformers down. With these few leads I set off, reading the Vietnamese press and talking to whomever I could make contact with. But how do you spot a reformer? After all, no one seemed very willing to say what they stood for, or at least politicians prefaced their comments about the 'importance of the private sector' with comments about the 'importance of their state sector' while, it appeared to me, being more concerned with making money by leveraging off their position as officials or taking advantage of Ho Chi Minh City's rapidly expanding land market. Failing to locate the so-called 'reformers' proved very formative and has had a profound influence on all my subsequent work.

As the millennium came and went, I gradually established myself in the academic community in the United Kingdom. Between teaching and writing, I continued to conduct fieldwork in Vietnam, branching out from my earlier exclusive focus on the south. I interviewed Vietnamese companies across a range of provinces in both the north and the south of the country in 2004. I talked to provincial and district officials – again across a range of provinces – responsible for overseeing the collection and spending of revenue in 2005, and in 2007 I interviewed small-scale traders operating on the northern border with China (the Lao Cai–Hekou border). By this time, I was fairly adept at operating in Vietnam in contrast to those awkward early years. I had a good sense of how the system operated. I knew when to ask questions and when not, and I had a good circle of friends, who continued to be a useful source of information and insight. While the more recent fieldwork has evidently kept me up to date, its main contribution – I think – has been to enable me to refine my view of Vietnam in the context of the wider world, which I had started to piece together as a doctoral student in the 1990s.

In 2005/6, I took leave of absence from Bristol University to work for the United Nations Development Programme (UNDP) in Hanoi. Though formally I was now an international civil servant, I was still an academic and I suspect the experience – and the access it gave me – was more beneficial for me as a researcher ultimately than it was for UNDP or Vietnam. However, such is the nature of donor projects, and I was grateful for the opportunity to observe aspects of Vietnam and particularly the international donor community more closely than I had ever done before, including being in Hanoi for the Tenth Communist Party Congress in April 2006.

So to this book. I tell you all this because inevitably it is my personal story which provides the context for this book. My involvement in Vietnam from 1990 to the present, and the experiences I have had, immediately make me part of a particular generation of Vietnam scholars. They frame my insights and to a great extent affect what I am going to say. I am not a scholar of the Vietnam War era (i.e. the American war in Vietnam). My interest in Vietnam did not emerge out of the war (either opposition or war service). I am mindful of the war's effects, although I have no memories of it, as I was a young child when it ended in 1975. I think this matters a great deal. Debates about whether the war was a civil war or the result of an act of foreign aggression belong to a different age. Equally, although I believe I caught a glimpse of the end of the central planning era in the very early 1990s, my engagement with Vietnam has been in the era of so-called marketization and ever greater 'engagement' with institutions and actors outside of Vietnam. My generation, although not exclusively my generation, is trying to come to terms with how Vietnam is changing – or not changing – socially, economically and politically in the era of so-called 'reform'. We are also asking questions about the future of Communist Party rule in an era, it would seem, of escalating pluralism.

This book is my snapshot of a country that I have been involved with for nearly twenty years. I hope what I have written will last. I am a firm believer that issues of power and political culture do not change very fast, and the aim of this book is to capture something of the more transcendent aspects of Vietnamese politics. Of course, some of its points of reference and its context are likely in time to become dated but then it will become a matter of historical record, providing insights into where Vietnam has come from, and offering a glimpse of one person's experience of a country.

★

Inevitably, I have incurred many debts over the years to those who have shared their understanding of Vietnam, and often their work, with me. To avoid missing anyone out, I am not going to name people individually. Suffice it to say I am extremely grateful to you all – especially those who passed many a happy hour debating the finer points of Vietnam's politics over *bia* and *muc kho* (dried squid) in Hanoi. I am grateful to the Taylor & Francis Group for granting me permission to reproduce the following articles (all single-authored by me): 'Ho Chi Minh City's Political Economy under Reform: Between Exception and Rule?' *Critical Asian Studies*, vol. 37, no. 3, 2005: 363–90; 'Slow, Quick Quick: Assessing Equitisation and Enterprise Performance Prospects in Vietnam', *Journal of Communist Studies and Transition Politics*, vol. 19, no. 1, 2003: 49–63; 'Corruption and the Politics of Decentralisation in Vietnam', *Journal of Contemporary Asia*, vol. 33, no.1, 2003: 69–84; 'Globalisation and the State Revisited: A View from Provincial Vietnam', *Journal of Contemporary Asia*, vol. 37, no. 1, 2007: 1–18; 'Privatisation as State Advance: Private Indirect Government in Vietnam', *New Political Economy*, vol. 14, no. 2, 2009: 257–74; and 'Present but Not Powerful: Neo-liberalism, the State and Development in Vietnam', *Globalizations*, vol. 7, no. 2, 2010. I am also grateful to University of California Press for granting me permission to reproduce 'Political Change in Vietnam: In Search of the Middle Class Challenge to the

State', *Asian Survey*, vol. 42, no. 5, 2002: 694–707; 'From Patronage to "Outcomes" and Vietnamese Communist Party Congresses Reconsidered', *Journal of Vietnamese Studies*, vol. 2, no. 1, 2007: 3–26 (both single-authored by me). Any errors of fact or judgement in the book are, of course, mine.

INTRODUCTION

If one thinks about Vietnam today, what images does it conjure up? It is not inappropriate to say that there is still a strong association in many people's minds with war and its aftermath, even if this is not a day-to-day preoccupation within Vietnam. However, for many people, the country also conjures up a multiplicity of other images: a vibrant street life, amazing food, a country in transition from plan to market, industrialization, continued Communist Party rule, a strange mixture of seemingly free-market capitalism and yet continued talk of socialism, an increasingly vibrant public sphere, leading, for some, to thoughts of political pluralism, and a ruling party which is struggling to come to terms with a changing society and economy.

Underpinning much of the commentary on contemporary Vietnam is also a heavy association with 'reform', usually understood as a set of policy changes associated with events which gathered momentum from the late 1970s and early 1980s. The much-celebrated Sixth National Communist Party Congress in December 1986, widely seen as the birthplace of *doi moi* (renovation), is strongly associated with such a position. Here, the policy changes are usually depicted in terms of increased economic openness, reflected in support for export-oriented trade and foreign direct investment, encouragement of the private sector, and alignment or partial alignment with various neoliberal-inspired policies. This book, however, encourages a move away from a preoccupation with 'reform' as necessarily being about change, or as somehow capturing what Vietnam is about, or the character of its politics, suggesting instead a need to get behind this overused label.

As a consequence of this, some of the dominant images of Vietnam which are explored throughout the book have relatively little to do with the sweeping away of what was there before but instead relate to the persistence, or reworking, of existing power structures. As will be seen, the book is not very sympathetic towards ideas of state retreat (although it is open to state change), arguments which imply the unmediated advance of neoliberalism or liberal democracy (even if not now but 'some time in the future', as is often implied), or positions which emphasize the very great power of external forces in relation to something more indigenous. However, none of this should be mistaken for a position which thinks that the Communist Party will always rule Vietnam, not least because no political party rules for ever.

An approach to studying politics

As well as being about Vietnam, the book also lays out an approach to studying and conceiving of politics. So what, in outline, does this approach to studying politics look like?

In one sense, it is correct to say that this is a book about the state – as is captured in the book's title. However, this is to raise some interesting and not necessarily straightforward questions about the relationship between politics (or power) and the state. For example, if one is interested in the state, is this synonymous with being interested in politics? Or, to turn it around, if one is interested in politics, must one automatically be interested in the state? This book advocates an approach which says that studying issues to do with politics, and more pertinently power, is the *means* by which we potentially shed light on the entity we call the state. In saying this, it is not being suggested that the political realm should be seen as being synonymous with the state (the book is open to the idea that the state is just one part of the political and not necessarily the most important part). However, in the approach to studying politics which is advocated here, it is argued that if we are to stand a chance of shedding light on the state it is important that as researchers we do not focus directly on it. This may sound a strange thing to say, but what are its implications in terms of method?

The problem with focusing directly on the state is that to do so is in fact to define the object of our study in advance, which is a common problem in political science. The widespread tendency of scholars, including those who study Vietnam, to describe themselves as working on 'state–society' relations illustrates the problem perfectly since it assumes there is something clearly identifiable called the state to study – with clear boundaries, and so on. Instead, this book argues that it is necessary to try and surrender any preconceptions as to what the state is and, put simply, trust that what the state *really* is will come back into view as we focus our attention elsewhere. Of course, this is trickier than it sounds, but we must try.

It is this desire to surrender our preconceptions about the state which lies behind the book's focus on business – as reflected in many of its chapters – as a particularly fruitful window onto the political, and ultimately the nature of the state, precisely because in the world of money-making questions of 'public' and 'private', or state and society, seem more mixed up. Central to the method for studying politics advocated in this book, and related to the previous point, is also a commitment to looking at 'actors' – whether formally of the 'state' or not, albeit operating in a distinctive, power-laden setting – and seeing what they tell us about the political and ultimately the state. Writing on Africa, Béatrice Hibou says something similar, arguing that to understand the state it is necessary to 'understand the people in power and, equally important, their games, their strategies and their historical practices' (Hibou 2004: 21). It is through such a focus, she suggests that the outlines of the state come back into view. This too is the approach taken in this book.

Continuity and change in politics

All the book's chapters seek – in their different ways – to advance us towards an answer to our key research questions, namely 'what is the nature of the state?', and 'what is the relationship of the state to the political?', both of which are revisited at the end of the book. Throughout the book's eight core chapters, which are based on fieldwork conducted from 1996 to 2007, it is clear that events in Vietnam are not standing still. This comes across most obviously in respect of changes affecting state enterprises (many of which have undergone significant organizational change in recent years), the growth of Vietnam's capital markets, and signs of a widening of the political space, or a more vibrant society.

However, at another level, one of the messages of the book is that while some of the actors and institutions may change, and while the relative weight between different dynamics may shift somewhat, certain things do not change very fast. This takes us to the heart of issues to do with the nature of the political, namely the way in which there is an underlying logic to Vietnam's political system – and not just Vietnam's – which means that power continuously seeks to re-create itself. Central here is the strong association in Vietnam between holding public office and making money, such that when certain institutions or money-making avenues are closed down, the logic of the system is such that they tend to spring up elsewhere. This can be seen most clearly in respect of public administration reform pursued by the international donor community in Vietnam since the 1990s, such that Vietnamese newspapers today are still full of stories about troublesome institutions, or the time that it takes to get things approved either as a citizen or as a business. Such complaints were widespread in the late 1990s. The only change more than a decade on relates to the institutions and, to some extent, the actors involved, *not* to the underlying practices themselves, which persist. While none of this necessarily makes for 'good governance', or any of the other normative labels commonly hung on the state, it does tell us something about power.

The inappropriateness of reform as an organizational motif

We will return to many of the issues raised in this introduction in the book's conclusion, when we pull together what we understand by the state and its relationship to the political in a more overtly theoretical sense. However, since this book is also about eschewing some of the stereotypes commonly bandied around in popular and academic discourse on Vietnam, we will conclude this introduction by revisiting the question of the appropriateness of 'reform' as a motif for making sense of what has occurred in Vietnam over the last fifteen to twenty years. In this book, the concept of 'reform' is not seen as having much utility as a window onto Vietnam. Instead, it is seen as preferable to refer to the more neutral 'marketization' or highlight a process of international economic integration. If the term 'reform' is used, it is usually followed by the word 'years' (i.e. 'the reform years'). In this way, the word 'reform' is being used to indicate an approximate period of time (largely the 1980s onwards) and there is an implied rejection of any of the other connotations usually associated with the term 'reform'. But why might the concept of reform be seen as distorting?

There are at least four key problems with the idea that 'reform' offers a satisfactory window either descriptively or in explanatory terms onto what has happened in Vietnam over the last fifteen to twenty years. First, to talk in terms of reform is immediately to place the emphasis on *change*. This, it has already been suggested, runs the risk of downplaying important areas of continuity, whether this is in terms of the persistence of existing power structures, elite control over the economy, or particular forms of rule. Some readers may retort that of course we know that reform is not just about change. However, in terms of emphasis, continuity tends to be neglected. Indicative of this is the way in which it is quite hard to tell the story of 'reform' without depicting contemporary developments in Vietnam in terms of everything the pre-reform years were not (i.e. not closed, not planned, not supportive of the private sector), and yet on closer analysis of the pre-reform years such a stark characterization is difficult to sustain.

Second, the focus on reform as change tends to place the emphasis on *policy* change introduced by Vietnam's elite, implying further that policy is the key driver of change. In fact, it is questionable that policy is a leading determinant of change in Vietnam (or elsewhere), or that change is something which elites are necessarily in control of. To talk in this way is to make a distinction between the formal and the informal, or what actually happens, and this is an important characteristic of this book. Writing on China, Barry Naughton has referred to accounts which place a heavy premium on elite-led *policy* change as the key to understanding the reform years as offering a sanitized morality tale with crucial details airbrushed out (Naughton 1995b: 22). These details, it is argued here, often relate to the more Machiavellian aspects of politics, which have to do with money, patronage, strong-arm tactics, and elite self-interest. By not mentioning or by downplaying these things, talk of reform serves a legitimating function in terms of those in power.

Third, accounts which place the emphasis on reform as somehow capturing what has happened in Vietnam rarely pause to consider what policy actually is. On closer inspection, what we find is that what people tend to call policy – a disparate collection of elite actions and counteractions – is often much less coherent than is thought. Moreover, policy coherence is something we ('insiders' and 'outsiders') like to impose upon the state in a bid to reinforce the state in the image of what we think it ought to be. That we behave like this, state theorists would suggest, reflects the way in which the state as an idea exerts power over us, as well as, in many cases, our own closeness to power (Abrams 1988; Mitchell 1991).

Finally, the inappropriateness of reform as a window onto Vietnam extends to assumptions about what constitutes politics, which is itself bound up with the use of the word 'reform'. Here, the tendency is to view politics in terms of disputes between rival factions grouped around distinct policy positions: traditionally the 'reformer' and 'conservative' language, which, the record shows, Vietnam scholars have found hard to jettison despite its many problems. However, what we find is that politics is much less about disputes over rival policy positions – elites in Vietnam hang loose to policy – than about money, patronage and loose political groupings linked to personalities. People often do not want to be identified too clearly with any particular policy position as this potentially restricts their freedom of movement, and prevents opportunism in terms of going after resources, particularly financial resources on offer from the international donor community.

Given the position being advocated here in respect of downplaying the significance of reform and/or policy, the question arises whether reform and policy offer any salience at all in explaining outcomes in Vietnam. The position taken in this book is that while it would be a mistake to dismiss them entirely, they are just one factor among many which determines outcomes.

Structure of the book

The rest of the book is structured as follows. Chapter 1 looks at why the Communist Party continues to rule in Vietnam despite rapid economic growth and social change. Chapter 2 seeks to challenge ideas about Ho Chi Minh City's distinctiveness vis-à-vis the rest of the country, highlighting a common 'reform' political economy in which state business interests are important. In this way, the chapter introduces crucial details about Vietnam's political economy which are relevant for the rest of the book. Chapter 3 seeks to understand the phenomenon of big corruption cases, asking what they teach us about politics and the state. Chapter 4 looks at equitization in Vietnam, specifically trying to account for why equitization suddenly speeded up in the very late 1990s after years of going nowhere. Continuing with the theme of equitization, Chapter 5 shows how the sale of shares in state companies should not necessarily be associated with state retreat, including highlighting the use of uncertainty as an instrument of rule in Vietnam. Chapter 6 on local politics considers the impact of globalization on the state in provincial Vietnam, suggesting that, as with equitization, it is a mistake to associate globalization necessarily with state retreat. Chapter 7 examines one of the key events in Vietnam's political calendar, namely the National Communist Party Congress, held every five years. Adopting a revisionist tone, it argues that Congresses are less about policy issues than an occasion when access to patronage and political protection are circulated. Chapter 8 looks at neoliberal ideas about the state, seeking to explain why they have been relatively uninfluential in the direction of state change in Vietnam. The book concludes by asking how, in light of the preceding chapters, we understand the state and its relationship with the political.

1

COMMUNIST PARTY RULE

Some two decades after the collapse of Communism in Eastern Europe in 1989 and the former Soviet Union in 1991, Vietnam is just one of a handful of states where Communist Party rule persists (the others being China, North Korea, Laos and Cuba). While Vietnamese society is undoubtedly witnessing new forms of political expression, and pressure on the state, against the backdrop of rapid economic development, the fact of continued Communist Party rule at this juncture – whatever the future holds – requires some explanation. This chapter considers this issue with reference to theoretical ideas which have their origins in Barrington Moore's now classic text, *Social Origins of Dictatorship and Democracy* (Moore 1966). Moore's writing has since been built upon by other scholars, including most notably Rueschemeyer, Stephens and Stephens (1992). These writers, who emphasize the importance of changing class relations, state power and transnational forces in explaining moves towards greater democracy or their absence, are to be contrasted with those who focus on such things as political leadership, culture and political parties to explain why democratization has or has not occurred (Potter 1992: 355–79).

BOX 1.1   Vietnam's formal political system at a glance

Vietnam is a one-party state headed by the Communist Party of Vietnam (CPV). The National Party Congress is the highest body of the CPV and meets every five years. The Party Congress elects the Central Committee, the party organization in which political power is formally vested and which meets in plenary sessions at least twice a year. The Central Committee elects the Politburo and the general secretary of the Party. Between plenums the Politburo runs party affairs. The general secretary of the CPV, the president, the prime minister and the chairman of the National Assembly, Vietnam's parliament, are all members of the Politburo. Formally speaking, the CPV sets policy direction, which the government implements, although the reality is far more complex. The government consists of the prime minister, three deputy prime ministers, ministers, and heads of organizations of ministerial rank. The government is accountable to the National Assembly and reports both to the National Assembly and to the president. The National Assembly is the highest ranking organization of the state and the only body with constitutional and legislative powers. Members of the National Assembly are elected through national elections held every five years. In terms of sub-national government, People's Councils are elected at the provincial, district and commune levels. The People's Council is the highest state institution at the sub-national level, responsible to the electorate at each level and the National Assembly at the national level. People's Councils elects People's Committees to serve as the executive institution at the local level, although historically the People's Councils have been weak.

This chapter, which looks at political change in Vietnam over the past twenty or more years, will do so primarily with reference to the first body of literature. This has the advantage of helping us move away from a heavy reliance on the so-called 'middle classes' as the standard-bearer of democratization, which in recent years has tended to become the *sine qua non* of whether a country democratizes or not. While not ignoring the potential role of the middle class, the writings of Moore and Rueschemeyer et al. situate it within a broader context. Drawing on historical cases from the seventeenth to the twentieth century, these writers between them single out five classes as being important as to whether a country democratizes. These are large landowners, the peasantry and rural workers, the urban working class, the bourgeoisie (or capital-owning class), and the salaried and professional middle class. The writers argue that it is not only the changing stance of individual classes brought about by economic development that has a bearing on whether a country democratizes but also the relationship among classes and their relationship with the state.

In terms of the focus of this chapter, some of the writers' most interesting findings concern the position of the middle class or bourgeoisie. Drawing on the historical record, they note that while the middle class has been a force for democratization, it has often as not sided with authoritarianism. According to Moore, what is important is not simply the existence of a large middle class but its relationship with the state. That is, if it is to support democratization, it needs to be 'vigorous and independent' from the state. This chapter explores what this means in relation to Vietnam, particularly focusing on business interests that have emerged during the reform years. Also important, according to Rueschemeyer et al., in terms of whether the middle class will be a force for democratization, is its relationship with the working class. In countries where there is a large and politically active working class, the middle class has tended to feel threatened, favouring instead the authoritarian status quo. This issue will also be considered in relation to Vietnam. In addition, the chapter considers the nature of state power in Vietnam and the impact of transnational forces on the Vietnamese political scene, because these issues are also emphasized by these writers as having a bearing on whether a country democratizes.

The danger with the approach being proposed here is that it can all too easily be taken to assume that all countries are travelling on the same historical road, ending with the establishment of liberal democracy. When looking at political change in authoritarian states, we, in the West, find it genuinely very difficult to conceive of any other end point. And yet the experience in Asia to date would seem to suggest that Western-style liberal democracy is one of the least likely conclusions. Even Thailand and the Philippines, often seen as Asia's most democratic states, display many features that suggest their democracies are more formal than substantive (Anderson 1988a; Hutchcroft 1991; McCargo and Pathmanand 2005; Sidel 1996). Moreover, Singapore, with its long-standing capitalist development and substantial middle class and yet the absence of a democratic transition, although perhaps explained by Moore's emphasis on the importance of middle-class independence from the state, nevertheless seems to point to the possibility of another kind of evolution. One only has to read interviews with Singapore's leadership to be aware of the very different philosophical and cultural tradition on which it draws (Rodan 1992; Heng and Devan 1992). We can, of course, dismiss the language of such politicians as simply a cover for authoritarianism. However, in terms of trying to gain a sense of how politics in Vietnam, or elsewhere in Asia, is likely to evolve, it seems worth taking this differentness seriously.[1] These issues will be considered further towards the end of the chapter. In the meantime, it is important to bear in mind that the issues discussed below have been chosen because they appear to have been significant in the evolution away from authoritarianism in other historical contexts. However, they are not deterministic; nor do they provide much insight into the nature of political systems that will emerge in place of authoritarianism.

Changing class interests under reform

The onset of reform in Vietnam is variously dated from 1979, when the first tinkering with the central plan was carried out; from 1986, when the Vietnamese Communist Party held its Sixth Congress; and from 1989, when rather more substantive structural economic changes were introduced. Whatever one prefers, Vietnam for twenty years or more has been undergoing a shift from a system of central planning to one that places greater emphasis on the market to allocate goods and services. During this period, the ruling party has eschewed making changes to the political system along multiparty lines, focusing instead on making one-party democracy work better. Nevertheless, driven by growing integration into the world economy, the past decade and a half has seen rapid economic growth in Vietnam and rising per capita incomes.[2] This has had repercussions nationwide and in all sectors of society. The chapter will now consider the impact of the last fifteen or so years of rapid economic growth on class formation and the relationship among the five different classes cited above.

LARGE LANDOWNERS

The first class mentioned in the theoretical literature is large landowners. Historically, they have been against democratization. In Vietnam's case, it would appear to be axiomatic to argue that such a class does not exist. Large landowners were purged in the Democratic Republic of Vietnam during the 1950s, with the process continuing in liberated areas of the south during the 1960s and after the Communist victory in 1975 (Porter 1993: 57–8; Dacy 1986; Beresford 1989). According to the theoretical literature, the fact of their absence would seem to work in favour of a democratic transition.

However, is it right to see Vietnam as a country devoid of a large landowning class? Despite continued formal restrictions on the maximum permitted landholdings in the countryside, the reform years have been accompanied by the growing incidence of landlessness with its obvious corollary, namely the re-emergence of large landowners (Kerkvliet and Porter 1995; Dahm and Houben 1999; de Mauny and Hong 1998). There is also a confluence of interest between the government's stated desire for foreign investment in agroprocessing and the need for large landholdings. Foreign investment in agroprocessing has not been huge, but foreign agroprocessors have been able to secure large tracts of land when desired.

One might also argue that while the large landowners of the *ancien régime* have been toppled, in their place there has emerged a new landlord class, namely Communist Party cadres and government officials. After all, it is very often they, or their family members, who dominate the rural economy (Kerkvliet and Porter 1995; Kerkvliet 2005). If this analysis is correct, the prospects for a widening of the political space look less good.

THE PEASANTRY AND RURAL WORKERS

The second class is that of peasantry and rural workers. According to the theoretical literature, the peasantry have historically had an interest in democratization but have not been much of a force for it, largely because they have been poorly organized. The fact that Vietnam continues to be a predominantly rural society two decades after reform would seem to imply a relatively weak impulse for democratization. Nevertheless, with urbanization proceeding apace the situation is changing. Only 20 per cent of GDP is now derived from agriculture, although some 73 per cent of the population is still classified as rural (World Bank 2008).

Since the 1990s, rural unrest has become more common. The causes of the unrest are multiple but they would appear very often to be linked to land disputes involving local elites, often with allegations of elite corruption (Kerkvliet and Porter 1995; Kerkvliet 2003). Although there is no evidence of direct foreign sponsorship of rural unrest, dissident non-government groups based overseas and foreign human-rights organizations have been quick to champion the cause of aggrieved rural communities, while foreign governments, including the United States, have criticized the government's handling of such incidents.

Beyond individual instances of unrest, it would, however, be misleading to speak of a rural opposition in Vietnam understood in terms of an organization with a common institutional base and a coherent critique of party rule. Some scholars have alluded to the growth of autonomous farmers' groups (Fforde 1996: 78–80).

However, while it is clear that some farmers groups are increasingly outspoken, whether this amounts to clear or aspirational autonomy from the Party is less certain.

THE URBAN WORKING CLASS

The third class mentioned is the urban working class. It is regarded as having been an important force for democratization. In Vietnam, the urban working class is still quite small, given the predominantly rural nature of the country. However, the reform era has been accompanied by rapid urban growth, and hence a growing urban population. This has been driven in large part by spontaneous rural-to-urban migration, as strict controls on the movement of population have broken down and as farmers have flocked to the cities in search of employment on construction sites and in the factories that have sprung up in the context of marketization. By 2010, it is expected that one-third of the population will be urban-based.

In terms of organized labour, the urban working class has yet to flex its muscles in a way which has moved the political goalposts significantly. Labour relations have certainly become more complex during the reform years, with the growth of private, including foreign, capital. Since the early 1990s, strikes have become more common, including 'wildcat' strikes and the emergence of self-proclaimed but as yet not recognized independent trade unions. Nevertheless, organized labour has been kept weak by a combination of an uncertain legal framework governing its activities and an official trade union, the Vietnam General Confederation of Labour, which, given political pressures on it, cannot represent workers adequately (Chan and Norland 1999; Clarke 2006; Hanson 2003: 45-67; Ying Zhu and Fahey 2000: 282-99).

THE BOURGEOISIE

The fourth class is the bourgeoisie, understood here as the capital-owning or business class. In the popular view, entrepreneurs are often viewed as being part of the middle classes, and hence seen as a force for democratization. However, in the writings of Moore, Rueschemeyer and others, bourgeoisies are typically viewed as taking an ambivalent stance towards democratization. Richard Robison, for instance, has referred to an effective 'pact of domination' between capital-owning classes and the authoritarian state in Suharto's Indonesia, based around perceived shared interests (Robison 1988).

In Vietnam, the reform years have certainly seen the emergence of a new business elite. However, while this elite is new in terms of its business interests, it is in fact rather old in terms of its political ties. That is, many of the new entrepreneurs have emerged from within the existing system, are currently serving or former officials, or are the children of the political elite. To succeed in business, companies are still very reliant on the state for licences, contracts, access to capital and land, and, very often, protection (Gainsborough 2003a). Moreover, while this may be changing in some areas with business becoming more confident and less 'dependent' (Cheshier 2010; UNDP 2006), Vietnam still lacks the 'independent or vigorous bourgeoisie' cited by Moore as a necessary element in democratization.

The theoretical literature also emphasizes the importance of the bourgeoisie's relationship with the urban working class in terms of whether it supports democratization or not. If the middle class feels threatened by the working class, it is likely to be more conservative. If not, it is likely to be bolder.

Given the small size of Vietnam's working class, the outlook would appear more positive in terms of the possible stance of the bourgeoisie. However, as has been noted, although organized labour has become more militant in recent years and although there is disaffection in parts of the business community, there is little evidence yet of pressure for far-reaching political change.[3] In calls for less red tape and a more open and transparent business environment, which can be seen coming from parts of the business community, one can perhaps see the early stages of a division between the bourgeoisie and the state. However, these calls are relatively muted in comparison with the vigour with which many companies, out of necessity, go after state largesse.

THE SALARIED AND MIDDLE CLASSES

The fifth social group considered in the theoretical literature is the salaried and middle classes. In Vietnam, this would include professional state employees holding positions of responsibility in the bureaucracy and state enterprises, although there is likely to be some overlap with the capital-owning classes or bourgeoisie. Another group in this category would be professional Vietnamese employed by foreign companies or the international aid community. A decade ago some scholars were emphasizing an emerging gulf between groups such as these and the state, arguing that people were increasingly organizing their lives without reference to the party (David Marr cited in Thayer 1992b: 128). While the fact of someone's employment by a foreign company may be significant, it is more appropriate to emphasize the continued close relations between these groups and the state, in terms of their relatively privileged background (i.e. securing the necessary education to make them employable by a foreign company or the aid community), and a primary loyalty towards the state, including a willingness in many cases to join the party. Thus, as with the bourgeoisie, professional Vietnamese employed by foreign companies or the aid industry are often, although not always, still 'very much of the system'.

In terms of possible change in this area, middle-class Vietnamese regularly travel abroad and hence are being exposed to different ways of doing things, which can make them less tolerant of certain practices in Vietnam. There is also a growing exasperation on the part of some professional Vietnamese with official corruption, but again professional Vietnamese are as likely to be playing the system as railing against it (Gainsborough et al. 2009).

State power

As well as analysing the position of different classes and the relationships among them, the theoretical literature under consideration in
this chapter also argues that the nature of state power has been crucial
as to whether a country democratizes. In countries where it is difficult
to identify clearly a distinct realm of authority separate from society
(some African states, for example), the prospects for democratization
are reportedly poor. However, a very powerful state – one which is
almost entirely autonomous in relation to society – is also seen as not
conducive to a shift away from authoritarianism. Thus, it is in the
middle ground between not too little and not too much state power
that a democratic breakthrough has the greatest chance of success.

Over the years, the nature of state power in Vietnam has attracted
quite contrasting characterizations. Joel Migdal, for example, has
described Vietnam as a 'strong state', putting it, rather surprisingly,
in a category with Israel and Japan but also alongside other state
socialist countries (Migdal 1988: 269). For Migdal, these states are
strong because they are able to deploy state institutions to perform
certain public policy functions despite the existence of other power
centres. In terms of the Vietnamese state's alleged strength, Migdal
is joined by a number of Vietnam scholars.[4] Others have disputed
the characterization of the Vietnamese state as strong, arguing
that its actual capabilities are far less than is often assumed.[5] In
this book, it is argued that the state in Vietnam is comparatively
speaking quite strong but it depends on the context, hence the con-
flicting interpretations. Looking at the day-to-day working of state
institutions and the bureaucracy, it is striking how particularistic
seats of power in individual institutions are the norm, and how the
ability of formally senior institutions in the hierarchy to galvanize
junior institutions to act is limited. Power is thus scattered. The
state is weak. However, looking at the role of the police in people's
day-to-day lives – their official ability to harass, extract rents, and
generally prevent dissent, for instance – the state appears stronger.

Moreover, in periodic clampdowns on certain types of speculative business activity, and in the prosecution of big corruption cases, the state (or particular echelons of it) shows that when it feels so moved, it can act decisively and effectively. The issue of state strength versus state weakness will be developed further later in the book.[6]

In sum, therefore, the relative autonomy of the state some fifteen to twenty years after marketization would seem to be rather unconducive to a democratic transition. The theoretical literature particularly emphasizes how a heavy military and police presence in the state apparatus bodes ill for a transition away from authoritarianism. In Vietnam, the military and police have always been well represented in key leadership positions.[7]

Transnational forces

The literature also emphasizes the importance of transnational forces in the success or failure of moves away from authoritarianism. Factors mentioned as being of potential importance include a country's size, its geographical location, and the nature of its relationship with the global economy. Looking at Vietnam, one is conscious of how there are pressures working in both directions at the same time. The end of the Cold War might be regarded as resulting in a climate in which Southeast Asian countries, no longer seen as potential dominoes in an anti-communist struggle, have come under increased pressure from the USA and European Union (EU) states on issues of human rights and governance. The extent to which such pressure results in substantive change in the target country is, of course, debatable. However, what is indisputable is that the ideological terms of the engagement between the West and Southeast Asia have changed substantially from the days of the Cold War (Anderson 1988b).

On the other hand, Vietnam seems less vulnerable to external ideological and cultural inflows than some countries – neighbouring

Laos, for example. This would appear in part to reflect Laos's small size and its very heavy economic and cultural links with more democratic Thailand (Evans 1988). However, this relative lack of vulnerability in Vietnam's case may also be a feature and consequence of its heavily nationalistic independence struggle, which has given it a degree of self-belief that Laos, historically more dependent on Vietnamese wartime support, does not possess to the same extent. Moreover, in terms of limiting external ideological and cultural inflows, the state in Vietnam is still well placed to do this, even in an era of globalization (see Chapters 5, 6 and 8 in this volume for an examination of this point from a variety of angles). This again is something which Laos, with its close integration with Thailand, has appeared less able to do. That said, urban Vietnamese are now able to access a far greater range of media sources, despite censorship, than they were ten to fifteen years ago, so the situation is not static.

Vietnam's location in Southeast Asia and its membership in the Association of Southeast Asian Nations (ASEAN) since 1995 offer a certain level of insulation from US and EU pressure for political change. After all, while there is considerable variation in the political systems of ASEAN states, this is a grouping whose members still display relative degrees of authoritarianism, and an organization which has by and large maintained its principle of non-interference in the domestic affairs of its members (Dosch 2006). Meanwhile, Vietnam's all-important relationship with China – much improved in recent years but still characterized by mistrust – has also arguably served to maintain authoritarian rule in Vietnam. Whatever differences Vietnam and China may have, they have in common a shared mistrust of US global power and the fact that they are some of the last remaining communist states seeking to reform their economies along market lines without losing political control. Thus, as the frequent party and government exchanges between the two countries illustrate, there is much they can learn from each other (Amer 1999; Thayer 1992a; 2008; Vuving 2006; Womack 2006).

In addition, the popular tendency is to emphasize how in an era of globalization, increased integration in the world economy tends to work to the detriment of authoritarianism, not least with the growth of the middle class on the back of economic development. However, what is also evident in relation to Vietnam is the way in which foreign aid and private capital inflows work to bolster state power, because it is state institutions and state companies that are the principal beneficiaries (see Chapters 2, 6 and 8 in this volume).

From one-party rule to what?

From the outset, this chapter has emphasized the importance of trying to break free from a mindset that sees Vietnam as necessarily embarked on a historical road that ends in Western-style liberal democracy. Indeed, it has been argued that this is probably the least likely outcome, based on the experience of other countries in Southeast Asia. Taking this as our starting point, the key is not so much to be alert for some kind of liberal democratic breakthrough but rather to ask how else might a broadening of political space occur in a country like Vietnam?

At least part of the answer would appear to lie in a re-examination of concepts such as state and society. Instead of looking for the emergence of a robust civil society standing as a bulwark against state power, as much of the literature does, it is also important to look at what is occurring within the state. A number of scholars have argued similarly. In *Towards Illiberal Democracy in Pacific Asia*, Daniel Bell et al. write:

> The impetus for political reform arises not from the autonomous assertion of independent interests by social classes but from conflict within the state; political reform is about the management of intra-elite conflict rather than about the fundamental restructuring of state–society relationships. Therefore, political liberalization

[in Pacific Asia] is manifested in the changing architecture of the
state with civil society remaining both limited and circumscribed.
(Bell et al. 1995: 14)

That this is the case is testament to the very different philosophical and cultural heritage on which Asian states draw. Illustrating this with reference to Indonesia, Mark Berger notes how
Suharto's New Order regime 'reinstated and reconfigured organicist
(and/or integralist) ideas which view state and society as a single
organic entity and the embodiment of a harmonious village or
family' (Berger 1997: 341). While Berger notes that this ideology is
in part a reconfiguration, and is used to deny oppositional activity,
it does highlight the different philosophical and cultural roots on
which many Asian leaders draw. Moreover, to the extent that such
thinking is influential in terms of what actually happens, it offers a
clue to likely political evolution. To illustrate the same point, one
suspects that when Lee Kuan Yew spoke in the 1990s of the need
to establish safeguards to limit the 'way in which people use their
votes to bargain, to coerce, to push and jostle' the government, or
referred to the need for the government to show that it 'cannot be
blackmailed', such rhetoric does not simply represent sheer cheek on
his part, but is actually indicative of a fundamentally different way
of understanding the relationship between state and society (Rodan
1992: 5). Similarly, when Vietnamese leaders go on record to say
that Vietnam will never have need for opposition parties, justifying
such a position on the grounds that the ruling Communist Party
knows the will of the people and only exists to serve it, this is not
just a crude defence of authoritarianism but represents heartfelt
opinion based on a very different view of state and opposition than
that of the West.[8]

The idea that one should look for a broadening of political space
within the state rings very true for Vietnam. For all the emphasis
in foreign journalistic and academic writing on civil society, the
emerging middle class, Buddhist and Catholic dissent, dissident
intellectuals, Internet bloggers, youth disillusionment, and rural

unrest – all of which are legitimate areas of study – the main arena of struggle in Vietnam remains closely focused in and around the state. Thus, if one points to some of the major political debates of the reform era, which have to do with the relationship between the party and the government, the role of the National Assembly, issues of centralization and decentralization, or the best way to manage state enterprises, it is clear that the extent of change or the widening of political space must be seen in relation to state institutions. For example, the party may still be the ultimate authority, but it now has to contend with more robust government institutions and a stronger National Assembly, as, notwithstanding their common party representation, they are alternative seats of power. Whether this was the intended outcome of the critique of the party emerging at the Sixth Congress in 1986 is unclear, but, as an illustration of how change is occurring within the state, it is revealing. Equally, many of the concerns of the business sector, rather than finding expression through an organization external to the state, are still channelled through the state-sanctioned institutions (Stromseth 1998). Even if one were to speculate that such organizations might one day spawn breakaway groups or evolve into something external to the state, it is inconceivable that they would not retain something of the different philosophical and cultural underpinnings in terms of how they conceive of the relationship between state and society.

Conclusion

With reference to writings by Moore and Rueschemeyer et al., this chapter has sought to offer a robust account of the nature of political change in Vietnam over the past fifteen to twenty years. In terms of why the middle class has not emerged to challenge the state, the fact of its still-close relations with the state – dependent on it, not independent from it – seems highly significant. Moreover, for all the popular emphasis on issues such as civil society and globalization, the Vietnamese state remains relatively autonomous in relation to society, and relatively impervious in relation to external ideas and influences. Furthermore, when political change occurs in Vietnam, as it inevitably will, one lesson from much of the rest of Asia is that a broadening of the political space is as likely to come from changes within state institutions as from the rise of an assertive civil society, as imagined in the West. Whether this will result in a sweeping away of authoritarianism is questionable. More likely is that we will see a gradual softening of its sharper edges, although even this might be optimistic.

2

NEW STATE BUSINESS INTERESTS

The previous chapter explored some of the reasons why Communist Party rule has persisted in Vietnam in contrast to the collapse of Communism in Eastern Europe and the former Soviet Union. One of the issues raised was the relative dependence of business interests on the state in Vietnam despite two decades of marketization and integration in the world economy. This chapter considers the nature of Vietnam's business class in more detail, charting its emergence from within the state sector, and exploring what this means for our understanding of what is conventionally called 'reform'. This is done through a case study of Vietnam's second city and business centre, Ho Chi Minh City during the mid to late 1990s, when many of the business interests which remain relevant to the present day began to be visible. Given the book's critical stance towards the notion of reform, it is especially helpful to focus attention on Ho Chi Minh City because of its strong association in the popular and academic imagination with 'reform'. What this chapter suggests is that we need to be much more precise in our characterization of the city's alleged 'reformist' credentials and the extent to which its political economy stands apart from the country as a whole.

The chapter is structured as follows. It first reviews the literature on how Ho Chi Minh City has been depicted during the reform era. It then critiques this literature, arguing that, even before we consider the chapter's principal findings, there are good reasons why we should be sceptical about the received wisdom on Ho Chi Minh City. Next, an alternative depiction of Ho Chi Minh City under reform is presented, highlighting the rise of new state business interests and the growth of the gatekeeping state as party-state institutions moved to exploit new opportunities that emerged with the dismantling of the central plan and the growth of the market economy. It is argued that rather than being inspired by reformist ideals, city officials have often been motivated by much more venal desires. Finally, suggesting that this depiction of Ho Chi Minh City is not unique but rather encapsulates something of the reform experience across Vietnam, the chapter concludes by calling for a rethinking not only of the legacy of 1954–75 for Ho Chi Minh City's latter-day development but also of the way in which the city's shorter period under central planning compared with northern Vietnam also left its mark.

Ho Chi Minh City's depiction in the literature

Ho Chi Minh City stands out from the rest of Vietnam in a variety of ways. It is Vietnam's largest city. It is the country's economic powerhouse. It is Vietnam's richest city. During the reform era, Ho Chi Minh City has attracted more foreign direct investment than any other province or municipality.[1] Compared with Hanoi, Ho Chi Minh City also feels different. Part of this has to do with climatic differences, but cultural differences – not uninfluenced by climate – are real enough. This is evident in the perceptions that Vietnamese commonly have of themselves – and readily share with outsiders. Southerners typically described themselves as more carefree, less risk-averse, more outspoken, and less formal than their northern counterparts. Moreover, a new generation of foreign companies operating in Vietnam have learned – often the hard way – to take these differences seriously. Marketing companies, for example, commonly devise distinct strategies depending on which part of the country they are seeking to communicate with.

Beyond this, many of the assertions about Ho Chi Minh City's distinctiveness – and that of the south more generally – centre on its political economy. This includes reference to the city's large private sector and its rapid economic growth rate.[2] Indeed, these two characteristics are usually seen as being related, with the city's rapid economic growth regarded as a consequence of its dynamic private sector. In terms of Ho Chi Minh City's private sector, reference is frequently made to the business activities of the city's large ethnic Chinese population, which accounts for around 10 per cent of the total population, compared with just over 1 per cent nationwide. During the 1990s, two ethnic Chinese companies in the city commonly singled out for attention were the shoe company Bitis and business interests associated with Tran Tuan Tai, who prior to his death in 1997 founded Viet Hoa joint stock commercial bank and financed the development of An Dong market in Ho Chi Minh City's Cho Lon district. Bitis also featured in the 2006 top 200 companies in Vietnam, along with a number of other ethnic Chinese invested companies (Cheshier 2010).

In addition, Ho Chi Minh City is widely associated with reform. 'Reform' is viewed as having originated in the city, while the city itself is seen as having been influential in the 'reformist' direction that the country at large took after 1986. That Ho Chi Minh City has performed such a role is usually attributed to the stance of the city's leaders, who are commonly depicted as 'reformers'.

Surveying the scholarly literature on Vietnam it is not difficult to find accounts that echo this view of Ho Chi Minh City. From Nguyen Van Linh to Vo Van Kiet, Phan Van Khai and Truong Tan Sang, nearly all Ho Chi Minh City's post-1975 leadership have at some stage attracted the reformist accolade. Commenting on Nguyen Van Linh's election as party general secretary at the Sixth

Party Congress in 1986, William Duiker described him as 'having earned a reputation as a reformer' during his time as party secretary in Ho Chi Minh City after 1975 (Duiker 1989: 244). Gareth Porter referred to one-time party secretary Vo Van Kiet as a 'southerner reformer' who had endeared himself to critics of central government policies in the south by supporting 'innovative economic schemes' in Ho Chi Minh City in the late 1970s and early 1980s when he was party secretary there (Porter 1993: 109). Derek Tonkin referred to Truong Tan Sang, who served first as People's Committee chairman in Ho Chi Minh City (1992–96) and later as party secretary (1996–2000), as a 'dynamic technocrat', highlighting another label commonly attached to the city's leaders (Tonkin 1997). Meanwhile, Zachary Abuza wrote that southern leaders have a reputation for being 'pragmatic and laissez-faire', adding that Hanoi's 'ideological rigidity and social conservatism infuriates the more freewheeling capitalist south' (Abuza 2001: 163–4).

Underlining the idea that Ho Chi Minh City has been influential in the reformist direction that Vietnam has taken since 1986, William Turley and Brantley Womack argued that southern leaders 'developed a comprehensive program' in the early 1980s 'whose basic elements foreshadowed Doi Moi [renovation]' (Turley and Womack 1998: 111–12). Later they argued that reforms adopted in 1988, which formally recognized the private economy, unified the official and open-market exchange rates, and separated commercial and state banking functions, 'had strong support from, and at times followed proposals made by the Ho Chi Minh City government' (Turley and Womack 1998: 112–13).

Other scholars have highlighted the existence of reform 'experiments' in Ho Chi Minh City during the 1980s, such as the Ba Thi model, named after the director of the Ho Chi Minh City food department, where sympathetic officials allegedly allowed experimentation with markets before such practice was officially sanctioned (Beresford 1989: 207; Beresford and McFarlane 1995: 58; Duiker 1989: 95–6; Porter 1993: 125; Thrift and Thorbes 1986: 159; Turley and Womack 1998: 111). The adoption of reform nationwide is also associated with the rise of Ho Chi Minh City leaders to national office, notably Nguyen Van Linh's appointment as party general secretary at the Sixth Party Congress in 1986 (Turley and Womack 1998: 111). Vo Van Kiet's appointment as chairman of the State Planning Committee in 1982 has also been seen in this light, as has his replacement by Phan Van Khai in 1989. Khai served as People's Committee chairman in Ho Chi Minh City from 1985 to 1989.

Ho Chi Minh City's distinctive political economy is commonly explained with reference to its history. As a result of the division of the country into the socialist Democratic Republic of Vietnam (North Vietnam) and the state-capitalist Republic of Vietnam (South Vietnam) between 1954 and 1975, Ho Chi Minh City (then Saigon) spent less time under central planning than the north, instead spending an additional twenty years 'in the capitalist orbit' (Beresford and McFarlane 1995: 54). Commenting on the legacy of Vietnam's division into north and south, the World Bank noted in 1993 that the south had more of the capital stock in light manufacturing, easier access to capital from overseas Vietnamese, and better infrastructure. It also argued that the south had 'greater entrepreneurial tradition' than the north (World Bank 1993: 3).

Other scholars have delved further back into Ho Chi Minh City's history to explain its perceived distinctive character. Drawing on work by scholars such as Terry Rambo and Martin Murray, some scholars have argued that the way in which the south was settled in the precolonial period (the so-called 'march south' or *nam tien*) along with the concentration of capitalist agriculture and commerce in and around Saigon under the French created a distinctive southern political economy, which continues to be relevant to this day (Beresford and McFarlane 1995: 53–4; Murray 1980; Rambo 1972). Gareth Porter writes:

> The contrast between a southern population that is relatively unafraid to assert its political interests and northern and central Vietnamese populations that remain politically more timid is

striking testimony to the divergence of social structures in the
south from the longer-settled north and center. The open villages
of the south have encouraged greater individual entrepreneurship
and political independence than the closed villages of the north
and the center. Moreover, the experience of southerners with a
relatively pluralistic political system in which political dissent
was widespread has undoubtedly contributed to greater boldness,
especially in urban areas. (Porter 1993: 163)

In sum, the received wisdom is clear. Ho Chi Minh City is
regarded as standing apart from the rest of Vietnam, a fact that can
above all else be attributed to its distinctive history. Moreover, Ho
Chi Minh City's distinctiveness has been especially in evidence
during the reform era – so it is argued – with the city having been influential in the reformist direction the country at large has taken.

Questioning the received wisdom

But how far do we accept this depiction of Ho Chi Minh City?
Clearly there are some things it would be foolish to take issue with.
Ho Chi Minh City undoubtedly has had a distinctive history. It
clearly is the country's economic powerhouse. However, there are
other areas, such as assertions about the city's alleged reformism or
the legacy of Ho Chi Minh City's pre-1975 history for its present-day
political economy, where claims made about the city are more open
to question.

Taking issue with the received wisdom about Ho Chi Minh City
is bound to be controversial. The Ho Chi Minh City 'as different'
camp is a large and influential one, incorporating scholars, development practitioners, business people, journalists and politicians. This
camp's views are strongly put and they permeate nearly all areas of
the literature both academic and popular. Nevertheless, there are
good reasons why we should challenge some of the sacred cows
associated with Ho Chi Minh City.

First, many of the claims made about Ho Chi Minh City rest on
weak empirical foundations. Consider, for example, the assertion

that reform had its origins in the city. This rests on the idea of reform 'experiments' pursued during the 1980s as the city made greater use of market mechanisms under the eye of sympathetic local leaders. However, a lot of this is based on hearsay.

No one has gone back and looked closely at these so-called experiments – and indeed the stance of the city leadership – to see exactly what was going on. Looking afresh at the public statements of Ho Chi Minh City's leaders during the late 1970s and 1980s what is striking is how little evidence there is to suggest any overt association with reform.[3]

Furthermore, interpreting these events is by no means straightforward. Greater application of the market cannot simply be equated with reform. It is quite possible that these 'experiments' were being pursued for much more venal reasons that have to do with the pursuit of personal profit rather than a quest for 'reform'. Motive is important and not easy to gauge. It is also unclear who precisely was pursuing these so-called experiments. Do they, for example, represent the spontaneous activities of 'societal' actors or are these so-called experiments the work of 'state' actors, more akin to the 'fence-breaking' described by Adam Fforde and Stefan de Vylder? (Fforde and de Vylder 1996). In addition, we need to be clearer about the role of the state in this. Did the state initiate the experiments? Did it sanction them after the event, or did they happen in spite of the state? Answering such questions is important if we are to come up with a more rigorous assessment of Ho Chi Minh City's alleged association with reform.

A similar criticism can be levelled at arguments that assert that Ho Chi Minh City has been influential in the reformist direction that the country has taken since 1986. As yet, no one has studied in depth a particular 'reformist' policy the centre adopted or looked at the role of Ho Chi Minh City in pushing for this policy. So far, scholars have uncovered only isolated references to Ho Chi Minh City's apparent support for policies that were later adopted nationally (Turley and Womack 1998: 112–13). However, it is important to show that other factors were not influential in the policy's adoption since it is possible that the centre would have adopted a particular policy anyway. Once again, motive is also important. If Ho Chi Minh City can be seen to be backing a particular 'reformist' policy, we need to know why it is doing so.

One area where Ho Chi Minh City is often depicted as champing at the bit of central control is fiscal policy. Ho Chi Minh City is said to resent having to subsidize poorer provinces on account of its more vibrant economy (Turley and Womack 1998: 114–15; Kolko 1997: 48). While anecdotal evidence can be found supporting this notion of resentment, academic studies have not scrutinized centre-province tax relations in detail related to Ho Chi Minh City, and especially not in ways which go beyond a quantitative assessment based on official data. This contrasts markedly with the large and complex literature on this subject for China. Until scholars have done such research we need to be much more circumspect in the claims we make.

Second, Ho Chi Minh City's strong association with reform in the literature is unsatisfactory because the term 'reform' is itself poorly defined. Although it is rarely stated explicitly, reform is usually taken to imply 'greater support for the market' or perhaps support for 'the rule of law' (Duiker 1989: 244–5). However, such characterizations are not straightforward. As we know from accounts that contrast US, German and Japanese capitalism, there are many different brands of capitalism or ways of structuring a market economy, none of which is necessarily better or 'more reformist'. Moreover, the seeming willingness of scholars to label Ho Chi Minh City's leaders as reformers sits uncomfortably with the fact that in practice it is often difficult to know where a politician stands. A good example can be found in the way in which politicians can in their public pronouncements combine support for the private sector and 'a leading role' for the state sector, without any apparent feeling that they are being inconsistent. Furthermore, reform is not static but changes over time, so what one leader advocated in the mid-1980s may seem distinctly mainstream by the late 1990s or the present day.

Third, the conjunction between scholarly accounts that trumpet Ho Chi Minh City's association with reform and the official Vietnamese view is striking. This ought to set alarm bells ringing regarding the political uses to which the term 'reform' has been put. In a volume published to mark the twentieth anniversary of Saigon's liberation in 1975, former Ho Chi Minh City party secretaries Nguyen Van Linh and Vo Tran Chi both penned articles that give weight to the idea of reform 'experiments' being pursued in the city before being adopted nationally (BTVTU 1996: 29-40, 511-32). However, this is a 'sanitized account' designed to show the good sense of the leadership – an account that 'distracts us from the real dynamics of the reform process' (Naughton 1995: 22). Thus, arguments about Ho Chi Minh City's reformism need to be treated cautiously because they may serve a wider political purpose, namely bolstering the state. Making claims about Ho Chi Minh City's reformism is also useful in order to attract foreign investment.

In the context of latent US guilt about abandoning Saigon to the Communists in 1975, upholding present-day Ho Chi Minh City as a paragon of reformism and free-market entrepreneurialism may at an unconscious level also serve a cathartic purpose for outsiders, with the city viewed as ultimately emerging triumphant from the ashes of defeat. Certainly, there is an air of triumphalism behind some of the early accounts that detail the persistence of market activity in Ho Chi Minh City or the south after 1975.[4]

Fourth, assertions about Ho Chi Minh City's reformism incorporate – at least implicitly – claims about the nature of the state, such as that it is more technocratic or governed by the rule of law. The character of the state in Ho Chi Minh City is considered later in the chapter. However, suffice it to say at this stage that if the bureaucracy in Ho Chi Minh City were qualitatively better than in other parts of the country, we would expect this to be reflected in the accounts of business people. It is not. While Ho Chi Minh City has attracted more foreign investment than other parts of Vietnam, doing business in the city is not easy. There is still lots of red tape. City officials do not appear particularly enlightened. Thus, simply at an intuitive level we ought to be wary of claims about Ho Chi Minh City since there is a mismatch between them and the experience of business people on the ground.

The rise of new state business interests

Conducting fieldwork in Ho Chi Minh City in the late 1990s, what stood out most clearly was not the freewheeling private sector often associated with the city but rather the emergence of new state business interests. In highlighting state business interests, it is not being claimed that other interests have not prospered in Ho Chi Minh City during the reform era. However, the rise of new state business interests during the reform years is an important phenomenon, and one that is in danger of being overlooked, not least because of the tendency to associate reform in Ho Chi Minh City with the rise of the private sector. Such business interests are also crucial because of the way in which they laid the foundation for the subsequent development of Vietnam's political economy. That is, much of what could be observed as standard business practice in late-1990s Ho Chi Minh City, notably how companies leveraged off their relations with the state, has been replicated the length and breadth of the country since, continuing to this day (see, for instance, Cheshier 2010).

'New state business interests' refers to business interests linked to state enterprises and/or bureaucratic institutions of the party-state which were at the forefront of moves to exploit commercial opportunities that emerged during the reform years. These interests are 'new' either because they involve existing state enterprises diversifying into areas distinct from those in which they were originally founded to operate, or because they involve the setting up of new companies.

Companies associated with new state business interests have tended to operate in a well-defined set of areas, although there has often been a bias towards the services sector. Sectors that occur with repeated regularity among the corporate success stories that emerged in the 1990s in Ho Chi Minh City, continuing to the present, include real estate, foreign trade, banking and finance, gold, retail trade, distribution, hotels, tourism and entertainment. Some companies have also operated in light industry, notably textiles and garments, food processing and construction. The sectors in which these companies are concentrated generally saw rapid growth during the 1990s and as a result the potential for profits was high.[5] They are also areas where marketization created new opportunities that did not exist under central planning, such as in foreign trade, banking and real-estate development.

New state business interests can operate as either state or private enterprises. Thus the approach advocated here emphasizes the importance of knowing who the shareholders of a given enterprise are rather than talking about the state and private sector per se. Therefore a nominally private company would be regarded as representative of new state business interests if it had state institutions as shareholders or if it can be shown to have had close connections with the party-state (e.g. through the employment or former employment of its owners).

During the 1990s new state business interests were operating in one of three ways in Ho Chi Minh City. First, existing state enterprises established before reforms began were diversifying out of their core business area into new sectors. Second, new state enterprises formed by party-state institutions began proliferating in the late 1980s. Third, new state business interests were moving to set up private companies, usually in the form of limited liability companies. The last phenomenon was observable mainly from the early 1990s. For a list of companies associated with the rise of new state business interests, see Box 2.1.

BOX 2.1　　New state business in Ho Chi Minh City in the 1990s

EXISTING STATE ENTERPRISES DIVERSIFYING INTO NEW AREAS
Saigon Tourist
Tan Binh Housing and Development Co.

NEW STATE ENTERPRISES FORMED FROM THE LATE 1980S
Ben Thanh Tourist
Eden Trading and Service Co.
Fimexco
Phu Nhuan Jewellery Co.
Saigon Jewellery Co.
Tamexco

STATE BUSINESS INTERESTS FORMING PRIVATE COMPANIES
Epco
Tribeco
Huy Hoang

Source: Vietnamese media.

Existing state enterprises diversifying into new areas

Some state enterprises established under central planning found
it difficult to adapt to the new era. Thus, diversification into new
business sectors by existing state enterprises is probably the least
common way in which new state business interests emerged during
the 1990s. Nevertheless, a number of companies have successfully
made the transition. One of the best examples is Saigon Tourist.
In 1995 it ranked seventeenth in the top 100 companies in Ho Chi
Minh City (by turnover), and continues to be prominent to this
day. Saigon Tourist was established soon after Saigon was liberated in 1975, at which point it took charge of a large number of Ho
Chi Minh City's hotels and restaurants. During the 1990s, Saigon
Tourist was controlled by business interests linked to the District 1
People's Committee.[6] Saigon Tourist has generally stuck to its core
business in the hotel, tourism and entertainment sector, successfully
exploiting the rapid growth in tourism during the 1990s. In 1999 it

ran fifty-three hotels and forty-one restaurants nationwide. However, the company also has interests in banking, where it is the leading shareholder in the joint stock commercial bank Oricom Bank, and in distribution, serving as a distributor for Ford in Vietnam.

The establishment of new state enterprises

Some of the most prominent examples of new state business interests that emerged in Ho Chi Minh City during the 1990s can be seen in companies established as marketization gathered pace in the late 1980s. Many of these companies were set up by the city's departments (*so*) or districts (*quan*). Indeed, there was scarcely a department or district in Ho Chi Minh City that did not have companies under its jurisdiction in the 1990s.

Good examples include Saigon Jewellery Company and Phu Nhuan Jewellery Company, which were both founded in 1988. Saigon Jewellery Company originated as a company under the city's Trade Department (*so thuong mai*). Throughout the 1990s the company's director was a former People's Committee deputy chairman in the city's District 10, Nguyen Huu Dinh. Six years after its founding, it ranked eleventh among the top 100 city companies based on turnover. Moreover, Saigon Jewellery Company was not just the dominant player in the gold industry in Ho Chi Minh City, but nationwide. Its gold taels, which have a distinctive dragon emblem, are considered the industry standard. The company also diversified into real-estate development, banking and retail trade. Saigon Jewellery Company was the leading local investor in the Diamond Plaza building, a prominent property development on District 1's Le Duan Street, and it also held shares in three joint stock banks: Exim Bank, Asia Commercial Bank and Danang Bank. Between 1989 and 1996 the company's turnover increased by an average of 43 per cent annually (CDNDNTD 1997: 16).

Phu Nhuan Jewellery Company was originally linked to a husband-and-wife team in Phu Nhuan district, although it was later brought under the control of the city party committee. The company's director, Ba (Mrs) Cao Thi Ngoc Dung, was active in the gold and jewellery business prior to forming Phu Nhuan Jewellery Company. Like Saigon Jewellery Company, Phu Nhuan diversified beyond the gold and jewellery business, developing interests in real-estate development, banking, tourism and distribution. Phu Nhuan Jewellery Company is a leading shareholder in Dong A Bank. The company has built villas in An Phu, a residential area popular with expatriates and wealthy Vietnamese. It also operated as distributor for Honda in Vietnam and had a small stake in the tourism sector. During 1988–94, Phu Nhuan Jewellery Company averaged 67 per cent annual turnover growth.

The formation of private companies

New state business interests also established private companies, often in the form of limited liability companies. A good example is the District 3 Seafood Production Import–Export Company, better known as Epco, which was founded in 1991. Epco's shareholders included business interests connected to District 3 People's Committee, the state-owned Bank for Foreign Trade (Vietcombank), along with a number of local ethnic Chinese business people.

Soon after its founding, Epco ran an advertisement in a Ho Chi Minh City newspaper, describing itself as offering import–export services to Hong Kong, notably the provision of live seafood and freshly cut flowers. However, it also developed interests in hotels, tourism, real-estate development and construction. In 1995, just four years after its founding, it had an annual turnover of 145 billion dong and employed some 790 people. This placed it sixty-eighth among the top 100 companies in Ho Chi Minh City at the time. Also in 1995, Epco opened offices in Los Angeles and Sydney. In the mid-1990s this was unprecedented for a private company.

Another limited company with strong state connections prominent in the 1990s was Huy Hoang, headed by a former government

official, Le Van Kiem, who came south in 1975. Kiem's wife worked
for a Ministry of Commerce company called Tocontap. Huy Hoang
was founded in 1990, operating initially in textiles and garments.
However, it later diversified into real-estate development and banking.
Huy Hoang held a leading stake in VP Bank and Asia–Pacific Bank
and was involved in the construction of luxury villas in District 2. In
1995 Huy Hoang ranked seventy-eighth out of Ho Chi Minh City's
top 100 companies in turnover.

While the companies profiled above have generally been very
successful, the picture surrounding the rise of new state business
interests is not one of unmitigated success. Despite appearances
to the contrary, some companies were not well run or at best were
pushing out the boundaries of what was legally or politically ac-
ceptable in terms of running a company. A number of companies
rose spectacularly for a period only to fall later. Epco, for example,
became embroiled in a major corruption case in 1997 that revealed
high levels of company debt. Moreover, most companies relied
heavily on their bureaucratic and political background for access
to licences, contracts and capital, and political protection. Nevertheless, despite the absence of a level playing field, entrepreneurial
skill and being responsive to the market were both important. Even
if entry to certain sectors was restricted, few companies enjoyed a
complete monopoly. Thus, if one company produced a poor-quality
product or service, customers could turn to another. The need
for companies to be responsive to the market can be seen in the
glossy marketing brochures and annual reports that were routinely
produced by companies like Saigon Jewellery Company or Saigon
Tourist during the 1990s in order to woo customers and investors.
This represents a major change from the days of central planning.

To sum up, the picture of a growing and often dynamic new state
business sector is a valid one for an important subset of companies.
This is far removed from the traditional view of a universally ailing
state sector – a point which will be further developed in Chapters 4
and 5. The analysis presented here also suggests that the true picture

doesn't fit the dominant view of Ho Chi Minh City as a bastion of private sector activity during the 1990s.

The growth of the gatekeeping state

With its emphasis on the growth of the market and the dismantling of the mechanisms of central planning, reform is often associated with the retreat of the state.[7] Given its association in the literature with reform and technocracy, Ho Chi Minh City might be expected to be at the forefront of such trends. Anecdotally, one can find references in the press to the closure or merging of state institutions whose role has become obsolete with the shift away from planning.[8] Moreover, the language of public administration reform is very much about streamlining the state (Fforde 1997; Vasavakul 1996, 1997b). However, it is hard to argue that much streamlining at all took place in practice in Ho Chi Minh City during the 1990s.

A good measure of whether the state is expanding or contracting is public-sector employment. Such data are collected annually by the government and include people who work in public administration, including for the Communist Party, for public-sector companies, or in areas such as health and education. The fact that it includes people who work both in state administration and in business means that it is a comprehensive measure of the size of the state. The data distinguish between those employed by the central authorities and those employed by the local authorities. Although there is an interesting story to be told in relation to trends in centrally managed employment in Ho Chi Minh City, the focus here is on those employed by the local authorities in order to uncover trends in the city administration. The data on public-sector employment are contained in Tables 2.1 and 2.2.

The data provide little support for the idea that the state was contracting in Ho Chi Minh City during the reform years. After falling in 1991–92, the number of people employed in the state sector managed by the city authorities increased in the next five consecutive

TABLE 2.1   Public-sector employment by local management
in Ho Chi Minh City (1,000 persons)

1990	1991	1992	1993	1994	1995	1996	1997	1998	1999	2000
178.3	174.5	171.5	186.6	194.7	194.8	207.1	211.3	210.1	208.6	208.6

Source: Official government statistics.

years to 1997. It fell slightly in 1998 and 1999 before stabilizing in
2000. Nevertheless, the number of people employed by the city
authorities in 2000 was well above the level recorded in 1990. More
detailed data provided by the Ho Chi Minh City statistical office
covering the period 1994–98 reveal that some of the largest increases
in public-sector employment were in the area of party and state
management and construction. How might this be explained?

Rising public-sector employment at a time when the central plan
was being dismantled makes sense in relation to the idea of state
institutions moving to take on new functions associated with gatekeeping the market economy. It also fits with the characterization
here of the rise of new state business interests with new or expanding
state or state-controlled companies increasing their workforces. The
rise of the gatekeeping state in Ho Chi Minh City can be seen in
relation to any number of areas where state institutions – both party
and government – were involved in carrying out inspections, issuing
licences or contracts, or overseeing access to resources regulated
by the state. For entrepreneurial public offices, such procedures
offered opportunities to supplement their income either through
the levying of legitimate administrative fees or through more blatant
acts of corruption.

Not surprisingly, interests quickly coalesced around such activities so that once a department had established itself in a particular
area it was reluctant to concede ground. This led to some trenchant
turf wars as state institutions sought to defend 'their patch'. When
not fighting each other, state institutions were very often making

TABLE 2.2   Public-sector employment in Ho Chi Minh City, 1990–98 (1,000 persons)

	1990	1991	1992	1993	1994	1995	1996	1997	1998
Local management	178.3	174.5	171.5	186.6	194.7	194.8	207.1	211.3	207.1
Central management	–	–	–	–	175.7	221.6	221.8	222.2	213.2
Total	–	–	–	–	372.8	419.8	422.5	439.3	420.3
of which:									
Industry	–	–	–	–	102.9	114.9	115.2	115.1	111.6
Education and training	–	–	–	–	73.1	76.6	98.3	101.1	103.5
Trade, hotel, restaurant	–	–	–	–	93.7	111.7	84.4	94.4	80.7
Public health and social affairs	–	–	–	–	32.7	35.6	37.3	34.5	34.9
Construction	–	–	–	–	21.4	26.0	30.4	32.1	33.0
State management, party, national defence	–	–	–	–	14.9	19.1	22.5	22.9	21.7
Transport, storage, communications	–	–	–	–	12.7	14.4	12.1	15.5	14.1
Agriculture, forestry, fishery	–	–	–	–	8.8	8.1	8.5	10.0	8.1

Source: Official government statistics.

life difficult for the city's residents or companies, who had to run the gauntlet of numerous offices to complete simple procedures. For example, getting a licence to renovate a house could take six months in the late 1990s. To complete house documentation, it was commonplace for a person to have to visit the district authorities some five times. Moreover, residents were very often required to pay fees at each stage of the process to ensure their application progressed.[9] Ten years on, the Vietnamese media are still full of reports of troublesome administrative procedures: all that has changed is that problem areas have simply shifted somewhat (Gainsborough et al. 2009).

Reformist or more parochial interests?

Returning to the question of motive, mentioned earlier, it is clear that where disputes occurred in Ho Chi Minh City during the 1990s, city officials were not arguing about the niceties of different approaches to reform – at least not for their own sake – but rather were seeking to defend business and bureaucratic interests associated with the rise of new state business interests and the emergence of the gatekeeping state, which had grown up over the course of the 1980s and 1990s. In practice, it is usually impossible to determine where bureaucratic interests end and business interests begin, either because they are one and the same or because bureaucratic institutions with gatekeeping responsibilities in one area have businesses operating in that same area.

Some of the most bitter infighting in Ho Chi Minh City in the 1990s occurred in relation to so-called enterprise reform, public administration reform, and land reform. One dispute that erupted in 1995 saw officials from the Trade Department, the Land and Housing Department, the Cadastral Department, the Go Vap district People's Committee and Tan Binh Housing and Development Company (controlled by interests connected to Tan Binh district People's Committee) and the Ho Chi Minh City branch of the state-owned Bank for Foreign Trade speak out strongly against the introduction of a central decree that sought to put a stop to speculative activity in the real-estate market.[10] The dispute was dressed up in terms of what was best for business and the land market in general. However, some of those who were most outspoken in their criticism of the decree could be linked directly to new state business interests active in the land market; they stood to lose most from the ruling. The shock of the decree was so great that the episode was remembered for many years afterwards in Ho Chi Minh City, like a stock-market crash might be recalled elsewhere.

Another dispute, which raged through most of the 1990s, pitted the chief architect's office in Ho Chi Minh City, backed up by the prime minister's office and the construction ministry, against the city People's Committee, the Construction Department, and the Land and Housing Department. The dispute centred on the jurisdictional boundaries between these institutions in urban planning. The chief architect's office was set up on the authority of the prime minister in 1993 to try to introduce a degree of central control over the rapid urbanization taking place in Ho Chi Minh City. Local institutions always resented the chief architect's office lauding it over them, particularly when it interfered with their business and gatekeeping interests. One particular bone of contention concerned who had the right to issue construction licences in the city.

A further conflict arose in response to an attempt in the late 1990s to restructure one of Ho Chi Minh City's general corporations, Saigon Trading Corporation (Satra). Although the proposed reorganization was depicted as a way to improve enterprise efficiency and competitiveness, the reality is that it represented an attempt by one institution (the city People's Committee) to wrest control of some of the city's most lucrative corporate assets from another (the Trade Department, which was the dominant influence at Satra).[11] One of the companies at the centre of the controversy was the Saigon Jewellery Company, profiled above. In the event, the results were mixed. Although a number of companies affiliated with Saigon Trading Corporation were moved, Saigon Jewellery Company remained under the auspices of Satra.

Conclusion: explaining Ho Chi Minh City's evolution under 'reform'

The portrayal of Ho Chi Minh City in this chapter – characterized by the rise of new state business interests, the expansion of the gatekeeping state, and the pursuit of parochial rather than reformist interests – is a far cry from the usual way in which the city is depicted. Equally striking is how, perceived in this way, Ho Chi Minh City is not so dissimilar from other parts of the country. For example, if one considers such landmark episodes of the 1990s in Hanoi such as illegal construction on the city's flood defences or real-estate speculation on West Lake and ask who was involved and what was at stake, it is clear that new state business interests and the activities of the gatekeeping state were very much at the heart of it (Vasavakul 1996; Koh 2000, 2001). This has profound implications for how we think about differences between north and south since it suggests that what has been described for Ho Chi Minh City may be reflective of a much more unified political economy than is commonly thought. That is, the rise of the new state business interests, the growth of the gatekeeping state, and the pursuit of parochial rather than 'reform' interests is not something unique to Ho Chi Minh City, but reflects developments in the country at large.

This makes it difficult to explain Ho Chi Minh City's evolution under reform since much of the literature to date has placed heavy emphasis on the city's distinctive evolution before 1975, particularly under the government of South Vietnam from 1954 to 1975. If on closer inspection we find that, in spite of its distinctive history, Ho Chi Minh City's political economy has evolved in ways quite similar to the rest of the country, then this suggests that something else is exerting an influence on the way in which the city has evolved under reform. (This is not to suggest that the pre-1975 period has left no legacy at all, but it does imply that we need to think more carefully about what precisely that legacy is.)

In addition, one of the implications of this chapter is that there is a pressing need to reassess the impact of the legacy of the first ten years after liberation – that is, 1975–85 – on Ho Chi Minh City's contemporary development, notwithstanding the fact that this represents a shorter period under planning than some other parts of the country. The remainder of the chapter offers a few pointers about how the fact of Ho Chi Minh City's distinctive history might be married with the reality of its undistinctive evolution under reform.

In thinking about the legacy of 1954–75 for Ho Chi Minh City's present-day political economy, it is important not to parody the former Saigon regime as a bastion of 'freewheeling capitalism' where the state rarely gets a look. After all, this was the era of state capitalism, where state regulation of the market was considerable and where state officials, including the military, were just as likely to be active in business as they are now.[12]

While many accounts emphasize the persistence of markets in Ho Chi Minh City after 1975, it is easy to underestimate the scale of the rupture that occurred with the Communist victory. The flight of both capital and people in the dying days of the old regime, and subsequently, is part of this rupture, not least that of the city's economically important ethnic Chinese population (Stern 1985; Khanh 1993; Unger 1987/8). However, the sense of disruption is also evident in other areas, such as re-education, two surprise currency changes in 1975 and 1978, and the policy of de-urbanization, which saw people resettled in New Economic Zones (Tan 1983: 12–13; Forbes and Thrift 1987: 114–19, 121–6; Khanh 1993: 26–7; Thrift and Forbes 1986: 126; Dau 1998: 178).[13]

Developing the point just made, it is therefore necessary to be cautious about arguments that assert Ho Chi Minh City's distinctiveness with reference to a 'reassertion' of pre-1975 capital. A whole range of factors make such an eventuality unlikely, apocryphal stories of business people recovering hidden gold from their garden aside.[14] These include complications associated with capital returning (witness the problems with *Viet Kieu* (overseas Vietnamese) business people seeking to invest during the 1990s); the continued cautiousness of the ethnic Chinese community in Ho Chi Minh City;[15] a tendency for those who underwent re-education not to be best placed politically to make a big impression in business; and simply the fact that by the 1990s many of those with pre-1975 business experience were no longer so young or at the peak of their careers. In the 1990s, a number of people in state business or in the banking sector in Ho Chi Minh City were said to have pre-1975 experience.[16] However, such people were not especially common and they tended to have been clearly aligned with the Communists before 1975. In this respect, they hardly represent the reassertion of pre-1975 capital as commonly imagined.

It is important also not to underestimate the legacy of planning for Ho Chi Minh City just because the period spent under planning was relatively short. In the aftermath of its defeat, the former Saigon witnessed a considerable investment of time and resources in the city – a latter-day 'march south' – during which northern officials and administrators were dispatched to Ho Chi Minh City and the surrounding countryside in order to construct and run the institutions of planning.[17] The period was long enough for careers to be made in the bureaucracy and quite long enough for the politics of bureaucratic socialism to take root in the city (Porter 1990, 1993). The depiction of Ho Chi Minh City's bureaucracy earlier in the chapter would seem to support this position.

Finally, we should not forget who has actually run Ho Chi Minh City since 1975. Most accounts hold great store by the 'southern' credentials of the city's leadership, suggesting that this somehow explains their 'reformist' outlook. While the southern origins of Ho Chi Minh City's leadership is indisputable, placing all the emphasis on this underestimates the extent to which the city's leaders are also members of a hierarchical Communist movement in which democratic centralism (i.e. the formal requirement that party bodies defer to the organization above them in the hierarchy) still counts for something, notwithstanding increased decentralization under reform.

Former city leaders such as Truong Tan Sang (People's Committee chairman 1992–96 and party secretary 1996–2000) and Vo Viet Thanh (People's Committee chairman 1996–2001) cut their teeth in this movement as young men. During the war, Sang was in the Youth Union and Thanh in military intelligence. During the 1960s and 1970s, when infiltration and betrayal by the enemy were part of everyday reality, the importance of Leninist discipline and loyalty was instilled into them. Their successors – for example, Nguyen Minh Triet (party secretary 2000–06), and Le Thanh Hai (People's Committee chairman 2001–06) – were similarly 'of the system' with origins respectively as a youth union organizer in the south during the war and in the Youth Volunteer Force. Moreover, since the end of the war, these leaders have successfully negotiated their rise up the party hierarchy – notably Triet, who was appointed Vietnam's president in 2006. To do this, central connections are important even for those pursuing a career in the geographically limited area of Ho Chi Minh City.

Former Ho Chi Minh City leaders Sang and Thanh also had good central connections at one time or another. Sang was variously reputed to be a protégé of former prime minister Vo Van Kiet or former party general secretary Do Muoi, while Thanh was a protégé of former interior minister Mai Chi Tho whose career he closely shadowed for a period. In 1989 Sang studied at the Nguyen Ai Quoc Institute in Hanoi (now the Ho Chi Minh Political Academy), an appointment commonly reserved for up-and-coming party leaders. He became a member of the party Central Committee in 1991 and a member of the Politburo in 1996. In 2003, Sang was reprimanded by the party Central Committee for failing to take 'appropriate action' to prevent the criminal activities of a notorious Ho Chi Minh City underworld boss, Truong Van Cam (alias Nam Cam), who was sentenced to death following a high-profile trial. The unstated implication was that senior politicians in the city had turned a blind eye to Cam's activities. Thanh is a former deputy interior minister and one-time Central Committee member.[18] Triet is a former provincial party secretary and member of the Politburo. Hai became a member of the Central Committee in 2001. In sum, therefore, the freedom for manoeuvre of politicians in Ho Chi Minh City is more circumscribed by the need to cultivate one's position at the centre than is sometimes suggested. This, once again, casts doubt on the tendency to depict Ho Chi Minh City, and those who led it, as simply blazing an alternative path.

3

CORRUPTION

For many elite and ordinary Vietnamese, foreign scholars and development practitioners, the reform years in Vietnam are to be associated – unquestionably – with an increase in corruption. However, what constitutes corruption, and in turn deciding what (or whether it) has actually increased, is less straightforward than is commonly thought. We live in an age which tries to assert that what constitutes corruption is a universal – that it is the same the world over – when there is plenty of evidence that this is not the case (Chibnall and Saunders 1977; Gorta and Forell 1995; Rivkin-Fish 2005). Meanwhile, to assert uncritically that 'corruption', understood with reference to some kind of 'objective' measure, is increasing fails to take account of both the domestic and the global political reasons, which may lead us to believe that this is the case even if the objective reality is somewhat different. Such problems are compounded – conveniently or otherwise – by the fact that by its very nature measuring corruption is fraught with difficulty.

This chapter addresses these issues through a study of a major corruption case – the so-called Tamexco case – prosecuted in southern Vietnam in 1997. Tamexco was one of a number of high-profile corruption cases that took place towards the end of the 1990s in which party and state officials, including bankers and businessmen, were tried in court on charges of alleged corruption. In nearly all such cases, the outcome was the same: the accused were found guilty, with the alleged ringleaders usually sentenced to death or given lengthy prison terms. The prosecution of big corruption cases like Tamexco has continued to be a feature of Vietnamese politics to the present day.[1]

In studying these cases, two factors stand out. First, there is the seeming frequency with which they occur in both the north and the south of Vietnam and especially from the second half of the 1990s. No sooner had one case finished than another was getting under way. As one case was going to court, another was breaking. Moreover, a survey of the secondary literature, and a look at some primary sources, suggests that there is no equivalent episode for the 1980s.[2] Part of the reason for this may lie in the fact that the party's way of responding to corruption within its ranks has changed. In the past, disciplining errant party members was the responsibility of a designated party institution, and dealt with as an internal party matter. Thus, the practice today of using the courts in a very public manner is new. However, this does not entirely explain the increase in such cases, since it appears that they became more common over the course of the 1990s. Furthermore, the use of the courts to prosecute these cases itself raises interesting questions in terms of how we understand the concept of 'rule of law'. Second, there is the ferocity with which the cases were executed: the painstaking nature of the investigation process, its regurgitation in intricate detail in the media, and the often lengthy court proceedings. These also beg explanation.

So how do we understand the phenomenon of big corruption cases? To view such cases simply as the state getting tough on corruption, as much of the journalistic and practitioner literature does, seems simplistic. Moreover, why did big corruption cases become more common during the 1990s and why does the state devote so much effort and so many resources to prosecuting such cases?

In an attempt to answer these questions and to shed light on some of the other issues raised, the chapter first briefly reviews some of the most pertinent literature on corruption. It then offers an alternative way in which we might understand the phenomenon of big corruption cases, arguing that they are best viewed as an attempt by the political centre to discipline the lower levels of the party-state in a climate of increased decentralization. To set this interpretation in context, the chapter will explore the logic of the reform years in terms of decentralization, but argue – against the tide of much of the literature – that while decentralization has occurred strong thrusts towards recentralization can also be observed in which the centre has sought to regain the initiative. The chapter will then seek to add flesh to the bones of this argument by looking in detail at the Tamexco case. The chapter will chart both Tamexco's rise and its fall, subdivided into investigation, trial and sentencing. A key question that will be considered is why Tamexco rather than another company found itself at the centre of a big corruption case – particularly since a common refrain at the time was that what Tamexco was being prosecuted for was not very different from what many other companies were engaged in. Answers to these questions have the potential to shed important light on the character of the Vietnamese state.

Although Tamexco was a Ho Chi Minh City-based company, the argument being advanced here is not first and foremost about Ho Chi Minh City. That is, recentralization, or moves by the centre to regain the initiative in relation to the lower levels, is a nationwide phenomenon. It is possible to argue that Ho Chi Minh City represents a particularly extreme case where recentralization is needed. However, this is not what is being suggested here.

The literature on corruption

The reform years have spawned a large literature on corruption. Its principal focus has been fourfold. It has sought to document the *changing nature* of corruption. It has looked at the *causes* of corruption. It has considered the *consequences* of corruption for political stability and economic development, and it has focused on finding *solutions* to the perceived problem. In terms of the nature of corruption, some commentators have referred – somewhat blandly – to the existence of administrative, political and judicial corruption in Vietnam (Anti-Corruption Resource Centre 2008). Others have made a distinction between public-sector and private-sector corruption. Others still have referred to petty and grand corruption, with the former tending to be understood as small-scale, everyday corruption, and the latter being larger scale and involving high-level officials either directly or by providing protection (UNDP 2008). It is grand corruption which is the focus of this chapter.

Thaveeporn Vasavakul (2008) has argued that during the reform period corruption has occurred in one of three ways, namely grease or speed money, the illegal privatization of state property, and the selling of state power. Grease or speed money refers to state officials offering a faster or better service to citizens or other officials who approach them for services in exchange for payment. The illegal privatization of state property refers to public officials exploiting their position for private gain through fraud, embezzlement, extortion, smuggling or illegal tax collections. The selling of state power involves the acceptance of bribes in relation to recruitment or promotion in respect of public office. The sale of state power, Vasavakul says, can also involve the sale of services normally carried out by public officials to private individuals, including organized crime. Meanwhile, other commentators have highlighted the rather predictable nature of corruption in Vietnam: that is, people know what the 'going rate' is – for example, to secure a public position or a construction tender (Salomon 2008).

In terms of the causes of corruption, most accounts posit a link with 'reform', whether this is understood to be insufficient reform, such as perceived regulatory loopholes resulting from the transition from plan to market, decentralization, poor implementation of the country's laws and related regulations, or a decline in ethical standards on the part of officials (Anti-Corruption Resource Centre 2008; Central Committee of Internal Affairs 2005; Davidson et al. 2008; Fritzen 2005). Others see corruption as a consequence of low salaries, a legacy of the state subsidy period, notably what is referred to as the ask–give (*xin cho*) mechanism, or dangerously close political–business relations (Beresford 2008; Government of Vietnam 2008; Transparency International 2006). A report published by UNDP in 2009 suggested that corruption needs to be understood as a systemic problem – that is, not as an aberration of the system but as how the system actually is. Here, the emphasis is first and foremost placed on the strong connection in people's minds in Vietnam between public office and moneymaking (Gainsborough et al. 2009).

In terms of suggested solutions, these tend to flow from the analysis of causes. Thus, if low salaries are seen as the problem, the suggestion is that they need to be increased. If corruption is viewed as the result of poor implementation of the country's laws, these need to be tightened up, and so on. The reality is that few of the interventions pursued since the 1990s have had much impact on behaviour (Anti-Corruption Resource Centre 2008; Central Committee of Internal Affairs 2005; Malesky 2008a; McKinley 2009).

In terms of the issue under scrutiny here, namely how we understand the phenomenon of big corruption cases, the scholarly literature seems to have much less to say, notwithstanding the attention afforded to such cases in the press. Moreover, in media coverage of big corruption cases, the response of the state in staging these cases is simply taken at face value, namely that they are viewed as an attempt by the state to crack down on corruption. The problem with such interpretations is that they seem to depict the state as a neutral actor, clamping down on corruption in the public interest. The politics has been largely extracted out. Moreover, if we are suggesting that big corruption cases represent something much more political, could it not be that a desire to get tough on corruption is not the main motivating factor at all?

In order to offer a more nuanced understanding of big corruption cases, it is suggested here that it is necessary to situate them in a broader context, viewing them in terms of the political centre seeking to maintain control over the lower levels of the party-state in a climate of increased decentralization which has emerged during the reform years. This would seem to make sense of why big corruption cases have become more common since the 1990s as the strains of marketization on the polity's cohesion have become more intense. Moreover, with the centre increasingly fearful of losing control, such an approach also sheds light on why the central state acts with such ferocity and thoroughness in executing these cases. Furthermore, seeing corruption cases in terms of a struggle between different echelons of the state brings the politics back in, helping us to move away from the idea of the 'neutral state acting for the public good'. To opt for such a structural explanation is to recognize that, although the central state is acting in this way, it is not reducible to the conscious reflections of any single politician.

In order to situate this approach in its broader context, we now look at the issue of centralization and decentralization during the reform years.

Decentralization

The reform period, or more specifically the shift from plan to market, is commonly associated with decentralization. This can be understood in terms of the underlying logic of the central plan where planners needed to have control over resources in order to allocate them. This necessitated a certain level of political control. Moreover, from the perspective of the localities, restrictions on market activities meant that they were relatively dependent on the centre for the top-down allocation of resources (Gainsborough 2003a). Marketization has created a new logic. Local governments have been given new authority. This has included greater control over local expenditure, notably on infrastructure, and increased freedom to approve foreign investment projects. Indeed, provinces and cities have been positively encouraged to pursue their own comparative advantage. For isolated, resource-poor provinces, the changes have not necessarily been advantageous as the downward flow of resources from the centre has declined but has not been replaced by alterative income sources. However, for a resource-rich port city such as Ho Chi Minh City, its authority vis-à-vis the centre has been strengthened.

At a more micro-level, the new logic of the market is evident in the proliferation of business interests at the lower level of the party-state – as we saw in Chapter 2. Looked at in this way, it is important to note that decentralization has occurred not just between the centre and the provinces and cities but also within provinces and cities.

Recentralization

However, decentralization is not the only logic at work. Seeing its ability to control the lower levels under threat, the centre could also be seen trying to reassert control, notably from the 1990s. This sense of recentralization was evident in Ho Chi Minh City in the late 1990s, notably in five key areas: the growth of the central state bureaucracy; the importance of central protection; attempts to influence appointments; the establishment of local-level institutions with a strong central mandate; and periodic clampdowns on speculative activity. We now look at each in turn.

THE GROWTH OF THE CENTRAL STATE

First, as we saw in Chapter 2, the reform years have seen the growth – not decline – in the size of the state bureaucracy as measured by public-sector employment. Moreover, the expansion of the *central* bureaucracy – that is, central institutions with a presence in the city – has been much faster than local institutions in Ho Chi Minh City. The rate of expansion has been most acute in the area official statistics list as 'party and state administration' (i.e. regulatory and inspection bodies), which again seems to concur with the idea that more attention is being paid by the centre to maintaining control (General Statistics Office 2009). Furthermore, when a central institution carried out an inspection of a local institution in Ho Chi Minh City, the local institution sat up and took note even if it tended to behave errantly when the centre's back was turned.

CENTRAL UMBRELLAS

Second, a key concept in Vietnamese political culture is the idea of the umbrella (*o du*) whereby lower-level institutions or individuals receive backing or protection from those higher up the political chain. The continued authority of the centre despite decentralization also comes across in this area, with one informant in Ho Chi Minh City arguing that a central umbrella generally provides more protection than a local one.[3]

CONTROL OVER APPOINTMENTS

Third, the centre could also be seen trying to gain greater control over political appointments in Ho Chi Minh City during the 1990s. In 1992, an attempt was made to give the prime minister the power to appoint (*bo nhiem*) the People's Committee chairman in the city. The chairman had previously been elected at the local level (i.e. by the city People's Council). In the end, the motion was narrowly defeated in the National Assembly. However, the prime minister's powers were partially increased in that he was given the right to approve (*phe chuan*) the People's Council election and was able to dismiss (*mien nhiem*) the People's Committee chairman (Constitution of Vietnam 1995). Since the change the tendency has been for there to be long delays in confirming the appointment of the People's Committee chairman in Ho Chi Minh City, although it is unclear the extent to which this is the result of blocking tactics by the centre.[4]

Other changes involving appointments in the city can also be viewed in terms of a greater assertion of central power. Since the early 1990s, the Communist Party secretary in Ho Chi Minh City has also been a member of the Politburo. This was not previously the case. The change has usually been viewed as reflecting the growing authority of Ho Chi Minh City. However, it can equally be interpreted as representing greater central control with the top politician in the city 'locked into the centre' by virtue of his Politburo position.[5]

LOCAL INSTITUTIONS WITH CENTRAL MANDATES

Fourth, attempts by the centre to assert its authority in Ho Chi Minh City were evident in the 1990s via its efforts to establish local-level institutions with a strong central mandate. A good example is provided by the creation of the chief architect's office in 1993. Formed against the backdrop of rapid and often uncontrolled urbanization in Ho Chi Minh City, the chief architect's office was, in the words of one official, established to stop city institutions 'doing whatever they liked'.[6] That the chief architect's office was a central creation was evident from the fact that the head of the office (the chief architect) was appointed by the prime minister. In matters to do with urbanization, the chief architect's office also claimed elevated status in relation to the city-level departments and even in certain circumstances in relation to the People's Committee chairman. However, from the outset, its powers were hotly contested, leading to a protracted turf war between the chief architect's office, on the one hand, and the People's Committee chairman and the city's departments, on the other. During the late 1990s, they campaigned for the chief architect's powers to be reined in. However, these calls fell on deaf ears as the centre continued – successfully – to back the chief architect.[7]

CLAMPDOWNS ON SPECULATIVE ACTIVITY

Fifth, the centre's authority in the city could be seen in relation to periodic clampdowns on certain types of market activity, usually involving speculation. A good example occurred in February 1995 with the introduction of Decree 18, which clamped down on real-estate speculation, notably in Ho Chi Minh City. At the centre of such activity were state business interests linked to the city's departments and districts. Decree 18 stopped the speculators in their tracks by announcing that land-use rights – which had come to be regarded as de facto private property – had to be converted to land leases, which companies had to pay for. One journalist writing at the time described businesses as feeling they had been 'dispossessed of power' (*bu tuoc doat quyen loi*).[8] Banks, which hitherto had been accepting land-use rights as collateral for loans, in turn fuelling the speculation, stopped lending. That the momentum for the clampdown came from the centre was evident from the fact that it was launched with the issuing of a decree (which is a central instrument) but also because of who came out and defended it.[9] Moreover, in its aftermath, the city authorities campaigned for the key tenets of Decree 18 to be reversed. However, as with calls for the chief architect's powers to be reined in, the centre was not easily swayed.

The preceding section has suggested that despite decentralization the centre retains a high degree of authority. Nevertheless, the lower levels have increased their power during the reform years and the centre is being tested more than ever before. It is in this context that the big corruption cases should be viewed: rising in number as the pressures of decentralization increase with marketization, and being executed with increasing ruthlessness, reflecting the centre's growing concern that it is in danger of losing control.

In an attempt to shed more light on these issues, the chapter now turns to look at the Tamexco corruption case. The Tamexco case, named after the company around which the case revolved, first came to light in Ho Chi Minh City in 1996. It went to court in early 1997 concluding with the execution of three businessmen a year later.

Tamexco's rise

Tamexco, or the Tan Binh Production Service Trading and Export Company as it is known in full, is a general trading company formed in 1989. It was nominally a state company founded by interests connected to the party committee in Ho Chi Minh City's Tan Binh district. In 1993, Tamexco was formally brought under the authority of the city Party Committee as part of a more general change affecting district companies. However, informants have suggested that Tan Binh district remained the dominant influence in Tamexco despite the change. This included people of solid political stock, notably two women: Truong My Hoa, who was party secretary in Tan Binh district 1986–91, and her deputy Le Thi Van, who in line with common practice was also People's Committee chairman in the district. Truong My Hoa has an exemplary war record. Destined for a career at the centre, Hoa became a Central Committee member in 1991, eventually rising to be Vietnam's vice president. Her deputy, Le Thi Van, never achieved such heights but rose to be deputy chairman of the People's Committee in Ho Chi Minh City in 1994. Tamexco's director was Pham Huy Phuoc. He was born in the Mekong Delta province of Tra Vinh in 1955.

Tamexco expanded rapidly. An advertisement for the company in 1991 described it as being involved in import–export, real estate and tourism. Products commonly imported by Tamexco included fertilizer, construction material and cars. Tamexco was also an exporter of seafood. Figures for 1992 show it recording an increase in import–export turnover of 60 per cent year on year, contributing 18.6 billion dong to the state budget and achieving after-tax profits of 7 billion dong.[10] In the same year, and reflecting a common trend at the time, Tamexco set up Tan Viet joint stock commercial bank, better known as Tacombank, becoming its leading shareholder. Phuoc was made chairman of the bank's management board (*hoi dong quan tri*).[11] Moreover, Phuoc was in demand elsewhere, serving as the deputy chairman of a Japanese–Vietnamese joint venture company, Neetaco. Tamexco's business interests did not stop there. An article in *Thoi Bao Kinh te Saigon* (*Saigon Economic Times*) in 1994 singled out Tamexco alongside seven other up-and-coming companies, saying it had 'good prospects of becoming a future business group' (*co nhieu trien vong chuyen sang tap doan tuong lai*). Apart from linking Tamexco up with Tacombank, the article also listed Cosimex and the Tan Binh Investment and Development Company (*Cong ty Dau tu va Phat trien Tan Binh*) as belonging to its group.[12]

Tamexco's fall

That Tamexco was at the centre of an emerging corruption case first became evident in 1996. An article in the English-language *Vietnam Investment Review* reported that Tamexco director Pham Huy Phuoc had been arrested in 'March/April' on charges of corruption in connection with losses at Tamexco estimated to be in the region of 350 billion dong (US$25 million).[13] According to the article, news of Phuoc's arrest prompted a run on Tacombank.

INVESTIGATION

Over the next few months, the investigation into the events at Tamexco, led by the Ho Chi Minh City police investigation authority (*Co quan can sat dieu tra cong an thanh pho Ho Chi Minh*), gathered momentum. Among the main parties in the case, Phuoc and the director of a limited company called Dolphin which had worked closely with Tamexco, Le Minh Hai, were charged with 'corruption involving socialist assets' (*tham o tai san xa hoi chu nghia*), 'offering bribes' (*dua hoi lo*), 'intentionally contravening state regulations causing serious consequences' (*co y lam trai qui dinh cua Nha nuoc ve quan ly kinh te gay hau qua nghiem trong*) and 'gambling' (*danh bac*). Hai had reportedly been instrumental in bribing the head of Notary Office No. 1 in Ba Ria-Vung Tau, Le Duc Canh, to verify artificially inflated land values. This enabled Tamexco to increase its bank borrowing. Canh, in turn, was charged with 'taking bribes' (*nhan hoi lo*) and for 'exploiting his public position for private gain' (*loi dung chuc vu quyen han trong khi thi hang cong vu*). Another prominent figure in the case, Tran Quang Vinh, who was the director of a limited company called Binh Gia which had also collaborated with Tamexco, was accused of corruption and intentionally contravening state regulations.

On 8 October 1996 the net was cast wider with three senior bankers charged with 'intentionally contravening state regulations' for continuing to lend to Tamexco despite its debts. This included Nguyen Duy Lo, the deputy general director at the state-owned Vietcombank; Nguyen Van De, a general director at Vietcombank and management board chairman of the joint-venture bank First Vinabank; and Tran Linh, who had headed Vietcombank's branch in Vung Tau and who was also the deputy general director at First Vinabank. Vietcombank was the main Vietnamese shareholder in First Vinabank. On 26 November, another senior Vietcombank banker, Nguyen Manh Thuy, was charged with the same crime of 'intentionally contravening state regulations'. The levelling of the charge against Thuy brought to twenty the total number of people facing charges.[14]

During the investigation, steps were also taken to remove from office serving politicians implicated in the case before their involvement became widely known. In late May, just a few weeks after the problems at Tamexco first came to light, *Sai Gon Giai Phong* (*Liberated Saigon*) reported personnel changes in Tan Binh district, including the departure of the People's Committee chairman and deputy party secretary in the district, Pham Van Hoa. Hoa, who had succeeded Le Thi Van when she had become deputy People's Committee chairman in 1994, was later questioned when the case came before the Court of Appeal. He was also censured in June 1997 along with six other city and district officials by the Standing Committee of the Ho Chi Minh City party for 'being connected to the [Tamexco] case' (*co lien quan den vu an*). Back in May 1996, *Sai Gon Giai Phong* described Hoa as going to a different job (*di cong tac khac*). However the new job never materialized.[15]

Another politician who left office as the case against Tamexco was being prepared was Le Thi Van herself. She resigned as deputy People's Committee chairman in August 1996, reportedly on 'health grounds'. Like Hoa, she was summoned to appear at the appeal court and was also later censured by the city party Standing Committee.[16]

The investigation was accompanied by extensive media coverage of the case. During the early stages of the investigation, press coverage was light. However, as the investigation proceeded through October and November, newspaper articles appeared with greater frequency. There seemed to be very little of a sense in the coverage of the precept 'innocent until proven guilty', or of concern among officials that such coverage could prejudice the accused receiving a fair trial. On 29 October, even before the investigation was complete, the deputy head of the People's Court of Investigation, Dang Cong Tam told journalists categorically that Phuoc had bribed thirty-eight or thirty-nine organizations but that his main crime was corruption involving over 20 billion dong.[17]

On 12 December, the People's Court of Investigation in Ho Chi Minh City (*Vien kiem sat Nhan Dan TPHCM*) transferred the Tamexco file to the People's Court in Ho Chi Minh City (*Toa an Nhan Dan TPHCM*). This marked the formal end of the investigation stage. At the same time, the People's Court announced that the plan was to 'settle the case' by the end of January.

TRIAL

The case came to court on 23 January 1997. Compared with other cases, it was a relatively short affair, lasting just nine days until 31 January. It took place in an environment of widespread public and media interest. Large crowds, including family members of the accused and other onlookers, gathered daily outside the courtroom to catch a glimpse of those in the dock. The media barrage also continued, with daily coverage in the press and on television.

The trial itself included the release of a fair amount of salacious detail about Phuoc's alleged playboy lifestyle. Phuoc was said to have personally embezzled 144 billion dong, spending money on lavish foreign trips and gambling. In one case, Phuoc was said to have

gambled away five of Tamexco's cars in a card game. He was reputed
to have given gold to his mistress to buy a luxury villa in Ho Chi
Minh City worth over US$200,000. The attention of the court was
also drawn to the fact that Tamexco operated different accounting
books – something Phuoc was said to have personally ordered his
chief accountant, Ngo Van Ho, to do. The manner in which Phuoc
bought shares in Tacombank using Tamexco money and registering
the shares in the names of his relatives was also scrutinized.[18]

Rather revealing in terms of the actual web of responsibility
which surrounded Tamexco's activities was the questioning in court
of former Vietcombank deputy general director Nguyen Duy Lo.
While the official purpose of the cross-examination appeared to
be to shift the burden of guilt onto the bankers, the episode also
highlighted the involvement of other institutions, including the city
party committee, in ensuring Tamexco's access to bank credit. Lo
was asked to explain why Vietcombank had continued lending to
Tamexco despite its debts:

COURT 'By December 1992, Tamexco's total debt at Vietcombank
was $15.6m, wasn't it?'

MR LO 'It was only $10m.'

COURT 'Why, then, did you continue to lend a further $3m?'

MR LO 'At this stage, we did not want to lend but because Tamexco
was a fertilizer importer – importing fertilizer for the winter–spring
harvest – this was a duty entrusted to us by the office of the
government.'

COURT 'Why did they not entrust it to a company which could do
business profitably?'

MR LO 'The court ought to ask this question to the Ministries of
Agriculture and Trade; why did they give [fertilizer import] quotas
to Tamexco?'

When Lo was pressed further as to whether he was aware that
lending to Tamexco, given the circumstances of its debts, contravened

bank regulations (*sai so voi phap luat ngan hang*), he said that lending to the company was guided by Document 8 (*van ban 08*), issued on 8 April 1991. Document 8 apparently permitted certain bank clients to borrow beyond the normal ceiling set at 10 per cent of a bank's legal capital for a single client. According to Lo, it was the result of collaboration between different institutions in Ho Chi Minh City, including the local party committee:

> Document 8 was signed by [deputy State Bank governor] Chu Van Nguyen, and was the result of a collaboration between the State Bank and the Standing Committee of the Ho Chi Minh City party committee. It had the ability to overcome obstacles [*no co gia tri thao go*].[19]

Lo did not say who had signed for the party and to this day it remains something of a mystery.[20] According to the prosecution, Document 8 had been superseded by new regulations issued twenty-eight days later by the then State Bank governor, Cao Sy Kiem. Called to give evidence, State Bank governor Chu Van Nguyen said that Vietcombank Ho Chi Minh City must have known about this. Lo, however, said that Document 8 continued to apply in Ho Chi Minh City even after the new regulations were issued.

SENTENCING

At the end of the trial, the court handed out four death sentences to Phuoc, Hai, Vinh and Canh. The other sixteen accused all received prison terms ranging from three years to life. Of the bankers, Lo and Linh were jailed for fifteen years while De and Thuy received four- and three-year prison terms respectively. Le Thi Van and Pham Van Hoa were not convicted of anything. Truong My Hoa, who had served as party secretary in Tan Binh district during the late 1980s and early 1990s, was never publicly associated with the case.[21] On 7 January 1998, eight months after their appeals had been turned down, Phuoc, Vinh and Canh were executed by firing squad. The fourth man sentenced to death, Le Minh Hai, had his sentence commuted to life imprisonment, on account of his father's heroic war service.[22] On 20 April 1999 Tamexco was declared bankrupt.[23]

Why did Tamexco fall?

Tamexco's fall caused a sensation. After all it was not just any company. It was a jewel in its time: a privileged, politically connected firm which expanded rapidly during the early 1990s. Moreover, those who ran it were nothing less than members of the elite. So why did Tamexco fall?

In official accounts, the Tamexco case is usually depicted simply as the state getting tough on corruption. As the Tamexco trial got under way in January 1997, the Politburo member and then National Assembly chairman (now party general secretary) Nong Duc Manh was quoted as saying that only by rooting out corruption could people's declining confidence in the state and the government be restored. Echoing this interpretation, one foreign news report described the trial as a 'showcase for the government's determination to punish graft'.[24] However, this type of explanation does not adequately explain why Tamexco and the people associated with it were brought down. After all, much of the behaviour on which the trials centred was fairly widespread: political involvement in credit allocations, for example; lending to companies even if they are in debt; operating multiple books or buying shares in the name of relatives. Others have sought to explain Tamexco's fall with reference to the fact that it ran up large debts.[25] However, the existence of extensive debts is not in itself a satisfactory explanation since many companies have debts.

One possible explanation for Tamexco's fall is that it was linked to high-level political manoeuvring. Certainly there were rumours to this effect, with the suggestion being that Tamexco was a casualty of the fall of Politburo member Nguyen Ha Phan prior to the Eighth National Party Congress in 1996. The official foreign ministry statement at the time of his expulsion from the party said that Phan had been expelled for 'abuse of power, authoritarianism and fanaticism'. In an explanation which was never very convincing, the statement said that documents had recently come to light implicating him in the revelation of the names of comrades and locations of bases during the war after he had been arrested by the South Vietnamese government in 1959. According to accounts linking Tamexco with Phan's fall, Tamexco director Pham Huy Phuoc was reportedly 'close' to Phan, who wanted to promote him to a higher position. However, when Phan was brought down in pre-Congress manoeuvring, Phuoc lost his umbrella and hence became vulnerable himself.[26] Prior to his fall, Phan was head of the central party's Economic Committee (*Ban kinh te trung uong dang*). One informant said that given Phan's position, he was certainly the right person for Phuoc to know if he wanted promotion.[27]

Although superficially attractive, the theory also has some inconsistencies. Phan's downfall was sealed at the 10th Plenum of the Central Party Committee held on 12–20 April 1996. Accounts of Phuoc's arrest are rather vague. However, some suggest he may have been arrested in March shortly before Phan's fall at the 10th Plenum. An article in August 1996 said that Tamexco had been under official investigation since October 1995. If these assertions are correct, it would make a direct link between Tamexco and Phan less likely. Moreover, if such high-level connections did exist, they did not come to light in either the investigation or the trial.

Nevertheless, the idea that there was more to the case than meets the eye persisted to the end. Some of the newspaper headlines were tantalisingly provocative in this respect. 'Who stands behind Tamexco?' (*Ai dung sau lung Tamexco?*) one article was headlined, although it offered no fresh insights. At the end of the Tamexco trial, the prosecutor, Tran Kim Tien, said that those still hiding in the shadows would be exposed (*toi tin chac rang nhung bong den con la se duoc dua ra anh sang*).[28] In the event, a few more people were called to give evidence at the Court of Appeal but there were no major revelations. Asked why the likes of Phuoc did not blow the whistle in court given the certain knowledge that they were going to be sentenced to death, one informant said that to do so would ruin what little chance their families and children had for a future.[29]

GATHERING MOMENTUM

While it is difficult to pinpoint precisely why the case against Tamexco developed, it is possible to map the contours of the process, particularly a sense of gathering momentum during the investigation stage. When news of the alleged misdemeanours at Tamexco first broke, it was as if it was genuinely not clear – from the point of view of the investigators or, more importantly, their political masters higher up – how much was going to be made of the case, the nature of the charges, how wide the net was to be cast and so on. This initial caution is reflected in the fairly muted initial press coverage. However, events soon developed their own momentum. The charging of the bankers on 8 October 1996 clearly signalled a new stage. The removal from political office of those implicated before their involvement became widely known also strongly gave the impression of people readying themselves for a wider storm. Intensified press coverage carried with it a sense that a point of no return had been reached. Echoing this interpretation, one informant described how initially the aim was to keep the Tamexco case fairly low key; as the case started to attract attention this was not possible and the Politburo felt a need to make an example of it.[30]

PROVING GUILT

Once a decision had been made to make an example of the accused, the investigation process then became an exercise in assembling the necessary evidence to prove their guilt, rather than a search for the truth. Moreover, the trial was simply the culmination of that process with the outcome never really in doubt. It was in this context that the press coverage – creating the impression of guilt – was important. Thus, as was evident from the remarks of Ho Chi Minh City residents, by the time the sentences were announced the public was widely convinced of the guilt of the accused. The fact that the media coverage may have painted a distorted picture was not so important. In the case of Phuoc and the bankers there was a distinct discrepancy between the media picture and that offered by knowledgeable informants who had insights which went beyond those published in the press in the months after their arrest. One source described Phuoc as 'good businessman' but said that responsibility – in terms of who was responsible when things went wrong – was not clear. The four bankers imprisoned in the Tamexco case were previously highly respected, referred to as the 'four pillars' (*tu tru*) in recognition of their role in overseeing Vietcombank's transition from monobanking to a two-tier banking system. The same source described Vietcombank's Nguyen Duy Lo as a 'victim', saying he took responsibility but that it was not he who signed Document 8.[31]

Conclusion

While there is much that remains hidden in relation to Tamexco, what is clear is that the company's director Pham Huy Phuoc once enjoyed close relations with politicians in Ho Chi Minh City and probably at the centre too. For reasons about which we can only speculate, a severing of these relations occurred some time in 1995 or 1996. What happened next is clearer. The businessmen and bankers connected with Tamexco were taken to court, and either sentenced to death or given prison terms. The city- and district-level politicians were censured but were not imprisoned. Meanwhile, no central-level politician was ever publicly implicated in the case. In terms of a reflection of the dominant hierarchy of power, this is revealing.

Putting aside the case's more opaque details, it has been argued that big corruption cases are best understood as an attempt by the political centre to discipline the lower levels of the party-state against a backdrop of increased decentralization as a consequence of marketization. Such an interpretation, it is argued, makes sense both of the increased frequency with which big corruption cases have occurred since the 1990s and also the ferocity with which they have been executed. It also represents a more authentically political account in so far as the centre is no longer seen as simply clamping down on corruption 'in the public interest' but rather is seen as representing one side in a struggle for influence between different levels of the state, where the prize is control over economic resources. Moreover, the successful prosecution of Tamexco and other big corruption cases, along with the centre's assertion of its authority in a number of others areas, as outlined in the chapter, suggests that the centre is not a spent force even if it is facing new challenges to its authority.

The argument put forward here also sheds light on another issue, namely how we understand the 'rule of law'. Prosecution of big corruption cases through the courts might be read as representing a positive development as the party, once regarded as being 'above the law', is now seen as willing to subject the disciplining of its own ranks to due process. However, given the emphasis of this chapter, more convincing is the idea that the 'rule of law' is in fact 'rule by law' – that is, utilizing law selectively to pursue the interests of one particular arm of the state, in this case the centre.[32]

4

HOLLOWING OUT THE STATE

Vietnam's partial privatization programme, known locally as equitization (*co phan hoa*), is a central plank of the government's approach to what is conventionally called state enterprise reform. An analysis of equitization is a useful way of probing the nature of Vietnam's emerging political economy. It is also helpful in further unpacking the character of so-called 'reform' in Vietnam. This chapter looks at equitization as it developed in the early 2000s. Underlining its importance as a rich area of investigation, equitization also provides the focus for Chapter 5 but there the spotlight is more on the insights equitization provides in relation to the use of uncertainty as an instrument of rule.

The main puzzle about equitization dealt with in this chapter concerns why, after proceeding so slowly for the first six years of the programme's existence, it suddenly accelerated, at least in terms of the numbers of enterprises formally completing equitization procedures. While there are many possible reasons, a key factor in the slow progress was an unwillingness on the part of the political and business interests associated with state enterprises to do anything that would remove them from what they regarded as the 'best space' for doing business.[1] During the period 1992–98, the majority of state enterprises calculated that this remained the state sector; however, a few years later this calculation had changed and hence equitization speeded up. The analysis sets out what led to the change in thinking, emphasizing a mixture of policy and non-policy developments. By way of supporting evidence, the chapter also presents new data which highlight the increasingly hard nature of the budget and credit constraint faced by provincial companies remaining in the state sector in 2001–02.

By pursuing equitization, Vietnam is very much associated with the gradualist approach to 'reform' – like China. Thus – as with China – there is much uncertainty in relation to exactly what equitization will produce in terms of the nature of the 'reformed' enterprise sector: in other words, equitization is no guarantee of enhanced dynamism or efficiency. This issue is addressed in the second part of the chapter when data on the performance of equitized enterprises are considered. The analysis also considers the likely prospects of equitized enterprises in Vietnam, comparing the manner of equitization in that country with World Bank conclusions on what worked and did not work in the former Soviet Union and Eastern Europe in the area of enterprise reform. The exercise is useful in highlighting areas of likely weakness in relation to Vietnam's equitized companies. Issues to do with enterprise performance are also developed in Chapter 5.

Why did equitization initially proceed so slowly before speeding up?

In the period from the launch of the government's equitization programme in 1992 until February 1998, just seventeen state enterprises completed equitization formalities (Webster and Amin 1998). Equitization picked up momentum in 1999 and 2000 so that by September 2001 some 700 state enterprises had reportedly completed equitization proceedings (World Bank 2000). However, even by that date, equitization had involved just 12 per cent of companies by number and just 2 per cent in terms of capital, highlighting the way in which it has so far mainly involved small and medium enterprises.[2]

The literature on Vietnam offers many reasons why equitization proceeded slowly in the period 1992–98. The most common include: reluctance on the part of enterprise managers concerned at losing privileges associated with being in the state sector; fear on the part of enterprise managers that asset-stripping or other corrupt practices would be uncovered if the books were scrutinized for the purposes of equitization; fear of enterprise workers about losing their jobs if the company underwent restructuring after equitization; the absence of tried and tested administrative procedures relating to equitization; and difficulties in valuing enterprise assets (for a review, see Freeman 1996).

There is probably an element of truth in all of this. However, much of the time, the reasons that are most commonly emphasized – such as unclear administrative procedures, difficulties in valuing enterprise assets, or opposition from workers – represent a distraction from more fundamental obstacles. Moreover, most explanations are simply too vague for it to be clear where the key obstacle or point of conflict is occurring. While opposition from workers was sometimes a genuine cause of delay, this was often put forward by company managers, their controlling institution, or both, to conceal or lend respectability to their own particular reasons for opposing equitization. For most of the 1990s, such opposition derived from the view that the state sector still represented the best place to be located in order to do business successfully. This in turn was linked to the belief that remaining in the state sector afforded a company the best chance of receiving state budget support, accessing other forms of protection, or avoiding the discrimination faced by private companies in obtaining bank credit, land use rights, licences or contracts.

The sources of opposition to equitization during the 1990s varied from one enterprise to another. In some cases, it involved enterprise managers-cum-owners; in other cases, where managers were merely political appointees, opposition could be seen coming from the bureaucratic institutions with authority over the enterprise (Gainsborough 2002).

The explanation favoured here for why equitization moved forward so slowly until the final years of the 1990s implies that difficulties relating to valuing enterprise assets or unclear administrative procedures could be overcome if there was the will. This is rather confirmed by the fact that seventeen companies did complete equitization proceedings before early 1998. That some enterprises did equitize underlines the fact that, while equitization was alarming for some companies, for others it represented an opportunity to clarify uncertain or ambiguous property rights, enabling them to do business with greater confidence. This, one suspects, lies behind the willingness of the Ho Chi Minh City-based company REE, along with some of the other early entrants, to equitize, although there is still much we do not know regarding their precise motives.

If equitization proceeded so slowly prior to 1998, what changed for it to accelerate thereafter? Part of the reason may be that many of the earlier bureaucratic obstacles had been overcome: procedures were simpler, incentives were clearer and there was now greater experience of the best way to go about valuing enterprise assets (World Bank 1999). There is certainly evidence that it took less time for the second batch of companies to complete equitization proceedings compared with the first (Webster and Amin 1998: 9). Moreover, it makes sense that, once companies started to equitize in larger numbers, the process developed a certain momentum as new entrants were able to draw on the experience of those that had gone before and draw reassurance from them.

However, these explanations are not sufficient on their own to explain why equitization accelerated. Returning to the issue cited above, namely that deciding whether to equitize or not involved a calculation on the part of the dominant interests associated with a given state enterprise on the best place for the enterprise to do business, then it is clear that by 1999–2000 the circumstances under-pinning this calculation had changed. This has to do with changes occurring in both state and private sectors, which exerted a 'push' factor and a 'pull' factor.

The push factor:
less hospitable conditions in the state sector

First, there is evidence that state control over enterprise assets began to be tightened in the second half of the 1990s. The passage of the State Enterprise Law, the creation of institutions such as the State Capital Management Department (*tong cuc quan ly tai san nha nuoc tai doanh nghiep*) under the Ministry of Finance, and the drive to establish general corporations (*tong cong ty*) from the mid-1990s, were part of this.[3] In a move that resembled the establishment of the *chaebol* in South Korea, the formation of the general corporations was designed to create economies of scale by grouping enterprises in a similar sector so that they could compete on the international stage. It also envisaged that capital could be moved around within the group to companies that needed it. However, the establish-ment of the general corporations created problems of its own, with member companies often finding the involvement of corporation management more trouble than it was worth (Gainsborough 2002; Cheshier and Penrose 2007). More rigorous state management of enterprise assets by the late 1990s also meant that the opportunities for asset-stripping had diminished, while the lesson drawn from major corruption cases such as Tamexco (see Chapter 3) or Minh Phung-Epco in 1997–99 was that there was now a greater danger of being penalized for such activities.

In addition, fiscal pressures associated with the Asian financial crisis of 1997–98 saw a tightening of access to budget subsidies or cheap bank credit for state enterprises, with the result that subsidies were now available for a much smaller core of companies. This tightening appears to have been sustained even after the immediate effects of the crisis subsided.

That conditions in the state sector were no longer so hospitable in terms of access to budget subsidies came across clearly in discussion of the state sector in both northern and southern Vietnam in the early 2000s. In the northern port city of Haiphong, for instance, where about a dozen companies had at this point been equitized, the state had 3,751 billion dong (US$245 million) tied up in the city's 211 remaining state enterprises in mid-2002, according to provincial statistics. This worked out at an average of just 33.7 billion dong (US$2.2 million) in centrally managed state enterprises and 7 billion dong (US$457,500) in locally managed companies. In many cases, companies had considerably less than this. Commenting on this situation, an article in the Haiphong newspaper noted that enterprises consequently had little scope to invest in or upgrade technology. Nevertheless, shedding light on the way in which enterprises were responding to harder budget constraints, the article said that companies were not just idle but rather had sought other sources of capital (*nguon von khac*):

> To talk in this way does not mean to imply that businesses are just waiting for state capital. In fact, there are a lot of companies which dare to think for themselves, dare to act on their own initiative and dare to borrow money from the bank in order to invest to upgrade technology, to expand production or produce new goods, and they get good results.[4]

A similar reliance on non-state sources of capital by state enterprises facing hard budget constraints was also evident in relation to the southern Can Tho province, where in June 2002 some fifty-six state enterprises and nine companies had completed equitization.[5] According to an article in the Can Tho newspaper, registered capital is 'just a legal calculation' and businesses actively utilize lots of different sources of business capital in order to operate (*su dung nang dong nhieu nguon von kinh doanh khac*).[6] If state enterprises could no longer rely on the state to provide them with capital and instead had to look elsewhere, it was a small next step for them to consider the possible benefits of equitization, particularly if the shift to hard budget constraints has occurred in tandem with a perceived improvement in the climate affecting the private sector.

The pull factor: improving the private-sector climate

The other side of the coin was that by 1999–2000 the climate for the private sector had improved, and was widely recognized to have done so. This represented the culmination of a whole series of changes introduced in the wake of the Asian financial crisis. Much has been made of the Enterprise Law (*luat doanh nghiep*) which came into effect in 2000, resulting (formally speaking at least) in the abolition of large amounts of red tape when setting up a private business. However, other changes, such as the ending of the ban on private companies exporting directly, and a gradual tempering of official hostility, were also important.

In the early 2000s, Vietnam's business environment was still not easy for any company regardless of ownership type. Moreover, discussions of the Enterprise Law in the provinces suggested that implementation of the law remained a problem as old regulations that contradicted it continued to be enforced.[7] However, it was reported in 1999 that non-state-sector industrial growth had eclipsed that of the state sector for the first time since the shift away from central planning. While these data were later revised, non-state-sector industrial growth has nevertheless continued to be significantly higher than state-sector growth every year since, bringing Vietnam in line with a trend that has been evident in China for some time (General Statistics Office 2009).

Moreover, it is no coincidence that the acceleration of equitization coincided with the shift to more rapid private-sector growth after 1999. Enterprise managers, the administrative organizations responsible for state enterprises (known as their 'controlling institutions'), and their labour forces all began to realize that, in the absence of budget subsidies and cheap bank credit and amid dwindling levels of protection, there were now few advantages to be had from remaining in the state sector.

At the same time, there were advantages to be had from not being in the state sector, such as the reduced danger of being accused of 'corruption involving socialist assets' (*tham o tai san xa hoi chu nghi*) and perhaps on balance the likelihood of less interference by state institutions with regulatory powers in the private sector compared with the state sector. (However, see Chapter 5 for the limits to this.)

With reference to the large state enterprises, including many associated with the general corporations which remained in the state sector, the fact that they were not all lining up for equitization can be explained largely by the fact that they had no choice. This is because in the early 2000s the government wanted to keep them in public hands. Moreover, being big and regarded as important, many of these companies were still eligible for benefits such as access to subsidies that were no longer available for their smaller counterparts, which were beginning to leave the state sector. [8]

Assessing the performance of equitized enterprises

Data on enterprises in Vietnam released soon after equitization generally pointed to improved performance, indicated by higher turnover, increased profitability, employment growth and higher wages (Webster and Amin 1998: 13). However, there is reason to treat such data suspiciously. First, all such data are provided by the companies themselves and released by the government; they were not independently scrutinized or reproduced via independent research. Second, some of the early data released covered a short time period following the completion of equitization procedures (often no more than a year). Third, of the companies that equitized first, all were profitable before equitization; most of these would probably have done well whether they remained in the state sector or not. Fourth, most of the data on enterprise performance were published, one suspects, in order to demonstrate the benefits of equitization to those enterprises unwilling to put themselves forward; this was especially the case during the mid-1990s, when equitization was moving forward very slowly. Fifth, the enterprises that equitized first were also small-scale, and privatization of small-scale enterprises has been generally successful all over the world (World Bank 2002). Furthermore, 'unscreened' data on the performance of provincial enterprises after equitization tended to reveal a more mixed picture. That is, while some companies did achieve better results, others were still struggling with debts and some saw business fall away (see Box 4.1).

BOX 4.1   Post-equitization performance in three provinces

TAY NINH

Cty co phan (CP) Khai Thac Khoang San Tay Ninh. In 2001 the company achieved turnover of over VND9 billion, which represents a threefold improvement on the period prior to equitization. Profits were VND1 billion, up eight times on pre-equitization.

Cty CP Cong trinh giao thong. Turnover in 2001 was VND40 billion, up 50 per cent on the period prior to equitization; profits were just under VND800 million, up 60 per cent on the pre-equitization period.

Cty CP Cap treo Nui Ba. Turnover in 2001 was VND12.3 billion, up 15 per cent on the period prior to equitization; profits were VND2.8bn, representing approximately a threefold increase.

Two equitized companies, *Cty CP Van tai and Cty CP Det bao bi*, encountered difficulties in 2001. Cty Van tai had the most problems, with turnover nearly half of what it was prior to equitization and profits roughly the same as previously (*dat xap xi truoc day*).

LAO CAI

Cty CP van tai Lao Cai. Completed equitization in July 1999. Since equitization turnover has begun to 'move in the direction of stability'. In 2001 the company had turnover of VND18 billion, remitted VND518 million in tax, and bought eight new vehicles and two boats and invested in building new factories. The average wage for the firm's 165 workers was VND524,000 per month.

Cty CP cong trinh giao thong. Completed equitization in September 2001. Since the beginning of 2002 the company has signed contracts worth VND10bn, including one for over VND4 billion with Lao Chau province relating to national route 4D. Turnover for the year is expected to be VND15 billion, double what was achieved before equitization. Average monthly wage is VND800,000 compared with VND100,000 before the company equitized.

Cty CP xay dung so 1 Lao Cai. Completed equitization in February 2002. Since the beginning of 2002 has signed twenty contracts with a value of VND6 billion. Turnover for the year expected to be VND12 billion.

CAN THO

According to the acting director *of So Ke hoach va Dau Tu tinh Can Tho*, Nguyen Van Duoc, some of the province's nine equitized companies are loss-making, with the province presently overseeing their consolidation (*tinh dang chi dao cung co*).

Source: Vietnamese media.

The manner of equitization: future implications

In the absence of more reliable performance data, it is helpful to look at other data – in this case gleaned from the Vietnamese press – concerning the manner in which equitization took place in Vietnam. This will be linked to lessons drawn from the privatization experience in the former Soviet Union and Eastern Europe in terms of what is believed to work or not work, and asking what, if any, are the implications for future enterprise performance in Vietnam. This will enable us to highlight potential problem areas, which are likely to have an impact on the performance of equitized enterprises in the future.

In its review of the lessons from the former Soviet Union and Eastern Europe, the World Bank (2002) identified a number of different criteria which, on the basis of experience up to that point, it judged to be important in determining the success or otherwise of privatization:

1. Privatization, it says, should be part of an overall strategy of discipline and encouragement.
2. Privatization in which enterprise assets are sold to 'insiders' (that is, enterprise managers and workers) or where post-privatization ownership is diffuse has generally not benefited enterprise restructuring and led to improved performance. Where privatization has worked best, the World Bank argues, is where assets have been sold to outsiders, notably foreigners, and where ownership is concentrated.
3. Enterprises sold through transparent tenders or auctions have generally attracted better owners, and have outperformed enterprises sold directly to politically connected parties, frequently at highly subsidized prices.
4. Where the state continues to hold a stake in a privatized company it is important to clarify the cash flow and property rights existing in the enterprise.

While some of the World Bank's conclusions are almost certainly self-serving – and they are certainly not the last word on the subject – the chapter examines each point in turn in relation to equitization in Vietnam as it was emerging in the early 2000s.

Discipline and encouragement

Discipline refers to such things as hard budget constraints, market competition, and the application of commercial rather than political criteria in bank lending. Encouragement refers to an appropriate regulatory and fiscal regime, security of property rights and opportunities to obtain business finance via the banking system or the stock market. Available evidence would suggest that Vietnam performed badly in many of these areas in the early 2000s, with many problems persisting to this day. The existence of monopolies or oligopolies in key sectors, large amounts of red tape, an unpredictable and often arbitrary tax system, and a poorly developed financial sector are all characteristics of Vietnam's business environment.

However, the climate is not all bad. As was indicated, budget constraints affecting provincial state enterprises were by the early 2000s quite hard in Haiphong and Can Tho. Moreover, data on property rights in Ho Chi Minh City suggest that, despite the absence of a law-governed framework upholding the security of property rights, they were secure enough, thanks to informal arrangements, to enable the emergence of new state business interests in the city during the 1990s. In this respect security depended on the ability of an enterprise's de facto owners to resist the encroachment of outside interests – something many were able to do quite effectively (Gainsborough 2002).[9] In addition, there were concerted efforts from the second half of the 1990s to tackle weaknesses in the business environment by reducing red tape, strengthening bankruptcy legislation and reducing anti-competitive practices. In sum, therefore, the outlook in terms of discipline and encouragement for equitized enterprises at this time could have been worse.

The nature of ownership: insiders or outsiders?

According to the World Bank, privatization has worked best where assets have been sold to outsiders, notably foreigners, and where ownership is concentrated. Where shares have been sold to insiders, there has been less enterprise restructuring, and enterprise performance has been less impressive. Government data on the ownership breakdown of 336 state enterprises that had completed equitization by 2000 revealed that outsiders had played a relatively small role compared with insiders and the state, which on average have bought more than 80 per cent cent of shares (see Box 4.2 for full details of the ownership breakdown of these enterprises). The state's role in equitization ranged from complete divestment to maintenance of an 80 per cent equity share. The average size of state equity in the 239 companies where it had retained a share (that is, just over 70 per cent of the 336 companies profiled here) was 32 per cent. The share of equity purchased by insiders ranged from none to 100 per cent, with an average of 59 per cent. The data presented here do not distinguish between type of insiders (that is, managers or workers), although generally speaking where workers have bought shares – as they often have – they have frequently been bought out later.[10]

The share of equity bought by (domestic) outsiders has ranged from none to 100 per cent. Where outsiders have obtained shares, the average share purchase has been 31 per cent, falling to 18 per cent overall. The data do not provide details regarding the identity of outside shareholders; however, outsiders are generally individuals rather than institutional investors. Foreigners, who face restrictions on their share ownership, have played a tiny role, with foreign share purchases equivalent to an average of 0.15 per cent of equity. Foreigners bought shares in just three of the 336 equitized companies profiled here, with the total foreign stake ranging from 10 per cent to 30 per cent.

The nature of ownership: concentrated or diffuse?

The World Bank also emphasized the importance of ownership being concentrated rather than diffuse. Discerning the situation in respect of Vietnamese equitized enterprises is difficult, mainly because the precise identity of the different shareholders remains hidden.[11] On the face of it, the average 59 per cent insider equity, 23 per cent cent state equity and 18 per cent outsider equity would suggest quite diffuse ownership. However, it is conceivable that they are all effectively the same people, with the state share held by

BOX 4.2   Ownership breakdown of 336 equitized companies

STATE

Complete divestment	29 per cent
Over 51 per cent	9 per cent
11–50 per cent	86 per cent
1–10 per cent	5 per cent
Average where state retains a stake	32 per cent
Average overall	23 per cent

INSIDERS

Complete divestment	0.6 per cent (2 companies)
100 per cent	19 per cent
51–99 per cent	38 per cent
11–50 per cent	40 per cent
1–10 per cent	3 per cent
Average where insiders retain a stake	59 per cent
Average overall	59 per cent

OUTSIDERS

No stake	41 per cent
100 per cent	1 per cent
51–99 per cent	9 per cent
11–50 per cent	38 per cent
1–10 per cent	11 per cent
Average where outsiders retain a stake	31 per cent
Average overall	18 per cent

FOREIGN

No stake	99 per cent
100 per cent	None
51–99	None
11–50 per cent	0.3 per cent (1 company)
1–10 per cent	0.7 per cent (2 companies)
Average where retains a stake	17 per cent
Average overall	0.15 per cent

Source: Official sources.

the former controlling institution, insider shares by managers appointed by the controlling institution, and so-called outsider shares by their business associates or relatives. This would point towards much more concentrated ownership and, in the World Bank's view, potentially better economic prospects. *x: easier to make decisions w/ 1 CEO*

Prior to equitization, some state enterprises suffered from disputes between different institutional interests with rival claims to rights over a particular enterprise. A key question is whether equitization has merely reproduced these rival interests or whether it moved forward only when such disputes were resolved, with the capitulation or buying out of one (or more) of the parties. There is some reason to suspect the latter. After all, it is questionable whether anyone would want to run a former state enterprise as a private company with disputes over property rights unresolved. Moreover, the fact that equitization initially took so long to advance may be explained by the fact that such disputes needed to be resolved before the process could move forward. Where equitization has resolved previous institutional disputes, this would suggest that ownership is more concentrated than first impressions might suggest.

Transparency

The World Bank suggests that enterprises sold through transparent tenders or auctions have generally attracted better owners, which have outperformed enterprises sold directly to politically connected parties, frequently at highly subsidized prices. Equitization in Vietnam appears to fall down in most of these areas since it cannot in any way be described as transparent. The process has largely occurred via closed, non-competitive bidding, with shares going to politically connected parties. In the late 1990s, the Haiphong People's Committee, with the permission of the central government, requested assistance from the World Bank's private-sector lending arm, the International Financial Corporation, to oversee the auction of a number of state enterprises in the city by way of a pilot project. However, the project failed in so far as no enterprises were ultimately auctioned. People connected with the project cited a range of reasons, including ambiguous or unclear political support. Vietnamese staff involved in the project said that state enterprises in Haiphong opposed the auction method because they feared that it might take ownership away from them.[12]

Valuing state enterprise assets

The lack of transparency in the equitization process is also evident in relation to the valuation of enterprise assets. Although there is a recognized formula for valuing assets (adjusted net worth ± advantage/disadvantage value + equitization expenses), we do not know the value put on each enterprise, nor what horse-trading was involved to get there (Webster and Amin 1998: 15). Even official information on this is not publicly available. However, it is generally accepted that equitization in Vietnam has not resulted in 'give-away' divestment, although assets have usually been sold at a discount to fair value.[13] The World Bank has not made explicit the thinking behind its assertion that, where assets have been sold at highly subsidized prices, enterprises have performed less well. However, where new enterprise owners have had to pay to obtain enterprise assets they are more likely to view the company as a valued resource and treat it accordingly. In this respect, the idea that the valuation process was not entirely without teeth may count in Vietnam's favour in terms of the future performance of equitized companies.

Continued state ownership:
cash flow and property rights issues

The World Bank also says that, where the state continues to hold a stake in a privatized firm, it is important to clarify the cash flow and property rights existing in the enterprise. Given the continued prominence of state ownership in equitized enterprises, this is clearly an important issue in relation to Vietnam. In particular, in the early 2000s it remained unclear what impact equitization was having on the relationship between enterprises and their former controlling institution. While equitized companies appeared to struggle like any other in obtaining long-term credit – reflecting systemic weaknesses in the banking sector – a number reported that the formalities for short-term borrowing have included a requirement from the banks that the company receive authorization from their former controlling institution before they may borrow. Although initially this was somewhat puzzling, it points to a less than complete severing of ties with pre-equitization influences. In addition, some 40 per cent of the first companies to equitize said that the state remained a significant influence in their company after equitization. These issues are explored further in Chapter 5.

Conclusion

By way of a window onto Vietnam's emerging political economy, this chapter has explored the reasons why equitization suddenly speeded up in 1999/2000, continuing through the decade. It has been argued that although simpler procedures and greater experience of the equitization process were one factor, more important was a change in calculation on the part of business interests associated with state enterprises as to the best place for them to do business. That is, reflecting less hospitable conditions in the state sector and more attractive conditions in the private sector, which emerged towards the end of the 1990s, companies which were once reluctant to equitize saw it as the way forward.

5

UNCERTAINTY AS AN
INSTRUMENT OF RULE

Staying with some of the issues raised in the previous chapter, this chapter re-examines the widely held view that privatization (or equitization) should be viewed in terms of a retreat of the state. Of course, there is recognition in the literature on Vietnam – and China – that equitization to date has been a partial affair or that state officials have very often been the beneficiaries of share sales. In Vietnam, comment is often made about the name – equitization rather than privatization – with the implication that this in some way reflects ideological resistance on the part of the state. Reference has also been made to the fact that the state in Vietnam often retains a high percentage of company shares even after equitization – again cited to suggest an unwillingness on the part of the state to 'let go'. Furthermore, it has been noted that equitization has generally involved only the smaller state enterprises and that, in terms of total state enterprise capital, only around 15 per cent has made the shift from state ownership to the equitized form since equitization was launched in the early 1990s.[1]

However, despite this, it is still argued that the dominant view remains that equitization – and privatization – should be equated with a retreat of the state, albeit a partial one in Vietnam's case and one that potentially has greater scope to run. Writing on the social impact of state enterprise reform in Vietnam, Gerard Clarke (2004) notes that even Vietnam scholars such as Gareth Porter and Gabriel Kolko, who Clarke notes are from different ends of the ideological spectrum, are in agreement that state enterprise reform marks the retreat of the state even if they differ on whether the retreat is a good or a bad thing. The Vietnam Development Report produced by the international donor community in 2004 also placed the emphasis firmly on state retreat when in respect of equitization it wrote: 'there is little doubt that the state share of economic activity will keep declining' (Vietnam Development Report 2004: 72).

However, is this interpretation right? Could it be that while the state share of economic activity may decline, equitization should be seen less as the retreat of the state and more as a new form of state interventionism in which we see not the state's retreat but its advance? Of course, the sale of state assets sounds – intuitively – like the retreat of the state, but 'political power' has an uncanny knack of reinventing itself or subverting practices, such as equitization, which on the face of it appear to threaten its grip. This, it is argued, is what is happening in Vietnam.

The chapter, which is based on in-depth interviews with eight equitized companies in four provinces in northern and southern Vietnam (Haiphong, Lao Cai, Tay Ninh and Can Tho) in 2003, is structured as follows.[2] First, a theoretical framework is introduced allowing consideration of the ways in which privatization may be associated with state advance. Next, data on the companies are presented, including details about their shareholding structure, how decision-making changed as a result of equitization, and about the business environment in general. The final section before the conclusion, entitled 'Equitization as Private Indirect Government', explores how uncertainty is used as an instrument of rule.

Privatization as state advance

Following the collapse of Communism in the former Soviet Union and Eastern Europe in the late 1980s and early 1990s, there was a surge in scholarly and policy interest in privatization. The interest was most intense around the time of 'big bang' privatization in Russia in the early 1990s but it continued for some years afterwards (World Bank 2002). However, the literature which emerged at this time tended to view privatization though a fairly restrictive lens, focusing almost exclusively on its economic impact, such as its effects on company performance or the wider macroeconomy (see Parker and Kirkpatrick 2005). Little, if any, attention was paid in this literature to the impact of privatization on the state. While there are a number of possible reasons for this, one suspects that in the political climate of the day it was felt that whatever else one might say about privatization and politics, the implications for the state were self-evident (i.e. that privatization should be associated with state retreat).[3]

Meanwhile and rather set apart from the writing on privatization, a different literature was taking shape in the 1990s that did scrutinize what changes in global governance might mean for state power. While some of the early writing in this field sounded the death knell of the state, it soon became apparent that in practice the picture was much more nuanced. Thus, across the globe, it was far from clear that the state was in retreat despite the rise of transnational forms of governance, 'globalization' or neoliberal reforms emphasizing liberalization, deregulation and a smaller state (Cameron and Palan 2004; Jayasuriya 2001; Nordholt and van Klinken 2007; Phillips 1998; Walker 1999; Weiss 1997). Nevertheless, writing that explores the way in which privatization may not in fact be associated with state retreat still remains relatively rare.

One exception to this is Béatrice Hibou, who in her 2004 edited book *Privatizing the State*, argued with reference to Africa that while state shares had been sold off, the recipients were kept in such a state of uncertainty by the authorities as to what they could and could not do with their new assets that the state continued to maintain a hold over them. Hibou called this 'private indirect government', writing:

> Privatization [for which we can insert 'equitization'] is in no way synonymous with the retreat of the state, or even the primacy of the private over the public.… [B]eyond the expanding role of so-called private bodies, privatization involves constant negotiation between dominant actors (whether they be public or private); the constant redrawing of frontiers between public and private; and the persistent hold of political relations and power more generally. Negotiations are always at the centre of this process of delegation and control which characterizes this mode of increasingly private indirect government. (Hibou 2004: 17)

In unpacking further what she means by this, Hibou is quick to say that we are not talking about 'total and exclusive' control. It is, she says, always possible for 'private actors' to find ways of circumventing control: 'Everywhere there are slip-ups and spaces where freedom can slip in, and if there are none of these, for astute actors it is always possible to invent ways of circumventing' (Hibou 2004: 19). We are also not talking – Hibou is clear on this too – about a single state authority. The state is not a monolith. Instead, what we see operating is a multiplicity of factions and power centres associated with the state or particular politicians.

Furthermore, Hibou offers a sharp riposte to all those who say 'this is not a sign of a strengthening of state power' but rather represents the 'ruses of those in power, indicating not the vitality of the state but its decline' (Hibou 2004: 19). Hibou claims that this is to fall into the trap of adopting a normative view of the state in which the state is defined in advance as a rational-legal and bureaucratic entity, of the sort usually associated with Max Weber. Hibou reminds us that Weber also worked on non-bureaucratic forms of the state with 'nonpermanent forms of intervention', where the cost of a major administrative apparatus is avoided (Hibou 2004: 19). Thus,

while we may need to make a distinction between state power and
state regulatory authority (i.e. the ability to design and implement
policy), Hibou says that we make a major error if we mistake the
absence of the latter for the absence of the former. This, it is argued
here, is an error frequently made in respect of much analysis of the
state. Concluding her thesis, Hibou continues:

> Privatization fits into this framework. Strengthening the power of
> this or that politician (or this or that faction) through appropriation
> of economic resources, or transfers of enterprises, obviously offers
> a personal opportunity for enrichment, or is a short term tactic
> to give a base to contested or delegitimized authority. But more
> than this, it traces the possible outlines of political action. It takes
> account of the interdependence of processes of economic accumula-
> tion and political control (and by the same processes maintains that
> interdependence); it is intrinsic to the negotiation of allegiances
> and loyalties. In other words, to understand the state, it is neces-
> sary to understand the people in power and, equally important,
> their games, their strategies and their historical practices. This
> mutual dependence defines the outlines of the state. (Hibou 2004:
> 21, 23)

Despite the fact that Hibou's research was conducted in Africa,
her theoretical framework speaks loudly to the reality of equitization
in Vietnam. The remainder of this chapter seeks to illustrate this,
looking at data collected on equitization in Vietnam. It is evident
that in the struggles that surround Vietnam's equitized companies,
there is no single victor. Everyone is as likely to be 'put upon' as
they are to try and 'throw their weight around', while any attempt
to separate out public interests from private interests is likely to end
in failure. Furthermore, there is also no single model of behaviour:
pretty much anything is possible.[4]

All companies profiled in this chapter are referred to by two
letters, which indicate the province/city and a number; for example
Haiphong 1 (HP1), Lao Cai 1 (LC1), Tay Ninh 1 (TN1) and Can
Tho 1 (CT1). All individuals are referred to by using a pseudonym
to ensure their confidentiality. Quotations from interviews in appear

in two forms: first, they are extracted directly from the interviews; and second, paraphrased information compiled from the interviews is utilized. The latter method is used where the precise way in which people have said things is not so important. Box 5.1 at the end of the chapter provides some additional background information on the companies while still concealing their identity. This information may be useful for readers wishing to relate the particular circumstances of the companies more closely to what they said.

The companies

All but one of the companies interviewed were established in the 1980s and 1990s (one was founded in 1979). They operate in a wide range of sectors, including services, trade, manufacturing, mining and construction. The companies were quite small: average annual turnover was 14 billion dong (US$825,000); average employment was 140 people. All the companies – except one, which was formally under a central ministry – began life as locally managed state enterprises (*cong ty nha nuoc dia phuong*).[5] Most of the companies equitized in 2000–2001.

Company attitude to equitization

In contrast to the popular view of widespread company resistance to equitization, the companies we spoke to were generally enthusiastic about equitization and many had put themselves forward as candidates. Some commented that they were among the first companies to equitize in their province or city. HP1 spoke for many when it said:

> We chose equitization because we felt it would suit our enterprise. If you have a lot of shareholders then you can draw on lots of different ideas, and people take responsibility if it's their money they have thrown in.
>   We saw equitization as a way of mobilizing the strength of workers. Do true, earn true! Mobilising capital is easier. The company

thought: should it borrow money or should it issue shares? Equitization also brought to an end the system whereby power was concentrated in a single director. We now have a management board, which is more democratic. We can also give everything to [that is, run everything past] the shareholders.

Among the companies interviewed, there were some cases where they were ordered to equitize, usually by their controlling institution responding to a target from the provincial People's Committee. However, even here, companies were not necessarily unenthusiastic about equitization, despite the fact that they had not taken the initiative themselves.

There were some examples of resistance to equitization among the companies interviewed. In one case, for instance, the deputy director was keen but the director and the firm's management committee (*ban quan ly*) needed persuading. The deputy director eventually won the day.

State attitude to equitization

Contrary to the common view of state reluctance to relinquish shares, it was not found that the state was always trying to retain a large stake in the equitized companies. In the companies interviewed, the state share after equitization ranged from 17 per cent to 70 per cent, with the average being 45 per cent. Admittedly the state was the largest shareholder in all but one company. However, it was not uncommon to find cases where the state wanted to relinquish a larger share of equity but was unable to find buyers (because no one thought the company was a going concern). In some cases, the state sold shares in two stages, with the second sale taking place after public confidence in the company had increased. In one of the companies interviewed, the state was planning to sell a further 20 per cent of its equity. However, the key point is that, as with enterprise attitudes towards equitization, the picture is not one of universal state reluctance. This is significant in relation to the argument here, which asserts that equitization should be seen not as the retreat of the state but rather as its advance. In a sense, what we are seeing with equitization in Vietnam is the state 'having its cake and eating it': that is, it is passing the buck in terms of who is responsible if anything goes wrong while continuing to share in the benefits when things go right.[6] In such circumstances, it is not surprising that the state was enthusiastic.

In emphasizing relative state (and company) enthusiasm for equitization, a somewhat different position is being adopted here compared with Vietnam specialists, such as Adam Fforde and Martin Painter, whose overall approach to understanding state ownership and hence the reality of state enterprise reform is nevertheless quite similar. However, even Fforde and Painter emphasize resistance to equitization either from interests inside or outside companies (Fforde 2004b, 2004c; Painter 2003). In this chapter, it is not denied that resistance exists or that there are not obstacles; rather, it is being suggested that always placing the emphasis on resistance risks a fundamental misunderstanding of what equitization is about. These points are explored further below.

How long did equitization take?

For the companies interviewed, equitization was generally completed in a year or less. However, it sometimes took much longer. The shortest time was 3 months and the longest was 37 months, with an average of 13 months. According to the enterprises spoken to, the hardest part of equitization was always valuing the company's assets. Moreover, disagreement between the authority overseeing equitization – usually the provincial People's Committee – and the company preparing to equitize was commonplace, the norm in fact. LC2 said that differences emerged over the 'account book value of the company' and the 'actual value of the company'. LC1 said that the People's Committee did not accept its definition of what it regarded as 'own capital' (*von tu co*), which the director of the company, Mr

Hoan, described as 'the fruits of the workers' own efforts'. Mr Hoan said that in the end the People's Committee got its way because the company 'did not want to push the matter given that they were the first company in the province undergoing equitization'.

CT1 said it also clashed with the People's Committee over how to value the company. This time, the dispute was over who owned the company office. Highlighting Hibou's point that we are not talking about 'total and exclusive' state control, the company came out on top on this occasion, according to CT1's director, Mr Ha.

The fact that valuing company assets proved so troublesome is also revealing as to how we should ultimately understand the process of equitization. Based on the data presented here, it would appear that a number of different things are going on. First, state officials tasked with overseeing the equitization of companies in their locale – usually the People's Committee and the Finance Department, which formally comes under the People's Committee's jurisdiction – are keen to undervalue the company's assets and generally place heavy emphasis on the liabilities of the companies. In this way, the state is able to obtain its share of the company without putting any new capital into it. At the same time, the interests associated with the company – that is, those looking to buy shares – are keen to claim as much of the company for their own as possible by asserting that assets and capital are 'own capital' or the result of the company 'growing' the resources originally entrusted to it by the state when it was first set up.

It is in relation to these differing perspectives that the disputes over preparing companies for equitization arise, but it is largely a political issue about control over assets, rather than, as most of the literature would have us believe, a technical problem. The complicating factor for scholars trying to make sense of equitization is that there are state interests on both sides, depending on whether they are 'state interests' representing the interests of the People's Committee/Finance Department or 'officials' connected with the company and looking to buy shares. However, either way, they are still the state, just, as Hibou says, a personalized, non-bureaucratic version of it.

HP1 offers a nicely graphic account of attempts by the authorities in Haiphong to acquire the company's assets on the cheap:

> City officials tried to grab the company at a cheap price ... in order to make money. They managed to sell some shares, which they resold to an equitized company in Hanoi [name withheld by the author]. But they did not fully achieve their schemes.

Concern about possible job losses in light of equitization is also mentioned frequently in the secondary literature as a reason why equitization has proceeded slowly. However, in relation to the interpretation of equitization favoured here – where equitization is viewed more in terms of (relatively orderly) primitive accumulation (understood in terms of state assets seeping out into de facto private hands) – concerns about unemployment appear as something of a red herring. The point is that in Vietnam's sensitive political climate people cannot talk about the real reason why equitization proceeds slowly – that is, a struggle for control over state assets – so they frequently mention politically 'safe' reasons like concerns about job losses, or the technical difficulties of valuing company assets. It is these kinds of 'obstacles' which are commonly mentioned in the Vietnamese media when difficulties with equitization are discussed. Among the companies looked at here, employment issues were only mentioned once (CT1). Here, the director, Mr Ha, said that he 'wrestled with who to keep and who to let go', adding that in the end he resolved the matter by keeping everyone!

Shareholding structure after equitization

There is nothing particularly out of the ordinary regarding the shareholding profile of the companies interviewed. As already noted, the state share of equity ranged from 17 per cent to 70 per cent, with an average of 45 per cent. Beyond this, share ownership was dominated by 'insiders', understood here as the company's management, workers, provincial officials and their friends. There was some institutional share ownership, including by state enterprises. However, in general, the shareholding structure of the companies interviewed was characterized by many small-scale individual shareholders alongside a few key shareholders. On account of their small stake, individual shareholders appeared to have little say in how the companies were run. In most companies, the company director held some shares although often not many, suggesting that in most cases the director was more a manager (on behalf of more powerful political interests) than an owner of capital. CT1 provides a representative example:

> Following equitization, the state retains a 67 per cent stake in CT1. The state share appears to be centred on interests at the provincial agriculture department even though the company began life under the former ministry of hydraulics. The remaining 33 per cent of the company's equity is in the hands of 57 individual shareholders, some of whom are company employees and some of whom are not. The largest shareholder with 10 per cent of the company's equity was referred to as *ong tinh* [Mr Province] and is clearly someone high up in the province. The smallest shareholder was said to have 'just a few million dong' worth of shares. The director, Mr Ha, has a 2–3 per cent stake in the company. There was no mention of institutional shareholders. In 2003, the state was planning to reduce its shareholding by a further 20–47 per cent. The resulting equity was expected to be bought by existing shareholders.

The shareholding structure of CT2 was slightly more unusual in so far as the state share was only 17 per cent and the largest shareholder was the company's director, Mr Nam. Mr Nam was clearly both a manager of capital and a significant owner of it. However, he still seemed to be acting on behalf of the state interests associated with the company:

> After the state share, the remaining 83 per cent of the company's equity is held by 65 shareholders, although four shareholders dominate. The largest shareholder is the director, Mr Nam, who

holds a 30 per cent stake in the firm. The smallest of the four main shareholders holds 7 per cent of the company's equity. Just 20 per cent of the company's shares are said to be held by outsiders.[7] Mr Nam said that in reality he has authority [*uy quyen*] over 80 per cent of the shares, including the state share and those held by his close friends.

A number of companies said that shares were constantly changing hands. In general, the trend appeared to be towards a concentration of shares into fewer hands, with officials and the politically connected typically buying out workers.

Company directors after equitization

The company directors of the companies interviewed were all men. Their ages ranged from 46 to 68 years. The average was 54 years. Most directors had served long periods in public administration and/or with other state enterprises before joining the company they were with at the time of the interview. Most directors had been with the company since it was founded. Often, they began working for it having previously held a position in the company's controlling institution. Many of the company directors had served in the army. All were either director or deputy director of the company before it equitized. Most were not native to the province they were working in. In the case of the two southern provinces where interviews were conducted, the company directors had all come south in the years immediately following Vietnam's reunification in 1976. Around half of the directors said that one or more of their parents had been state officials, while the remainder said that they were the children of farmers.

Firm decision-making after equitization

Generally speaking, there were clear signs of the emergence of a 'working' post-equitization decision-making structure in the companies interviewed, comprising a director, a management board and a shareholding council (*dai hoi co dong*). In most cases, the company director was the chairman of the management board as well. On a day-to-day basis, decisions were taken either by the director or by the management board or by the two together. The shareholders were consulted on 'big decisions' such as making a new investment, selling company assets, or overseeing the division of profits. As Mr Khang of TN2 said:

> The company operates according to what the shareholders and the management board say. If the director has any sense he will run things past the shareholding board.

In some of the companies interviewed, there was conflict within the company over how it was managed. In the case of HP1, for instance, the company was on to its third management board chairman in as many years. The problem was only resolved when the company's director, Mr Luong, took the job himself. It appeared that Mr Luong and the Haiphong industry department, which was the company's controlling institution prior to equitization, did not see eye to eye. The industry department, which traditionally had been the key player in company appointments, had chosen the company's first two management board chairmen before it finally allowed Mr Luong to take the post.

In most cases, however, the companies interviewed spoke highly of equitization in terms of the impact it had on decision-making and company morale. The following three extracts illustrate this well:

> Before [equitization], the director made a decision based on the opinion of the controlling institution; now the director bases his decision on what the management board and the shareholding council say [*theo nghi quyet cua Hoi dong Quan tri va Dai ho Co dong*]. Also [before equitization], the business production plan was decided by the controlling institution but now it is the shareholding council which decides. (Mr Ly, director of TN1)

> [Now] the director decides everything ... . When we were still a state company, we didn't take the initiative on anything, because

everything was under general ownership, so no one dared
decide.... [Now] everyone works diligently because it is their
capital they have put in and it is the livelihood of their close friends
[which is at stake]. (Mr Nam, director of CT2)

Previously, when we were still a state enterprise, the company's
capital belonged to the state. The state had public works projects
which it entrusted to our company. We carried them out, did our
accounts, and repaid the state. Since equitization, the capital now
belongs to our shareholders.... Before, when capital belonged to
the state, whether we made a profit or a loss, the state absorbed
it.... Now, if the company makes a loss, it is my loss and everyone
in the company's.... Whatever the company does is down to the
company; we look for jobs ourselves, we organize production,
customer relations, and we do our accounting ourselves. At the end
of the year, the state shareholders check the profit-and-loss balance
sheet. (Mr Danh, director of LC2)

In sum, therefore, what we see is greater dynamism and initiative
on the part of equitized companies. There is a sense that decisions
are generally made more quickly, and that everyone knows what they
are working for. These are all positive developments, one would have
thought, in terms of enterprise performance. Yet, looking again at
the data, one finds that this picture of change for the better – or
change at all – is only part of the story.

Equitization as 'private indirect government'

While talking about change, the directors of many of the companies
interviewed still referred in the same breath to their 'controlling
institution' (that is, the state administrative unit with formal jurisdiction over them when they were a state enterprise) as *their* controlling institution – despite equitization. Moreover, while companies
reported changes in decision-making practices in some areas, many
also continued to report to a wide range of state authorities on a
regular basis. Across the companies interviewed, this generally
included the provincial People's Committee, the firm's controlling

institution, the finance department and the tax department. Most companies reported quarterly and annually, although some made monthly reports. Moreover, when companies were asked who they reported to (*cap tren ma ong phai bao cao la ai?*), they nearly always reeled off a list of state institutions. Only one company director, Mr Ha of CT1, replied that since he was both the company director and its management board chairman he did not have a *cap tren* (higher level).

In addition, nearly all companies now had a representative from the provincial department of finance, or an equivalent body in their company, representing the state interest in the company. The representative (and sometimes representatives) usually sat on the company's internal audit board (*ban kiem soat*). The following examples capture well this pattern of continued extensive reporting to the state, despite equitization:

> Even after equitization, Mr Ly [of TN1] says he still has to report to the provincial People's Committee [which he continued to refer to as the company's controlling institution] both quarterly and annually.
>
> The provincial People's Committee is still involved in making higher level appointments in the company. Mr Khang [of TN2] says the company's relations with the transport department have not changed since equitization and that it is 'still the company's controlling institution'. He also said that he had been entrusted by the provincial People's Committee directly to represent their interests in the company together with an official from the provincial finance department's office responsible for managing the capital of state enterprises[*phong quan ly von cac doanh nghiep nha nuoc*].
>
> Where big decisions are concerns, the company consults [*xin y kien*] the provincial People's Committee and then afterwards meets with the shareholders [*Hoi dong Co dong*].
>
> Since equitization, the company [CT1] continues to refer to itself as belonging to the provincial agriculture department. The company still reports to the agriculture department once a quarter.
>
> [Despite equitization] Mr Hoan [of LC1] says that the company is under the direct management [*truc thuoc quan ly*] of the

provincial People's Committee, the transport branch [as its specialist organ] and the statistical department. However, it the People's Committee and the transport branch that are the most important.

Mr Thanh [of HP2] still describes the city People's Committee as the company's controlling institution, despite equitization.

Part of the explanation for this pattern of extensive reporting to the state even after equitization is that equitized companies are hybrids. Their attitudes, how they operate and what they expect from the state are beginning to change, but it is a gradual process. Old habits (of reporting) die hard. This is not surprising. After all, when the interviews were conducted, the majority of companies had been equitized for three years or less. Most had spent somewhere between ten and twenty years in the state sector. Moreover, as was evident from the profile of the company directors outlined above, these were men who had all spent long periods of time working for state enterprises or in the state bureaucracy. They had all reached adulthood by 1975, so their formative, working years were spent under central planning.

Furthermore, as noted above, the average state share in the equitized companies interviewed was 45 per cent. The state was bound to be interested in what was going on in the companies in which it had a stake – as many of the companies interviewed indicated:

> [If a regulation is unclear the local authorities will help us] because it still has a 42 per cent stake in the company. (Mr Hoan, director of LC1)

> [The local authorities pay attention to us] a lot because they are worried that they would lose their capital. (Mr Thanh, director of HP2)

In addition, some companies said that, although they were still reporting to the state authorities, the character of the meetings had changed. Mr Ha of CT1, for example, said that unlike previously when the company had to get the opinion of the department and the branch (*nganh*), the meeting is now 'just a discussion, and on all matters the company decides itself'.

Nevertheless, while the situation is inevitably nuanced, the fact that the equitized companies are still reporting to the state is highly significant. Not only does it shed light on the quasi-nature of 'private' property rights in equitized companies, but it also shows that this pattern of extensive reporting to the state is consistent with Hibou's notion of private indirect government (i.e. shareholders kept in a state of uncertainty so that the state maintains a hold over them). The director of CT2, Mr Nam, who said the company reported to the provincial People's Committee, the trade department and the tax department, captured this climate of uncertainty very clearly when he said: 'We are not compelled to [report] but we do so in order not to offend them so that when we have a problem then they will support us.'

Listening to other companies, a similar feeling of unease was sensed, with directors wondering whether their relations with the authorities were as 'friendly' as they once were, or stressing the need for connections to get things done. HP2's Mr Thanh, for instance, said he spent a lot of time worrying about how to deal with the higher levels, which for this company included the city People's Committee, the industry department and the tax department.

More than this, it is clear that the companies interviewed were operating in a highly unpredictable regulatory environment. This is precisely the kind of environment in which, according to Hibou, private indirect government flourishes. The list of company complaints was as predictable as it was long: laws and regulations that were not implemented, frequent changes in policies, delays, tax officials who refused requests for information, having to pay for information, customs officials who wanted extra money to do anything out of the ordinary, and government-promised 'incentives' for equitized companies that failed to materialize on asking.

Furthermore, the environment in which the companies interviewed were operating was not just unpredictable, it was frequently predatory. State institutions consistently sought to do the companies harm, often in an attempt to extract money from them, as the following examples show:

> In general, the city party committee supports the company. The director of the city industry department and the office of the provincial People's Committee do not support us ... Mrs X [name withheld by the author] at the provincial reform committee is afraid of taking responsibility so she takes a long time to do anything, resulting in lost opportunities for the company. (Mr Luong, director of HP1)

> Generally the local authorities are bad, especially after we equitized: the industry department, the department for managing financial capital, the city enterprise reform committee ... The management board and the state representatives give me grief whenever I am weak. (Mr Thanh, director of HP2)

However, as Hibou (2004: 19) says, it is not a zero-sum game: companies lose some but they also win some. Moreover, companies rarely take what is thrown at them lying down. Instead, they seek to outwit, to manoeuvre and generally use everything at their disposal to 'invent ways of circumventing'. As the director of LC2, Mr Danh said:

> We have both good and bad local authorities. We want to have good ones but naturally we have some bad ones. But people are still wary of me because I am a member of the [Communist] party and used to work at a former state enterprise.

Conclusion

In this chapter, it has been argued that equitization should be seen not as the retreat of the state but rather as a new form of state interventionism. Moreover, this is not said simply because state officials are buying shares ('officials lining their pockets'), which is the standard 'cynical' view of what equitization is about. The argument goes much further than this. Equitization represents a new form of state interventionism because the people who are ostensibly letting go (that is, authorizing the sale of state assets) are doing so in such a way that they continue to exert a hold over the recipients: 'private indirect government', as Hibou has referred to it. Keeping people in perpetual uncertainty is a key part of this. As has been shown, living in such conditions of uncertainty, equitized companies have no choice but to continue to report to the state.

The interesting remaining questions have to do with the sustainability of this model. That is, what are the stress points of private indirect government in Vietnam today? Also, what does this mode of operating mean for enterprise performance? Finally, how are things likely to evolve in the future? To conclude this chapter, some brief thoughts will be offered on these questions.

There are many tensions inherent in private indirect government, of course. Enterprise directors and owners of capital do not like it if officials mess them about, seek to do them harm, or generally behave in ways that cut into their bottom line. However, by and large, these people are far too busy trying to survive to develop any kind of systematic critique of such practices. Moreover, although the emergence of private indirect government on the back of equitization has been characterized as a 'new' phenomenon, what is new is less 'private indirect government', but more how it has combined with a contemporary neoliberal-inspired practice, namely equitization, to ensure the survival of existing power structures. Making people dependent by keeping them in a state of uncertainty is one of the oldest political tricks in the book. Thus, from the perspective of equitized company directors, it is not as if they are experiencing anything very different: *plus ça change* (that is how life is).

On the other hand, looking at equitized companies as hybrids, it is possible that we are observing the early stages of the emergence of a new class, one whose origins are clearly from 'within the state' but who over time will become less and less 'of the state' (Heng 1999).[8] It will therefore be interesting to see the extent to which interests between the state and capital start to diverge more markedly in the future.

In terms of enterprise performance, the neoclassical position is that in so far as private property rights are still not fully secure, companies will underperform. This may be true. However, based on these interviews, equitization does seem to have created new incentives where previously there were none (or few). Moreover, while the business environment is predatory and enterprises continue to have to fight to defend their patch, they are capable of doing this. This is not to say the situation is perfect – it is distinctly suboptimal, to use the jargon – but where in the world is it perfect?

Thus, in terms of performance it is suggested that equitization does represent a step forward, even if we have to be cautious about official surveys on the matter and recognize that, in the spirit of old-fashioned primitive accumulation, some people are obtaining assets on the cheap. Nevertheless, there are plenty of examples from around the world where the divestment of state assets has occurred in a much more disorderly fashion (such as in Russia) and it is testament to the relative coherence of the Vietnamese state that this is not the case in Vietnam.

In some respects, the coherence of the Vietnamese state is puzzling, given what we have seen in terms of diverse actors acting in a diverse variety of ways. However, the coherence of the Vietnamese state goes back to what Benedict Anderson (1983) once said about the state: 'harbour[ing] self-preserving and self-aggrandizing impulses, which at any given moment are "expressed" through its living members, but cannot be reduced to their passing personal ambitions'. For reasons that are poorly understood, these impulses appear strong in Vietnam.

Finally, how are things likely to evolve in the future? The trajectory of Vietnam at the moment is undoubtedly one that, among other things, involves further equitization (Cheshier and Penrose 2007; UNDP 2006). For instance, according to the government's draft five-year plan for 2006–10, about 1,000 companies are scheduled to complete equitization by 2010.[9] In this respect, Vietnam's international aid donor community is probably right when it proclaims that the state share of economic activity will keep declining (Vietnam Development Report 2004: 72). However, the received wisdom is very much mistaken when it comes to thinking about what this means. As the state share of economic activity declines, private indirect government – a new form of state interventionism – increases.

BOX 5.1   Additional background on companies interviewed

TN1

Area of business	Mining
Founded	1997
Equitized	2000
Control before equitization	Provincial People's Committee
State share after equitization	51 per cent
Largest shareholder	State
Annual turnover	VND8.6 billion (2002)
Employment	54 people

TN2

Area of business	Transport
Founded	1986
Equitized	2000
Control before equitization	Provincial Transport Department
State share after equitization	70 per cent
Largest shareholder	State
Annual turnover	VND9.0 billion
Employment	70 people

CT1

Area of business	Water engineering company
Founded	1992
Equitized	2000
Control before equitization	Ministry/Department Agriculture
State share after equitization	67 per cent
Largest shareholder	State
Annual turnover	VND4 billion (2002)
Employment	40 people

CT2

Area of business	Import–export
Founded	1995
Equitized	2001
Control before equitization	Department of Trade (since 1997)
State share after equitization	17 per cent
Largest shareholder	Company director (30 per cent)
Annual turnover	VND30.2 billion
Employment	50 people

LC1

Area of business	Transportation
Founded	1991
Equitized	1999
Control before equitization	Department of Transport
State share after equitization	42 per cent
Largest shareholder	State
Annual turnover	VND9 billion (2002)
Employment	150 people

LC2

Area of business	Construction (roads and bridges)
Founded	1979
Equitized	2001
Control before equitization	Department of Transport
State share after equitization	35 per cent
Largest shareholder	State
Annual turnover	VND16 billion (2002)
Employment	Not available

HP1

Area of business	Printing and packaging
Founded	1983
Equitized	2000
Control before equitization	Department of Industry
State share after equitization	30 per cent
Largest shareholder	State
Annual turnover	VND22.3 billion (2002)
Employment	371 people

HP2

Area of business	Garment manufacturer
Founded	1988
Equitized	2001
Control before equitization	People's Committee
State share after equitization	45 per cent
Largest shareholder	State
Annual turnover	VND 15.7 billion (2002)
Employment	Not available

Source: Author interviews.

6

LOCAL POLITICS

This chapter looks at local politics at Vietnam. However, it does so with reference to a specific body of writing, namely literature on globalization and the state which explores how the state is being affected by contemporary global influences. This is an important literature, which flags a key theme of the book, namely the way in which the state in Vietnam appears to be holding its ground in the face of powerful external forces, notwithstanding a certain amount of adaptation. Underlining the importance of this theme of state resilience, it will be pursued further in Chapter 8 when we look at the interaction between Vietnamese elites and their counterparts in the international donor community.

Two overarching questions lie at the heart of this chapter. First, accepting the likelihood of diversity, what conceptualization of the state makes most sense for the state at the sub-national level in Vietnam? Second, against the backdrop of the various claims made about so-called globalization and its impact on the state, how do we explain what we observe in Vietnam? With regard to the first question, the chapter considers whether it is most appropriate to conceptualize the state as retreating, emerging strengthened, or being reconfigured. Regarding the second question, the chapter

considers what importance should be attached to the two key
explanatory variables which are given prominence in the 'national'
globalization literature, namely the changing nature of cross-border
flows and the rise of private and transnational actors. To put it
another way, the chapter considers the way in which these two
variables are mediated to produce the effects they do.

The chapter is based on research conducted in 2003 in two
largely rural Vietnamese border provinces: Lao Cai in northern
Vietnam on the border with China, and Tay Ninh in southern
Vietnam on the border with Cambodia. The chapter draws
principally on interviews with Vietnamese companies as well as
other publicly available material relating to the so-called Greater
Mekong subregion (GMS), of which Lao Cai and Tay Ninh form
a part.[1] This includes official statistical yearbooks, material provided by multilateral institutions, and private and state-owned
news media.

The chapter proceeds as follows. To set the discussion of local
politics in context, the chapter first reviews some of the salient
features of the globalization and the state literature. It then offers
an analysis of the state based on research in Lao Cai and Tay
Ninh. Based on the evidence, it is argued that there is little to
suggest that the state is losing ground. Instead, the data point
to a relatively powerful state, which may even be extending its
reach in some areas. The chapter then explores whether in relation to changing cross-border flows and the rise of private and
transnational actors – that is, the two key variables for explaining
change in the nature of the state – we really do see the changes
in Lao Cai and Tay Ninh that the globalization literature suggests
we should. Arguing broadly speaking that we do, the final section
of the chapter asks how we reconcile the fact of a state which, at
the very least, appears to be holding its own, with the apparent
growth in cross-border flows and the rise of private and transnational actors.

Globalization and the state

From Kenichi Ohmae's book *The End of the Nation State* (1995) to Linda Weiss's *The Myth of the Powerless State* (1998) – with numerous other texts in between – much ink has been spilt on the subject of globalization and the state. While early writing on this subject was often polarized between the two diverse positions just highlighted, some of the most exciting scholarship has coalesced around a third position, which argues that neither position is correct. Rather than saying the state is retreating or becoming stronger, scholars in this third camp prefer to argue that the state is being 're-configured' (Held et al. 2000: 7–9; Hibou 2004). Although this begs the question 'Re-configured to what?' these authors are right to suggest that when considering changes to the state, it may not be a question of either stronger or weaker. Alternatively, it may be a case of stronger in some realms and weaker in others – all in the same state – with the challenge being to identify where this is the case (Phillips 1998).

While this would appear to offer a profitable line of enquiry in terms of description, there remains the tricky issue of how one explains change. Here, much obviously turns on how one views globalization. Scholars who adopt a relatively uncritical stance towards globalization – accepting it as a 'given' and not probing the ways in which it operates at the level of a discourse – naturally place rather more emphasis on globalization (however defined) as an explanation of change (Holm and Sorensen 1995). Alternatively, another way to understand so-called globalization is to say that we need to be more open to the idea of globalization operating at the level of discourse (Cameron and Palan 2004; Rydin 1998). To adopt such a perspective is not to deny that powerful global forces exist – largely associated with the creation of conditions conducive to the expansion of transnational capitalism dating back to the 1970s (McMichael 1996) – which may push states to act in particular ways. However, it is to suggest that part of globalization's power lies simply at the level of ideas, so that when states push at the door of alleged constraints on their actions – which they inevitably will – they will find the door comes ajar, revealing rather more room for elites to manoeuvre than the rhetoric of globalization suggests there should be.

Such a conceptualization of globalization seems especially relevant with respect to the so-called developing world, including Vietnam. Here, globalization is often depicted as an 'authorless' force, all-powerful and irresistible, creating a sense in which states have no alternative but to bend to its logic. Paul Cammack (2001: 403–7) makes just this point writing about the UK Department for International Development's 1997 report *Eliminating Poverty: Making Globalization Work for the Poor*. While the 'there is no alternative' view of globalization may make sense as a political project, it patently fails to capture reality. In a climate in which we are constantly bombarded with messages about the irresistibility of globalization, such an assertion may seem overly bold. However, one does not have to spend very long in developing countries to come to see the 'paper tiger' aspects of globalization. The very mixed picture of developing-country 'compliance' with respect to structural adjustment and its successor programmes – contrary to the 'there is no alternative' aspect of the globalization discourse – would appear to be an excellent case in point. Seen in this way, the challenge for the academic becomes ascertaining what aspects of the 'global reality' get though to developing states and then documenting what happens to it when it meets the 'local reality'. That is, how does the 'global reality' metamorphose as it winds its way to developing countries and what impact does it have on developing-country states?

To adopt such an approach is to explore what Tickner (2003) refers to as 'hybridity', which for this author embodies an *a priori* commitment to the idea that even before one factors in issues to do with power or interests, neoliberal processes of change such as liberalization, deregulation and privatization will by definition turn out differently in diverse historical and cultural settings. How states react to such processes – and in turn are changed by them – will also vary from place to place, although there may be some common themes, which it may be possible to map.

In seeking to pin down both the nature of the changes affecting the state and what underpins them, parts of the globalization literature make bold claims regarding the changing nature and significance of national borders. Indeed, borders and globalization are often inextricably linked, as any textbook definition of globalization shows. For instance, part of what globalization is said to embody is a change in the nature of flows across national borders, whether this is of goods, people, information or money. Held and his colleagues talk in terms of changes in intensity and velocity (that is, the speed at which they occur) of cross-border flows, among other things (Held et al. 2000: 14–16). The most commonly cited example relates to financial flows, where the financial sector is depicted as being integrated across national borders, such that massive amounts of money can be moved quickly around the world, simply at the press of button (Beeson 2003: 361). This, in turn, is said to have implications for state autonomy, particularly in terms of the ability of markets to discipline states which make the 'wrong' policy choices, potentially closing off certain policy approaches altogether. However, the extent of such discipline – assuming it applies at all in some places – is contested. Looking at Malaysia after the Asian financial crisis of 1997–98, Beeson (2000) offers an excellent case study of the way in which some states can still blaze an alternative economic policy path even in an age of global financial markets.

Beyond changes in the nature of cross-border flows, globalization is commonly associated with two other key developments: first, the rise of private and transnational actors; and second the emergence of new 'transnational' problems, many of which, it is argued, are the result of changes in cross-border flows. Although cause and effect in relation to these developments are not always clear, the implication is that the state is no longer the only authority in the land. Instead, there are now new 'jurisdictions' or sites of power – both private and transnational – on which, it is suggested, nation-states increasingly have to contend as they seek to tackle the new challenges that have arisen with globalization (Hughes 2001: 420). Nevertheless, once again, the precise way in which these changes have impacted the state, if they have, is in need of more thorough investigation.

While complexity in respect of the way in which variables such as changes in cross-border flows or the rise of new actors may be impacting the state is justification enough for us to revisit these debates, there is another important reason why a fresh look at these issues is needed. Looking at the kind of examples cited in some of the prominent texts on globalization and the state, it is notable how they often betray a bias towards the West, developed countries, or at least the 'more developed' developing countries, along with national governments and capital cities (i.e. the places heavily populated by international business and transnational institutions). By contrast, there is very little reference to sub-national or provincial government, or places far from the capital city, such as border areas, and yet – it is easy to forget – these are the areas in which the vast majority of the developing world's population live (and die).

Such an omission raises important questions in relation to the literature's conceptualization of change affecting the state and the weight it gives to certain causal factors (i.e. globalization versus other more local dynamics). For example, do the assertions in the globalization literature regarding the changed nature of cross-border flows stand up to scrutiny when one gets off the beaten track? Also, does the literature's emphasis on the rise of private and transnational actors apply to the same extent, or in the same way, once one moves away from capital cities? And, if they do not, what are the implications in terms of how we explain observed changes in the nature of the state?

Of course, not all the literature dealing with globalization and the state can be tarred with this brush. There is now a growing literature which makes a distinction between national and local states and considers how the questions posed above may be answered differently at the local as opposed to the national level. Put another way, such literature asserts that 'place' continues to matter even in an era of globalization (Dicken and Anders 2001; Sheppard 2002). Scholars writing on the local state in China, India, Indonesia and Thailand, for example, highlight the way in which local power is often highly 'unreconstructed', entrenched and unaccountable, and that civil society – to the extent that it exists – is either weak or decidedly 'uncivil' and hence unable to play a countervailing role in relation to the state (Hadiz 2004; Jeffrey and Lerche 2000; McVey 2000; Sargeson and Zhang 1999). Furthermore, even where 'globalization' or 'marketization' is making its presence felt at the local level, the state is frequently able to hijack or subvert reforms in such a way that existing power structures are maintained (Hadiz and Robison 2005; see also Chapters 5 and 8 of this volume).

We now offer a conceptualization of the local state based on research conducted in Lao Cai and Tay Ninh.

Conceptualizing the state

Naturally there is a large and sophisticated literature on conceptualizing the state. This includes the literature on whether the state should be seen as 'strong' or 'weak', incorporating a debate about whether such labels are useful at all (Koh 2001). There is also the literature which distinguishes between an East Asian-style developmentalism – where the state is depicted as authoritative and insulated from society – and the model derived more from Southeast Asia, where the state is still viewed as developmental but less insulated and less capable (Booth 2001). The literature on the state also encompasses analyses of the state where the effects of changes in the international realm are scrutinized according to different kinds of 'impacts': the impact of global forces on government policy choices (decisional impact); whether certain policies are not even considered because of the prevailing international climate (institutional impact); the effect of global forces on the class structure of society, including as it pertains to the state (distributive impact); and the extent to which international forces are precipitating new forms of rule (structural impact) (Held et al. 2000: 18).

While all this literature offers useful insights, the aim here is a more modest one, namely to set out a characterization of the state in Lao Cai and Tay Ninh provinces which makes sense of the data collected there. Other scholars working on Vietnam have sought to draw distinctions between provinces (Malesky 2004b). Here, we are operating at a level of abstraction whereby the characterization of the state is applicable to both provinces. This way of conceiving of the state may also have theoretical reach elsewhere in Vietnam – a point which will become apparent later in the book.

Some scholars who have written on the state have noted that rather than being immobilized by international forces associated with globalization the state seems to be at the heart of the regulation and promotion of economic activity, including cross-border activity (Held et al. 2000: 5–6). Thus, far from being in retreat, it is holding its ground, and possibly even extending its reach. This characterization seems to make sense of the state in the provinces of Lao Cai and Tay Ninh. In these two provinces, not only were state institutions at the heart of regulating economic activity, but they were also active participants in economic activity through the running of state and private companies. In Lao Cai the share of industrial output derived from state-owned enterprises was a hefty 86 per cent in 1999. The percentage share in Tay Ninh was a smaller but still significant 28 per cent (General Statistics Office 2001, 2009).[2] A large number of private companies in both provinces also had state institutions or officials as shareholders.

State institutions in Lao Cai and Tay Ninh often did not work well together (that is, the state was not normally an especially coherent force). Consequently, the state in these provinces often appeared to lack 'infrastructural' power (i.e. the ability to get things done) (Mann 1984). However, the state was not without teeth. The provincial party committee could force wayward government institutions to toe the line when it felt its interests were threatened or circumstances demanded it, such as pressure from central government. The performance of Lao Cai and Tay Ninh in respect of elections to the National Assembly, the country's legislature, in 2002, and again in 2007, represented a well-organized and tightly choreographed affair, where provincial elites could be seen transmitting the central Communist Party's message about the legitimacy of Vietnam's brand of one-party 'democracy', and vetting prospective, election candidates to ensure that they were suitable (Gainsborough 2005). In sum, therefore, it was clear that the state remained a force to be reckoned with, even if this has both positive and negative ramifications.

BOX 6.1   Why the state matters: views from enterprises in Vietnam's Lao Cai and Tay Ninh provinces

1. The state is a source of:
   - capital, including preferential interest rates
   - information
   - contracts
   - legislation, which can make a difference (good and bad).
2. The state makes demands of companies, requiring companies to:
   - submit regular reports
   - seek permission to expand the business/increase investment
   - undergo equitization.
3. The state can help solve problems (e.g. land disputes).
4. Who you know and how much you pay matters.
5. The forces of control are alive and well:
   - conducting inspections and checks (e.g. transport police)
   - restricting what people say
   - monitoring foreign researchers.
6. The state is still actively involved in equitized companies.
7. Companies have expectations of the state.

Source: Author interviews with Vietnamese companies.

This picture of the state as a force to be reckoned with also came across clearly in the way that Vietnamese companies in Lao Cai and Tay Ninh spoke about the state (Box 6.1). The state made demands of them – sometimes of an onerous nature. At the same time, it was a source of things they wanted (e.g. capital, contracts, information). It was able to solve problems. Thus, being well connected to the state mattered. In interviews, company directors frequently explained their success, or why the state did not make trouble for them, by reference to their connections to provincial leaders or their reputation because they used to work for the provincial government. That is, accessing resources, whether it be money, contracts or information, did not depend on a set of rules which were the same for everyone. Instead, it depended on who you knew.[3]

Beyond the business realm, there was also little sense of the state being in retreat. Rather, the forces of control were alive and well. This could be seen in the activities of the security forces, checking up on companies (and foreign researchers).[4] It was also evident in the way in which interviewees were careful about what they said, suggesting that they believed there was a danger of repercussions if they spoke out of line. In both Lao Cai and Tay Ninh, it was not uncommon for interviewees to decline to answer certain questions, or to answer in a vague manner, if they were felt to be politically sensitive. In this sense, we may say that while the state in Lao Cai and Tay Ninh may lack infrastructural power, it is not without despotic power (Mann 1984).

The chapter now looks at the two key variables commonly privileged in the globalization literature for explaining changes in the state: cross-border flows and the rise of private and transnational actors. To what extent do we see changes in respect of flows and the emergence of new actors, as the literature suggests we should, in Lao Cai and Tay Ninh?

Cross-border flows

Earlier it was noted that changes in cross-border flows could be measured in terms of intensity and velocity among other things. In this section the focus is on intensity. Velocity is looked at later in the chapter.

In terms of changes in the intensity of cross-border flows, it is possible to identify two contrasting interpretations within the globalization literature. Those who question whether globalization really captures something qualitatively new about the world are inclined to argue that in historical terms flows have not grown significantly (cited in Held et al. 2000: 5). Another perspective can be identified specifically in relation to the official multilateral institution literature on the GMS, although the view is more widespread than this. This perspective is implicit in references to the subregion 'opening up' since the early 1990s, a term which clearly incorporates ideas about increased flows. Such a view is very much the one held by the Asian Development Bank (ADB), which has supported a series of initiatives designed to enhance economic integration among the GMS countries since 1992. (For a critical look at the nature of the 'regional market economy' being promoted by the ADB in the Greater Mekong Subregion, see Oehlers 2006.)

But are the ADB and others right? Have provinces like Lao Cai and Tay Ninh seen an increase in the intensity of flows since the early 1990s? Or is this in fact mistaken – the result of insufficient attention to the historical record, as the first perspective highlighted suggests? Alternatively, it may be wishful thinking designed to support a normative position (i.e. that 'opening up' is a good thing).

Here, it is suggested that in relation to the GMS it is hard to argue against the view that there has been a significant increase in the intensity of cross-border flows of goods, people, money and information since the early 1990s. In the first instance, the context for an intensification of flows is clearly political, namely improved political ties in the GMS since Vietnam withdrew from Cambodia

TABLE 6.1   Expanded trade flows in the Greater Mekong Subregion
(US$ million)

Two-way trade	1991	1995	2000	2003	1995–2000 (% annual increase)
Vietnam and Cambodia	30–40*	118.1	178.9	300	10.3
Vietnam and China	300	691.6	2937.5	4800	64.9

* Early 1990s.

Source: Official government statistics; Vietnamese media.

in the late 1980s and the Paris peace agreements on Cambodia were
signed in 1991 (Roberts 2001; Peou 2001). Moreover, the emergence
of pockets of prosperity in parts of the GMS along with improve-
ments in infrastructure – in part brought about by the initiatives of
the ADB – have created both the demand and the means by which
flows have been able to increase. Table 6.1, which contains data for
two-way trade between China and Vietnam and between Cambodia
and Vietnam, clearly confirms this position in respect of goods,
notwithstanding the usual doubts about the accuracy of the data.[5]

On the other hand, there are important questions to be asked
about the precise extent to which cross-border flows have risen. To
some extent, ideas about 'opening up' distort our notion of how it
was before (i.e. before the early 1990s). Even in the 'bad old days' of
strained relations between China and Vietnam and between Vietnam
and Cambodia during the late 1970s and 1980s, flows continued to
occur, even if they were often illegal or more appropriately informal
(Chau 2000). A similar point has been made in respect of the way
in which Vietnam's neighbour Laos is often depicted as 'emerging
out of isolation' with the opening of the cross-Mekong Mitraphab
(Friendship) Bridge linking Laos with Thailand in 1994 (Walker
1999). However, isolation from Western or state-capitalist Asian

capital is not necessarily isolation. Moreover, to make these points is not simply to try to put the historical record straight, it is relevant to our discussions of causation. That is, how significant does the change in the intensity of flows need to be for it to have an impact on the state, assuming it has an impact at all? Moreover, how precisely do changes in the intensity of flows impact on the state?

These questions will be addressed later in the chapter after consideration of the position of private and transnational actors in Lao Cai and Tay Ninh. To what extent is it appropriate to talk in terms of their rise?

Private and transnational actors

In the context of the shift from central planning to a more market-oriented economy, provinces like Lao Cai and Tay Ninh have seen an expansion of the domestic private sector, particularly at the household level. Table 6.2 contains data which illustrate this, although

TABLE 6.2 Private-sector growth in Lao Cai and Tay Ninh

	GDP (%)		Industrial output (%)		Industrial output (%)	
Lai Cai	1991	1995	1991	1995	1995	2000
State	26.9	31.9	100.0	35.7	80.0	81.8
Non-state	73.1	68.1	0.0	64.3	20.0	18.2
Tay Ninh	1995	2000	1995	2000	1995	2000
State	29.7	33.7	7.9	17.2	26.2	30.4
Non-state	70.3	66.3	92.1	82.8	73.8	69.3

Note: There is a large inconsistency between national and provincial data sources used in this table. The national data also show an increase in the state share of industrial output 1995–2000 despite the inclusion of household industry. However, I find this plausible.

Source: Official government statistics.

as the figures indicate it has not always been an unqualified rise.[6] Nevertheless, there is more private business activity in absolute terms in Lao Cai and Tay Ninh now compared with the late 1980s or early 1990s. Both Lao Cai and Tay Ninh have also recorded increases in foreign private investment since the early 1990s even if compared with some other provinces in Vietnam they have lagged behind.[7]

In relation to the rise of transnational actors, one of the arguments commonly advanced in sections of the globalization literature is that globalization has precipitated new 'transnational' problems which are beyond the ability of states to solve on their own, hence precipitating greater collective activity. Certainly, the GMS states are not immune to such problems, whether they relate to migration, environmental issues, disease or crime (Emmers 2003). Lao Cai and Tay Ninh also have their fair share of such problems. The provincial newspapers in Lao Cai and Tay Ninh frequently run articles on people trafficking and other forms of cross-border smuggling in the provinces, including sometimes the participation of state officials or people connected to them. In November 2002, for example, the son of the deputy police chief in Tay Ninh province was arrested on charges of operating an illegal smuggling ring shipping goods from Cambodia into Tay Ninh.[8]

For the purposes of this chapter, the question is whether GMS states can be seen to be participating more extensively than they were previously in subregional, regional and transnational organizations. A review of media and other publicly available information on this subject certainly suggests that this is the case, particular since the early 1990s. This not only includes the establishment of the GMS subregional cooperation project under the auspices of the ADB in 1992, but also a veritable treasure trove of tripartite, quadripartite and pentapartite initiatives. At the subregional level, this includes the tripartite conference on drug control cooperation involving Vietnam, Cambodia and Laos, which held its third meeting in Hanoi in December 2003; the five-nation narcotics cooperation

BOX 6.2   Transnational organizations in Lao Cai and Tay Ninh

LAO CAI

- World Bank (participatory poverty assessment, 1999 and 2003)
- UK's Department for International Development (DFID) (participatory poverty assessment, 1999 and 2003; pilot commune-level projects, 2001–03)
- UN Development Programme (participatory poverty assessment, 2003)
- Vietnam Consultative Group Mid-term review (held in Sa Pa, Lao Cai, in June 2003)
- Oxfam GB, New Zealand (co-funding education project Sa Pa since 2003)
- Danish International Development Agency (conservation project 2002)
- Danish Red Cross (primary health-care project, 1995)
- Enfants et développement (ethnic minority education project, 1999)
- UN Office on Drugs and Crime (study on ethnic minority drug use, 2003)

TAY NINH

- UN Development Programme (public administration reform, 1998)
- Asian Development Bank (road and water supply/sanitation projects, 1999, 2005)
- Japan International Cooperation Agency (public health, legal projects)
- Danish International Development Agency (conservation, 2001)
- Centre for Asia–Pacific Law, University of Sydney (training course for People's Court judge; project supported by UNDP and Danida)
- UN Office on Drugs and Crime (training courses on preventing human trafficking, 2004)

Sources: Official donor agency sources, media and Internet.

meeting, which first met in July 2003, bringing together officials from China, India, Laos, Myanmar and Thailand; and the 'Economic Cooperation Strategy' meeting involving Thailand, Myanmar, Laos, Cambodia and Vietnam, which also first met in 2003. In terms of regional power politics, the key issue is often which state is in and which state is out for any particular grouping.

The IMF and the World Bank resumed operations in Vietnam in the early 1990s, as did many international non-governmental organizations. The UK's Department for International Development has had a presence in Vietnam since 1992, but has been more active in the country since 2000. The work of these organizations has, in turn, precipitated an increase in overseas development aid-funded projects in provinces like Lao Cai and Tay Ninh, as illustrated in Box 6.2. Such data broadly confirm the thesis in the globalization literature regarding the rise of transnational actors, and also of greater participation of the state in initiatives which involve cooperation beyond its borders.

The next section of the chapter explores how we reconcile the persistence of state power in Lao Cai and Tay Ninh with increases in cross-border flows and the rise of private and transnational actors.

A stronger state in the era of globalization explained

The first point to make in relation to the observable data is that it is not being argued that one should necessarily expect a different outcome (a weaker state, for example). In contrast to some traditional Asian conceptions of power (for a discussion of this, see Anderson 1990), power here is not viewed in zero-sum terms. That is, with advances in technology or the development of new surveillance mechanisms, the reach of the state – the total sum of power – can be extended. Equally, increased participation by national governments in transnational initiatives should not necessarily be seen as leading to a diminution of state authority – not least at the sub-national level – although some scholars seem to imply that it should.

What is being suggested here is that the causal mechanisms between increased cross-border flows and the rise of private and transnational actors, on the one hand, and the persistence of state power, on the other, are poorly understood. Therefore, the aim in this section of the chapter is to offer some clarification.

In order to do this, it is necessary to consider two factors. First, we must look again at the way in which cross-border flows are conceptualized in parts of the globalization literature. Do the changes in relation to flows which some of the literature identifies as a feature of globalization really accord with what we see in provinces like Lao Cai and Tay Ninh? Second, we must look more closely at the position of private and transnational actors in these provinces. How might the rise of these actors in fact bolster the state? Cross-border flows are looked at first.

In terms of flows, it was argued earlier that one can indeed point to an intensification of flows in provinces like Lao Cai and Tay Ninh since the late 1980s or early 1990s, even if there is a debate to be had about the precise extent of the rise. However, flows are also measured in terms of velocity. Is it appropriate to argue that there has been an increase in the velocity of flows crossing Lao Cai's and Tay Ninh's international borders?

In some respects, the velocity of flows has probably increased: opportunities for information flows via the Internet or expanded air links have added to the velocity of cross-border flows even for provinces like Lao Cai and Tay Ninh where Internet access and air travel is limited.[9] However, much of what crosses Lao Cai's and Tay Ninh's borders continues to do so in ways which have occurred since time immemorial (i.e. on foot) or at least since colonial times (with the introduction of the motor car).

It is in relation to global finance that arguments about changes in the velocity of flows are most commonly made, including assertions that state authority is undermined as a result. However, such a depiction of the financial sector represents a poor fit with the situation in Lao Cai and Tay Ninh. Money – as well as gold

– clearly crosses their borders in large quantities, but it is more likely to be carried across on the person or smuggled in shipments of other goods (Chau 2000; Gainsborough 2003b). There are some sophisticated, informal financial-sector arrangements in place under-pinning cross-border trade, but it is still far from the 'press of a button' capitalism described in the mainstream literature. In terms of the impact of these kinds of 'informal' arrangements on state authority, it is considerably less than that described for global foreign exchange or stock markets, even if controlling informal financial activity is notoriously difficult.

Thus, some of the arguments in the globalization literature about changing nature of flows, and their impact on the state, may not have the same salience for states not integrated in global financial markets. Moreover, if one incorporates sub-national governments in the analysis – as we are doing here – it is clear that we are not just talking about a handful of reclusive states, such as North Korea or Myanmar (Burma), or those countries without a stock market.

The chapter now turns to how the rise of private and trans-national actors might in fact bolster the state.

Earlier in the chapter, it was noted that it was indeed possible to argue that border provinces like Lao Cai and Tay Ninh have seen the emergence of new private and transnational actors over the course of the 1990s. However, simply documenting an increase in the number of these actors is not enough. Rather, it is necessary to look more closely at the political standing of such actors, particularly their relationship with the state, in order to deduce what, if any, impact they are likely to have had on state authority. Looking at the discussions of private and transnational actors in the mainstream globalization literature, both in terms of how they are conceptualized and in terms of the claims made about their impact of the state, much of it seems quite inappropriate for provinces like Lao Cai and Tay Ninh.

With reference to Southeast Asia, Mark Beeson talks about private-sector actors 'taking responsibility from governments in specific … areas', citing "the regulation of online commerce, the management of intellectual property issues, or the impact ratings agencies have on government policy"' (Beeson 2003: 362). However, these kinds of example simply do not capture the nature of state–private-sector relations in Lao Cai and Tay Ninh, where there is little or no online commerce, where intellectual property rights are routinely flouted, and where ratings agencies have little, if any, direct influence over sub-national government even if they have started to impinge on national government thinking.[10]

In addition, it is not enough simply to assert the existence of private actors; it is important to know something about their relationship with the state before one can draw conclusions about their likely impact on the state (Moore 1966). In Lao Cai and Tay Ninh, where there are still large numbers of state companies, private-sector companies still have close relations with the state: that is, private companies have state institutions or officials as shareholders; the people running private companies are often former officials; and nominally private companies are still operating with a considerable degree of state involvement. This is not to suggest that the interests of those who head state institutions and private companies are always identical. However, they are generally members of the same class, who know each other, drink together, went to school together, and have often worked together.[11] Box 6.3 contains details of the career background of private-sector actors in Vietnam's Lao Cai and Tay Ninh provinces, illustrating the way in which the majority are closely connected to the state.

BOX 6.3   Origins of private-sector actors in Vietnam's Lao Cai and Tay Ninh provinces

LAO CAI

Lao Cai Joint Stock Transport Construction Company   Former state company founded in 1979. Equitized in 2001. Director born in 1955 in Ha Nam; parents both farmers; served in the army 1978–83; deputy director of company when still a state enterprise.

Cuong Linh Construction Company Limited   Founded in 1994. Director born in Lao Cai in 1969; son of retired government officials; graduate of construction university.

Lao Cai Joint Stock Transportation Company   Former state company founded in 1991. Equitized in 1999. Director born in 1956 in Yen Bai province; father worked for the government; deputy director of company when still a state enterprise; formerly worked for another state enterprise.

Minh Duc General Construction Company Limited   Founded in 1993 although registered as a limited company in 1999. Director born in Lao Cai in 1954; parents farmers; worked for the government in finance and accounting in the late 1980s; husband a senior official in provincial government.

TAY NINH

Tay Ninh Joint Stock Mineral Company   Former state enterprise founded in 1997. Equitized in 2000. Director born in Ninh Binh in 1957; son of a state official; career in state industry and provincial department of industry; also director of the company before it equitized.

Dong Nguyen Trade, Service and Production Company Limited   Founded in 2000. Director born in Tay Ninh in 1957; parents farmers; graduate of finance university in Ho Chi Minh City; worked in the provincial department of finance in the 1980s; worked in a state export company from 1988 until set up Dong Nguyen.

Tay Ninh Joint Stock Transportation Company   Former state enterprise founded in 1986. Equitized in 2000. Director born in Haiphong in 1948; came to Tay Ninh in 1979 to work in district government; bulk of his career was in state business; served as director of the firm prior to equitization.

Minh Trung Limited Company   Founded in 1993 but registered as a limited company in 1999. Director born in Tay Ninh in 1952; son of state officials; worked for provincial organization department (*ban to chuc chinh quyen tinh*) 1978–99.

Source: Author interviews with Vietnamese companies.

Writing on China, Dorothy Solinger (1992: 123-4) talks of a 'stratum of people exclusively pursuing business who are inextricably entangled with cadre-dom and an official class increasingly corroded by commercialism'. As a result, exchanges such as the issuing of licences or contracts, which are often depicted as occurring between distinct groups, in fact take place 'within a single blended class' (Solinger 1992: 123-4). Also with reference to China, Jean Oi (1989: 232) writes that it is not always easy to distinguish between the regulators and the regulated because the latter are the 'former colleagues and friends and relatives of the regulators'. Such a depiction of the political and business elite in China fits well with respect to the data for Lao Cai and Tay Ninh.

In light of these observations about the relationship between the private sector and the state, it makes sense that the rise of private-sector actors might not readily be associated with a diminution of state power.

So far, these arguments have only been made with reference to domestic private capital. However, they can be extended to include both foreign private capital and transnational institutions. With reference to foreign private capital, the picture in Lao Cai and Tay Ninh was less one of 'all-powerful' transnational corporations making demands on the state – although up to a point foreign companies clearly have influence – but more a picture of rather vulnerable companies, struggling to negotiate an alien and often confusing political and business environment. The clearest evidence of this derives from the endless tales of woe that foreign companies frequently recounted concerning the difficulties they have encountered with the state. Such a picture is clearly far removed from the image of all-powerful transnational capital.[12] Thus, if one asks who has the upper hand, it makes more sense often to give the benefit of the doubt to the state rather than the company.

Similar reservations underlie some of the arguments made about the strength of international institutions in relation to the state. David Held and his colleagues cite scholars who view state power as increasingly 'juxtaposed' with the 'expanding jurisdiction of institutions of international governance' and the constraints and obligations of international law, citing the activities of the World Trade Organization (WTO) as an example (Held et al. 2000: 8). Mark Beeson (2003: 362), meanwhile, writes of states 'increasingly falling under the purview of ... the legitimate authority of international organisations'. However, this kind of language seems inappropriate when trying to capture the influence of transnational actors in Lao Cai and Tay Ninh, who, like their counterparts in the foreign business community, are as inclined to highlight the obstacles to their activities put in their way by the state, including at the sub-national level. This was as commonplace for the World Bank as it was for international non-governmental organizations (NGOs).[13]

There is also a tendency to view the expanding presence of transnational organizations as equating to a diminution of state power. This too seems misplaced. The most appropriate characterization of the presence of transnational organizations in Lao Cai and Tay Ninh is where the state welcomes such institutions in because of the resources they can offer, is on the receiving end of large inflows of financial and other assistance as a project is rolled out, but where the impact of the project as measured in terms of the extent to which practice or behaviour really changes is limited. Anecdotally, it is noticeable, however, that state institutions which manage such projects are often able to employ new staff, buy new vehicles or refurbish their offices, or simply reap the reward of enhanced prestige associated with being the local partner for an international project. Thus there is a sense in which the state power is being augmented – not diminished – even whilst the presence of transnational organizations is expanding. Furthermore, much of the 'participation' in regional and international forums is at the rhetorical level with states hanging back from actually implementing the many declarations and agreements they sign (Emmers 2003).

References to state power being constrained by international law also seem out of place in Lao Cai and Tay Ninh. One of the dominant themes which came across in interviews with companies in these provinces was the prevalence of clientelism – understood as who you know, how much you pay, and the extent to which your reputation goes before you. Thus, these are the 'rules' by which companies operate. The rule of law – whether domestic or international – seemed not to have penetrated very deep.

In addition, during the period in which this research was conducted, Vietnam was not a member of the WTO; although Vietnam has since joined, the influence of the WTO in provincial Vietnam is not yet significant. This again highlights the way in which arguments about the authority of international organizations in relation to the state need to be qualified, particularly at the sub-national level. Furthermore, such arguments underline the way in which the formal advance of transnational institutions may not be incompatible with the emergence of a stronger state.

Some of the arguments in the globalization literature about challenges to state power centre on the rise of transnational social movements. For provinces like Lao Cai and Tay Ninh, which by and large are led by politically conservative leaders and where opposition is not tolerated, the influence of transnational social movements is negligible to non-existent (Gainsborough 2005). In Lao Cai and Tay Ninh, there is even less evidence of nascent civil-society-type activity compared with Hanoi and Ho Chi Minh City. Among the citizens of Lao Cai and Tay Ninh such concerns seem considerably further down the agenda. Thus the impact of transnational social movements is simply not something that the state in Lao Cai and Tay Ninh has to contend with.

Conclusion

This chapter has explored ways in which mainstream arguments about the impact on the state of changes in cross-border flows and the rise of private and transnational actors may need to be qualified when the focus is shifted to the state at the sub-national level. It has been argued that where provincial governments are less integrated in the global financial architecture, and where domestic private capital has close relations with the state, the impact of both changes in flows and the rise of private actors is likely to be less in terms of precipitating a diminution of state power. Equally, there seems to be a tendency in some of the scholarly literature to overstate the influence of foreign private capital and transnational institutions in a way which seems inappropriate, certainly with respect to the data uncovered for the two provinces analysed in this chapter. It has also been argued in this chapter that there are important ways in which the growth of private and transnational actors may be associated with a strengthening – not a decline – of state power in some areas.

7

SHARING THE SPOILS

The Tenth National Congress of the Communist Party of Vietnam, which was held on 18–25 April 2006, was preceded by the mother of all corruption scandals, namely PMU 18, so-called after a project management unit in the Ministry of Transport that was alleged to have embezzled millions of dollars of public funds, mainly by awarding public works contracts to private companies owned by family and friends. The corruption case, which cost the transport minister his job and saw his deputy put in prison pending an investigation as well as implicating countless other officials, created a certain frisson around the Congress, which is a key event in Vietnam's political calendar and happens every five years. How many political scalps would the corruption case claim? Who was pushing the scandal, and to what end? What, if any, were the connections between PMU 18 and the Congress? And, what would the consequences be for the anticipated changes to the Politburo and Central Committee line-up at the Congress? Of course, rumours abounded in Hanoi – most of them, it became apparent, wrong or simply reflecting wishful thinking by officials lower down in the political hierarchy.

Aside from the speculation about prospective leadership changes expected at the Tenth Congress, the Vietnamese-language press

---

BOX 7.1   What is the Political Report?

The Political Report is the key policy document that accompanies a party congress. It reviews the country's political and economic performance over the past five years and sets out objectives for the next five years. The national Political Report is compiled by centrally drawing, at least formally, on inputs from the party at different levels. Provincial party committees, which hold their own congresses in advance of the national congress, also produce Political Reports. A draft of the Political Report is circulated for comment from all sectors of the state and society before being revised and presented to the party congress for approval.

At the Tenth Congress, the Political Report had twelve sections setting out official party thinking in areas such as industry, education and training, social welfare, culture, national security, foreign affairs and party leadership.

---

and the Internet were packed full of Congress-related stories and debate. Given PMU 18, corruption inevitably featured heavily in the debate, but there were many other issues on the agenda, too – from how to make the Communist Party more democratic, to the rights and wrongs of party members doing business, to the future of socialism.[1] Some of the discussion was formally sanctioned – like the official feedback on the party's Political Report (see Box 7.1), a draft of which was circulated in advance of the congress – but whether it was officially sanctioned or not, much of the coverage was outspoken, seeming to push at formally approved boundaries. This was especially the case with Internet coverage, which, even if it was regulated 'onshore', seemed to invite a more full and frank expression of views than that contained in some of the newspapers.

Outspoken coverage took many forms. Some of it was predictable – like dissidents calling for multiparty politics – but there were also mainstream politicians who appeared to go further than usual in their criticism of the way the party was operating. The former party general secretary, Le Kha Phieu, for instance, called for an end to what he called the 'illness of partyization' (*benh dang hoa*), in which the party dominates everything.[2] Continuing the same debate, the former deputy prime minister, Vu Khoan, said that talent and moral stature were more important when deciding appointments, including ministerial appointments, than whether someone was a party member.[3] To be sure, ideas like this are not entirely new: echoes of them can be traced all the way back to the Sixth Party Congress in 1986 (Thayer 1992b). What was significant in the run-up to the Tenth Congress was the way in which such voices were being heard against the backdrop of a more vibrant society, where pressure on politicians to turn words into action appeared to be growing.

Congress coverage also included some tantalizing newspaper editorials that asked provocative questions such as 'What do we want?' (*Ta muon gi?*) or 'What do the people want and who would they choose?' (*Dan muon gi va chon ai?*), the latter in reference to prospective leadership change at the congress.[4] There was also some outspoken comment on the 'readers' views' pages of some of the newspapers. One reader, for example, said he was afraid that party members would engage in 'under the table' business (*kinh te chui*) if the ban on party members owning private companies was lifted.[5] Another reader touched on the highly sensitive issue of the children of Vietnam's elite (*con ong chau cha*), making unflattering remarks about the behaviour of Vietnam's new rich.[6]

While the leadership changes that occurred at the Tenth Congress and the issues that were discussed were undoubtedly interesting, there is an implicit assumption in the analysis of party congresses past and present that congresses matter. However, to make such an assumption without subjecting it to critical scrutiny seems a mistake. This is not to say that congresses are not important, but before we assume they are it is necessary to ask how precisely they matter.

To date, most analysis of Vietnam's party congresses has focused on the presumed policy significance of a particular congress, with the analysis itself heavily based on extrapolation from leadership change and a reading of the Political Report. This is often referred to as Kremlinology – or Ba Dinh-ology in Vietnam's case, after Ba Dinh square in central Hanoi (Templer 1998: 81). In defence of Kremlinology, it is often argued that although everyone knows the defects of this approach, academics continue to engage in it because in the absence of better information they have no choice. However, scholars do have a choice. Of course, access to information is a problem, but it is not just a problem of insufficient data. Even with the best intelligence in the world, this type of analysis is flawed because it assumes that 'policy' is what scholars ought to be interested in. Even leaving aside the question of what policy is, this chapter argues that much more important than policy are 'outcomes', or what actually happens on the ground. Put like this, policy is just a minor element in a much more complex equation that determines outcomes. Consequently, rather than focusing on the policy signifi-cance of Vietnam's congresses, a more fruitful way to assess their significance is to view them first and foremost as occasions when access to patronage and political protection are circulated and then to consider how outcomes emerge as a result of this.

To explore these issues, the chapter is divided into six sections. Following this introduction, the next section reviews the existing literature on Vietnam's congresses, highlighting the tendency to focus on the presumed policy significance of a given congress. The third section offers a critique of this literature, drawing attention to both the flimsy empirical foundations on which the mainstream approach is based and the reason why the focus on policy is mis-placed. In the fourth section, the case is made for seeing congresses as occasions when access to patronage and political protection is circulated. In the fifth section a conceptual framework is mapped for understanding how outcomes emerge, emphasizing the importance of seeing congresses in as broad a political and economic climate as possible. The conclusion revisits the question of how congresses matter, as well as considering the wider implications of the findings presented here.

We now turn to the question of how previous party congresses in Vietnam have been analysed.

How have past congresses been analysed?

Over the years, most congress analysis has been concerned principally with two things: first, changes to the Politburo and the Central Committee line-up made at a congress; and, second, the content of the key document that accompanies a congress, namely the Political Report. Writing just after the Eighth Congress in 1996, Brantley Womack embodies the dominant approach to analysing congresses:

> Official history is reckoned by these conclaves, and they provide the temporal bottom line for major realignments in policy directions and leading personnel. The Congress is preceded by more than six months of organized discussion of draft documents, most importantly the 'Political Report', at all party levels; before that process begins, the central leadership must struggle over what direction to take in writing the drafts. (Womack 1997: 83)

Both the leadership changes that result from a congress and the Political Report that accompanies it have been scrutinized largely with a single goal in mind, namely what it tells us about Vietnam's future. Thus, in the post-1986 period, the key question associated with any congress has been 'What does it tell us about the outlook for reform?' This emphasis on a predictive analysis has been a key hallmark of writing on Vietnam's congresses.

The assessment of those elected to the Politburo and the Central Committee at successive congresses has taken the form of trying to ascertain what particular leaders stand for based on their public pronouncements or their place of birth or career background, and then, in the post-1986 period, trying to draw conclusions about what this might mean for reform. Hence, the question on everyone's lips at the time of a congress is 'Does the new Politburo mark a boost or a setback for reform?'[7]

Scholars have also relied heavily on the use of labels to characterize particular politicians. 'Reformer' and 'conservative' are the best known and have shown the greatest longevity, although over the years the repertoire of labels used has become much wider. The late Douglas Pike, for example, referred to no fewer than seventeen labels in his assessment of the Seventh Congress in 1991, namely reformers, pragmatists, neoconservatives, conservatives, ideologues, military, modernizers, technocrats, bureaucrats, economists, jungle fighters, self-reliants, interdependents, low risk takers, high risk takers, young and old (Pike 1991: 81; 1992: 75).

Others have classified politicians according to blocs or sectors. Carlyle Thayer (1988, 1997), for instance, classifies Central Committee members according to senior party, central party-state, military and provincial categories. Thaveeporn Vasavakul (1997a) has done something similar, although she introduces new categories based on information that became available in the 1990s.

Politicians have also been clustered according to generations. In his book *Vietnam: The Politics of Bureaucratic Socialism*, Gareth Porter (1993) highlights three generations of politicians distinguished according to when they joined the party. The first generation included Le Duan, Pham Van Dong, Vo Nguyen Giap and Le Duc Tho, among others. They were members of the Indochinese Communist Party when it was established in 1930 but had ceased to hold formal office by 1986. A second generation of leaders, fifteen years younger than the first generation, joined the party around the time of the August Revolution in 1945. They started to take over state and party positions in the early 1980s. Porter includes former prime minister Vo Van Kiet in the second generation. Porter then highlights a third group of leaders, including Nguyen Van Linh and Do Muoi. They are similar in age to the second generation but they joined the party a little earlier and hence generally reached high office sooner. Nevertheless, whether it is labelling politicians as reformers or conservatives or talking in terms of sectors or generations, the goal is the same, namely to provide insights into what politicians stand for in relation to the policy issues of the day.

A further attempt to ascertain the policy significance of a congress has been based on analysis of the Political Report. The Report reviews the country's performance since the last congress and sets out the party's policy orientation across a range of areas for the next five years. In the reform period, analysis of the Political Report has prompted scholars to try to deduce such things as the degree of the party's commitment to maintaining a 'leading role for the state sector' in the economy, the extent of official enthusiasm for the 'multisector economy', or whether there are any signs of a political loosening up, or indeed to search for any clues as to what the party's priorities are or how it proposes to deal with the problems of the day.

Congresses also tend to get remembered in policy terms. Thus, in the collective memory, the Sixth Congress is associated with the launch of *doi moi*, the Seventh Congress with the closing off of multiparty politics, and the Eighth Congress with a reform slow-down ahead of the Asian financial crisis. Not all congresses are so easily pigeonholed: the Ninth Congress, for instance, seems to have resisted easy labelling. The Tenth Congress is arguably associated with corruption and its fallout.

Amid accusations that congress analysis is often speculative, Thayer has attempted to place it on a firmer empirical footing with a quantitative analysis of changes in the make-up of the party Central Committee. Based on this analysis, Thayer argued in 1985 that the process of leadership change had become 'regularized', by which he meant that a previously rather ad hoc process was becoming institutionalized, including the development of a more predictable time frame. Thayer also noted the rise of provincial-level leaders on the Central Committee in the period up to 1985 and forecast that the position of economic reformers in the political system would likely be strengthened (Thayer 1988). In 1997, Thayer updated his 1985 analysis to see whether his predictions had stood the test of

time. Generally, they had, although Thayer also noted that in so far
as the rise of provincial leaders on the Central Committee prior to
1986 had been suggestive of decentralization, changes to the Central
Committee after that date pointed to a process of recentralization
(Thayer 1997).[8]

Thayer (1997: 187, 190) has also sought to link changes to the
Central Committee – understood in terms of sectors – with policy
change, arguing that the policies of central-level 'reformers' have
found support at the provincial level. Building on Thayer's analysis,
Vasavakul (1997a: 87) has also explored the policy significance of
congresses, arguing that policy differences are the result of 'competition among different sectoral interests within the party'.

Past congress analysis critiqued

In the previous section, the following observations about congress
analysis to date were made: first, that it has sought to be predictive (i.e. it seeks to provide clues as to where Vietnam is going);
second, that it has been concerned with the policy significance of
a congress explored through analysis of leadership changes and
the Political Report; and third, that congresses have tended to be
remembered in relation to distinct policy positions (e.g. resisting
multiparty politics or launching or decelerating reform). What is
wrong with this?

The first problem with much of the congress analysis lies with
the foundations on which the predictive analysis is based. In terms
of leadership change, many of the assertions about what politicians stand for is based on thin evidence and, indeed, is often pure
speculation. Faced with a lack of information, it is common practice
for scholars to jump to conclusions regarding what a particular
politician is alleged to stand for. As a result, southerners are classed
as reformers (Abuza 2001: 163–4), people with a military or security background are labelled conservatives (Sidel 1998: 81), while
politicians who cannot easily be pigeonholed on one side of the

reformer/conservative divide are referred to as being at the 'ideological center' of the party (Thayer 2002: 83).

In reality, politicians – like everyone else – are simply too complex to be summed up with reference to a simple label such as 'reformer' or 'conservative'; it weakens the ability of such labels to help us predict how someone is likely to behave, which is why they were deployed in the first place. Nguyen Van Linh, for example, who rose up the ranks in Ho Chi Minh City before becoming party general secretary in 1986, was widely trumpeted as an economic reformer. However, he was as capable as anyone of tightening the screw politically when he felt things were in danger of getting out of hand (Thayer 1992b: 115-17). Le Kha Phieu, who served as party general secretary from 1997 to 2001 and has a military background, has often been referred to as a conservative, but, as was noted at the beginning of the chapter, he was associated at the Tenth Party Congress with some very outspoken language about problems in the party.

The Political Report is scarcely any more reliable as a guide to where Vietnam is heading than speculation about what politicians stand for. Even those who utilize the Political Report in their analysis recognize that it is a 'bland and conciliatory' document (Womack 1997: 83). This makes it very difficult to discern what it is saying and often results in some hair-splitting analysis of the language used.

Against this backdrop, it is perhaps not surprising that the predictive value of much congress analysis has been poor. On the whole, commentators have veered between making generalizations that are too sweeping, based on the available evidence, and hedging their comments so severely that their analytical or predictive value is next to useless. The following quotations provide examples of this:

> While the pragmatists were expected to increase their influence after Le Duan's death, any expectation of a swift policy shift in favour of leadership by pragmatic reformers quickly evaporated. (Esterline 1987: 103)

> It can be expected to be a more conservative group but leading reformers have also retained their seats. (Womack 1997: 84)

> Vietnam is entering a critical period with the approach of the five-yearly congress of the ruling Communist Party due to take place in early April. Continued inter-party factionalism could undermine the country's political stability and set back the course of reform. Alternatively, delegates to the Ninth National Congress could decide to jettison the ideological baggage of the past and adopt a renewed programme of reforms. (International Institute of Strategic Studies 2001)

The last quotation provides an example of both hedging and an analysis which is arguably too sweeping: the stakes at the Ninth Congress were never that high.

Ultimately, however, the problem with this kind of analysis is not one of insufficient information but rather its assumption that it is the policy significance of a congress that we ought to be interested in. Even with first-class intelligence on Vietnam's political elite, such an approach would be mistaken. Policy, if it is meaningful to talk of policy at all, is only an intermediate step on a complex road that leads to outcomes, and it is outcomes – and how they emerge – that we should be interested in. This is especially the case if we wish to move towards a more reliable predictive analysis.

Furthermore, it is not actually very clear what policy is. Writing on China, Barry Naughton says that during the reform period, the Chinese elite were never able to 'articulate a vision of the post-reform system' and that rather than 'groping for stepping stones in order to cross the river' – to use the common analogy – they were for significant periods 'slogging around in a swamp' (Naughton 1995b: 22). Something very similar could be said about Vietnam. The idea that there was a coherent policy blueprint that the elite were set upon in 1986 and then sought to implement is a fallacy. It may be possible to attribute some coherence to reform *ex post facto*, but this is very different from saying there was something identifiable called 'reform' at the outset. Furthermore, there is always a danger that in a bid to create some clarity scholars attribute too much coherence to reform *ex post*.

Mainstream congress analysis has historically asserted the existence of rival policy positions on the part of Vietnam's elite (Vasavakul 1997: 81–3). However, it is far from clear that politics in Vietnam is as much about carefully crafted policy positions as it is (or appears to be) in the West. Rather, to the extent that distinct policy positions can be identified – and often they cannot – they are distinctly secondary. Moreover, it is always an open question whether it is the analysts who are superimposing a particular position on politicians, rather than the politicians claiming it as their own. In this sense, the Political Report may be bland not just because it is a 'consensus' document, as is usually said, but because there genuinely are not any firm policy positions. This line of analysis chimes with what is frequently said about politics in other parts of Asia, namely that politicians or political parties do not differentiate themselves from each other in terms of distinct policy positions. Instead, politics is about personalities and money (Robison and Hadiz 2004; Slater 2004; Phongpaichit and Baker 2005; McCargo and Pathmanand 2005; McVey 2000; McCargo 2005; Sidel 1999, 2001). In fact, being identified with a particular policy position is politically compromising and can be dangerous.

So, if a focus on policy is misplaced, what then should we focus on? First, the focus should be on outcomes and trying to understand the complex process by which they emerge; and second, the starting point for assessing the significance of Vietnam's congresses should be seeing them as occasions when access to patronage and political protection is circulated and then seeing how outcomes emerge in the wake of this.

Such an approach makes senses for a number of reasons. First, it is much more in tune with how Vietnamese people experience politics or congresses, where the focus is clearly more on leadership change, and its repercussions, than anything else. Second, this approach does not rule out the existence of policy positions, but it does not start with them and it allows for a much more 'sketchy' notion of what policy is. That is, if policy positions do exist, they should be seen as distinctly secondary to patronage, which, given what has been argued regarding the uncertain position of policy within the political system, would appear to make sense. In other words, who you are aligned with comes first; policy comes second. Finally, the approach being advocated here redresses the balance in congress coverage from an analysis overly focused on policy to one in which informal politics is brought more centre stage.

We now develop these points further, beginning with the idea that congresses are occasions when access to patronage and political protection is circulated. Following this, we will consider the process by which outcomes emerge.

The circulation of patronage and political protection

Writing on the Philippines, Benedict Anderson (1988a) argued that the political system there allowed for the periodic circulation of elite families in and out of the upper echelons of the state. The potential for elite disgruntlement and eventual possible protest was thus reduced as, over time, all had access to the spoils. The problem with President Ferdinand Marcos (1965–86), Anderson says, was that he centralized power much more exclusively in his own hands, thus upsetting this equilibrium. While accepting the very different political conditions between the Philippines and Vietnam, such an analogy is relevant for Vietnam, where every five years access to patronage and political protection is circulated via changes to the Politburo and Central Committee.[9]

For Vietnamese officials, the key question at a congress is whether someone you are connected to personally or through your workplace moves up or out as a result of the circulation of positions, and what this means for you, your institution or your family in terms of the provision or loss of protection and access to patronage. In Vietnam, holding public office gives you access to patronage, which can range from access to the state budget and the ability to make decisions about how to spend public money, to the authority to issue licences or other forms of permission, to carry out inspections, or to levy fines. The result is that people come to you hoping for services or favours or generally to try to influence you. Equally, if you hold high office, people do not want to cross you for fear of what you might do to them. Whether such fears are really justified is debatable, but certain positions carry with them a reputation that gives the office-holders and people close to them a degree of protection in what can be a nasty and brutish political environment. Against this backdrop, it is no wonder that public office in Vietnam comes with a price tag, since it is well understood that buying a seat is an investment that can be recouped.[10]

At the Tenth Party Congress in 2006, it was clearly the anticipated circulation of access to patronage and political protection resulting from leadership change rather than the finer points of policy that was exercising people and generating the outpouring of speculation and rumour noted at the beginning of the article (see Box 7.2). This was especially clear with respect to PMU 18. As the corruption case escalated and more officials were drawn into its net, PMU 18 generated a frenzy of speculation as to who might pick up the posts on the Central Committee that were now expected to be vacant – since the case claimed the political scalps of a number of high-level people originally destined for places on the new Central Committee – and what further repercussions this might have further down the hierarchy.[11] Support for this position of seeing congresses as occasions when access to patronage and political protection is circulated can be seen in work by Abrami et al. (2008), who have identified a clear increase in public spending in Vietnam in the year before a congress.

The unfolding of PMU 18 and its subsequent momentum in the run-up to and during the Tenth Party Congress was also viewed by informants, without exception, as being directly linked to the congress. Various theories circulated as to who was pushing the case

BOX 7.2   Changes to the Politburo at the Tenth Congress

UNCHANGED

Nong Duc Manh (party general secretary)
Le Hong Anh (minister of public security)
Nguyen Minh Triet (president)
Nguyen Tan Dung (prime minister)
Truong Tan Sang (head of the party's Central Economics
    Committee)
Nguyen Phu Trong (chairman of the National Assembly)

UP

Pham Gia Khiem (deputy prime minister and foreign minister)
Pham Quang Nghi (secretary of the Hanoi Party Committee)
Nguyen Sinh Hung (deputy prime minister)
Nguyen Van Chi (head of Central Inspection)
Ho Duc Viet (chairman of the National Assembly Committee on
    Science and Technology)
Phung Quang Thanh (defence minister)
Truong Vinh Trong (first deputy prime minister)
Le Thanh Hai (secretary of the Ho Chi Minh City Party
    Committee)

OUT

Tran Duc Long (former president)
Phan Van Khai (former prime minister)
Nguyen Van An (former chairman of the National Assembly)
Phan Dien (former secretary of the Danang Committee)
Pham Van Tra (former defence minister)
Troung Quang Duoc (former deputy chairman of the National
    Assembly)
Tran Dinh Hoan (former head of the party's Central Organization
    Committee)
Nguyen Khoa Diem (former head of the party's Central Culture
    and Ideology Committee)

DIED IN OFFICE

Le Minh Huong (former interior minister)

and to what end, although – as is usual – none of the theories came accompanied by particularly convincing evidence. Some informants said that PMU 18 represented an attempt to undermine the then party general secretary Nong Duc Manh. Others said it represented an attempt to undermine the then prime minister, Phan Van Khai. The former appeared marginally more convincing because of an alleged connection between Nong Duc Manh and PMU 18, but inasmuch as Nong Duc Manh was given a second term as party general secretary at the Tenth Congress the tactic failed, if indeed that was what it was. When questioned as to why it was necessary to undermine Phan Van Khai since he was due to step down anyway, informants said the intention was to prevent Phan Van Khai from putting his supporters in key positions when he retired.[12]

The approach to understanding congresses advocated here suggests that it may make more sense to remember past congresses in terms of the politicians who fell from grace, where once again the struggle was less about policy and more about access to patronage and political protection. This emphasis appears particularly apt in respect to the Eighth and Ninth Congresses, where the fall of Politburo member Nguyen Ha Phan in 1996 and the replacement of party general secretary Le Kha Phieu in 2001 make little sense in policy terms.

The official reason put forward to justify Nguyen Ha Phan's ejection – that he had provided information to the enemy during the war nearly thirty years earlier – was clearly dredged up to provide justification for a piece of political manoeuvring.[13] Equally, the accusations against Le Kha Phieu – of ineffective leadership and a failure to revive the economy or root out corruption – sound equally hollow, suggesting political expediency (see Thayer 2002 for a discussion). Of course, the ejection of top leaders is sometimes justified in policy terms, but this is often just a fig leaf.

The Seventh Congress in 1991 has traditionally been understood by Western scholars as the point at which the party made clear its opposition to multiparty politics against the backdrop of what had recently occurred in Eastern Europe and the Soviet Union. More-over, support for multiparty politics has also been identified as the reason for the fall of Politburo member Tran Xuan Bach (Womack 1997: 84). However, no one has ever produced any hard evidence to corroborate either interpretation, and it is unclear what exactly Tran Xuan Bach said to whom and when. So did Tran Xuan Bach fall because he breached a sacred policy line in advocating multiparty politics, or was it more the result of a struggle for spoils?[14]

Even that most 'sacred' of post-1975 truths, namely the associa-tion of the Sixth Party Congress in 1986 with the 'launch' of *doi moi*, would merit fresh investigation in relation to the revisionist interpretation of congresses being advocated here. Revisiting the literature written immediately in the wake of the Sixth Congress, it is striking that *doi moi* often does not get a mention. Writing in January 1987, John Esterline (1987: 96), for instance, quotes a *Newsweek* journalist as saying that 'reform is on everyone's lips', but Esterline himself seems distinctly uncertain where the country was heading, saying 'the state ... continues to live in the past'. The fact that *doi moi* is not mentioned in analyses written during or shortly after the Sixth Congress reinforces the idea that the association of the Sixth Congress with *doi moi* is something that occurred after the event for political ends. According to this interpretation, finding the origins of 'reform' is not simply a question of getting one's historical facts right. Rather, it connects directly to the issue of party legitimacy, which is intimately bound up with the idea that the party 'devised' and 'launched' *doi moi*.

We are not yet in a position to put flesh on the bones of this argument in terms of a full rendering of national patronage networks, either for the Tenth Congress or for earlier congresses. However, the analysis above and other analyses provide clues as to where a more substantial investigation might begin and what such networks might look like. For example, during the 1990s there was evidence for two major political groups centred respectively on the one-time party general secretary Do Muoi (1991–97) and the former prime minister

Vo Van Kiet (1988–97).[15] One way in which rival interests between these groups appeared to be played out in the 1990s was in respect of the reorganization of state business in Ho Chi Minh City. While superficially this could be construed in terms of rival industrial policies, it was ultimately a struggle for control over companies and economic resources (Gainsborough 2002).

As we saw in Chapter 2, research on Ho Chi Minh City in the 1990s showed clearly the existence of political–business groups in the city linked to local politicians associated with corporate and banking interests. However, it was impossible to distinguish between the different groups on policy grounds. Politicians in Ho Chi Minh City could also be seen looking 'upward' to the umbrella of a national politician for protection in a way that suggests we should expect national patronage networks to extend 'downward' from Hanoi to the cities and provinces.

Research on patronage networks in Ho Chi Minh City also suggests that when considering such networks at the national level we are more likely to encounter loose political groups centred on personalities, wherein allegiances are not fixed but shift over time as the authority and standing of key politicians wax and wane. This is very different from the idea of factions grouped around distinct policy positions, or a notion of 'reformers' and 'conservatives', which is also linked to policy rather than personalities. In Vietnam, if policy features at all, it is distinctly secondary and can easily be jettisoned or adjusted to suit the circumstances. Relevant here is the way in which government agencies go about seeking international funding, where (policy) positions are adjusted according to what is required. What people really think in such situations is often unclear.

How outcomes emerge

If congresses are first and foremost occasions when access to patronage and political protection is circulated, what can we now say about the process by which outcomes emerge?

Earlier, the shift from a focus on policy to an understanding of how outcomes emerge was justified by saying that policy is only a minor element in a much more complex equation that determines outcomes. In order to understand the process by which outcomes emerge, it is necessary to think as broadly as possible. Thus, we are interested in both the economic and the political, the domestic and external environments, and, importantly, the formal and the informal. Put another way, we are interested in the full range of influences that determine what Vietnam's leaders advocate in the first place and how their ideas or actions are refined, embellished, knocked off course, or blocked on the road to outcomes, or what actually happens on the ground. This broader context rarely, if ever, features in mainstream congress analysis, given its focus on policy and the alleged position of individual politicians in respect of the (policy) issues of the day. However, this context is essential if we are to improve the quality of our predictive analysis and, importantly, if we are to come to a more considered view of how congresses matter.

Writing on China, Naughton has argued that over the longer term the pattern of reform was shaped more by 'economic conditions and the interaction between economics and politics than it was by ideology or politics' (1995b: 23-4). This observation is equally applicable to Vietnam and is relevant to the argument here about the importance of viewing in a broader context what happens at a party congress. What Naughton is saying is that policy decisions usually occurred either in response to underlying economic conditions (i.e. how the economy is structured), which poses limits on what is feasible, or, equally importantly, as a consequence of the underlying political economy (i.e. who holds economic power). Decision-makers, the people promoted at congresses, have to work within these constraints, which operate both domestically and externally. It is this broader environment, much of which operates informally – not 'who is up or down' or what the Political Report says – that one needs to understand in order to attempt to predict where Vietnam is going. This is not to say that politicians do not matter, but they matter less than much congress analysis has implied.

When we talk about the broader environment in respect of Vietnam, we are thinking of the full range of domestic and international relationships in which the country and its leaders are embedded institutionally and personally. Externally, this would include Vietnam's relations with multilateral agencies, such as the World Bank, the International Monetary Fund and the United Nations, along with the various bilateral donors with which it interacts. We would also need to consider the international economic agreements that the country has signed, such as the ASEAN Free Trade Area, the bilateral trade agreement with the United States, and membership of the World Trade Organization. These relationships and agreements all impose constraints within which domestic policymakers must operate, although in the typology being put forward here we are interested in what the actual constraints are as opposed to what the formal rules or treaties say. This is because there is usually more room for manoeuvre than the official position suggests, as rules, even in international trade, are open to interpretation, and non-compliance in respect of international agreements does not always result in sanction (see Chapter 8).

In terms of the domestic environment, the focus is on the structure of the economy, which, as Naughton says, exerts an influence on elite behaviour by determining what is possible. The structure of the economy is affected by Vietnam's comparative advantage in terms of industrial production, for instance, which in turn is determined by the country's resource endowment, labour and other business costs, and level of technology. These all provide broad parameters within which elites must operate.

At this point, the focus of our analysis needs to shift to Vietnam's domestic political economy, or, as Naughton says, the interaction between economics and politics. Here, we are concerned with who controls the commanding heights of the economy, although, as with the international political economy, we are more concerned with the actual or informal arrangements that ultimately govern what happens. It is here that identifying who has access to patronage and political protection, as highlighted in respect of party congresses, becomes important. However, this is just one of a number of factors that determine outcomes. Those who are in a position to act have to do so while taking into account other 'networks of power' in the form of other political–business interests operating both domestically and internationally. The calculations that are likely to ensue are myriad and complex (e.g. Who can we not afford to offend? Who must we win over before we act? Who do we not need to worry about?). Given the complexity of this process, it is inevitable that how outcomes emerge needs to worked out – and mapped – on a case-by-case basis. The key point is that within this process, congresses and what they decide are just one element in a complex equation that determines outcomes. Chance, luck and skill are as important as economic conditions and the interaction between politics and economics operating both domestically and externally.

Conclusion

This chapter has mapped out an alternative approach to assessing the significance of Vietnam's party congresses, which historically have been analysed with too much focus on their alleged policy significance. In keeping with other parts of Asia, politics in Vietnam is more concerned with personalities and the associated access to patronage and political protection than with policy. As in other parts of Asia, politicians in Vietnam generally do not distinguish themselves from each other on policy lines, although struggles for control over resources are sometimes dressed up in policy terms. To support these arguments, data on the Tenth Party Congress held in April 2006 were presented showing that it was prospective leadership changes and their implications that held the attention of the country's political elite. The finer points of policy were much more secondary, although lively debate in the press on a range of contemporary issues again suggests that 'policy' may provide the context in which struggles for 'position' occur. In light of these findings, it may be fruitful to revisit earlier congresses, which have tended to be remembered in terms of policy, and to consider whether they too could be seen in a similar light. Some pointers have been offered in this direction, but further research is required.

Having raised doubts about the policy significance of Vietnam's congresses, the chapter has then sought to assess their significance by considering how outcomes – or what happens on the ground – emerge, and seeing what role congresses play in that process. The chapter has argued that the circulation in access to patronage and political protection that occurs at party congresses is only one factor among many that go towards determining outcomes. To gain a full understanding of the process by which outcomes emerge, it is also necessary to take into account the structure of the domestic and international economy and the relationship between politics and the economy, also operating domestically and internationally. In all of this, special attention needs to be paid to the informal realm so we are not duped into taking formal rules for granted.

Taking all these things into account is undoubtedly a tall order, and it is clear that how outcomes emerge and why need to be mapped on a case-by-case basis. Refining and embellishing this analytical framework, which could be applied to analyse other set-piece political events, is again a task for further research. However, based on the arguments presented in this chapter, Vietnam's party congresses are only important in so far as they put people in a position to act. After that, actors are buffeted by a wide range of factors, some of which are entirely beyond their control, making what congresses 'decide' only tangentially important.

8

ELITE RESILIENCE

This chapter explores what happens to neoliberal ideas about development when they encounter Vietnam's distinctive political and cultural context. In particular, it seeks to understand neoliberal thinking about the state and the extent to which it can, in any way, be seen to have left an imprint on Vietnam some twenty years after the onset of marketization. The chapter also serves as something of a stock-taking exercise prior to the conclusion, particularly around the issue of continuity and change, in light of what we have discovered in the book so far. Furthermore, this chapter, like the conclusion, starts to try and talk about 'the state' at a level of abstraction which we generally resisted in previous chapters. It is not that we are forgetting what we have learnt in the book so far – namely the importance of taking into account the interactions and preferences of actors within the entity we call 'the state' – but we are exploring the extent to which it is possible to generalize in light of these insights.

While the literature on neoliberalism is varied and diverse, it is not an exaggeration to say that the tendency in much Western scholarship is to emphasize – implicitly or explicitly – the very great power of neoliberalism in our world today. Dag Einar Thorsen and Amund Lie, for instance, describe how neoliberalism has been viewed as the 'dominant ideology shaping our world today', adding that for others we live in 'an age of neoliberalism' (Thorsen and Lie 2006). Meanwhile, Jamie Peck and Adam Tickell, who offer a useful geographers' perspective, are in no doubt of the power of neoliberalism, arguing that the 'transformative and adaptive capacity of this far-reaching political-economic project has been repeatedly underestimated' (Peck and Tickell 2002). Not everyone, of course, takes this perspective (see, for example, Hadiz and Robison 2005; Hamilton 1989; Hibou 2004; Harrigan 1996; Thirkell-White 2007 for authors who adopt a contrasting position), but as the authors cited above indicate, the 'neoliberalism as powerful' camp is an influential one nevertheless.

This chapter, as much of the book, is firmly in the camp of those who question the power of neoliberalism, specifically leading to the argument that despite twenty years of reform, which has involved extensive engagement with a wide range of neoliberal actors, the state in Vietnam remains little changed in terms of its underlying political philosophy and many of its practices. This is in stark contrast to large swathes of the literature on Vietnam, which, while acknowledging that the Communist Party is still in power, sees reform instinctively as being synonymous with change, including political change. Now, obviously, we need to be very careful and precise regarding the balance between continuity and change – and the chapter will be – but there is at least enough of a sense of continuity to suggest a puzzle which needs explaining. That is, what does it say about this 'dominant' ideology we call neoliberalism, if its impact on one developing country is at best marginal?[1]

The chapter first looks at how neoliberalism is understood, paying particular attention to its perspective on the state. It then looks at the issue of continuity versus change, focusing on the state's self-image, its relationship with its citizens, the influence of patronage and money in political life, and the extent to which power is centralized or more scattered. The final section prior to the conclusion seeks to make sense of the findings through an account which is attentive to both structure and agency. It is argued that while at least part of the explanation for the relatively small impact of neoliberal ideas about development on the Vietnamese state must lie in the way in which it has fashioned the nature of its engagement with external institutions to its advantage, a more complete account lies in exploring the way in which elite interests both inside and outside Vietnam converge. This emphasis on a convergence of elite interests is important since this point is often missed in the literature, which places the emphasis on elite resistance (see, for example, Dixon and Kilgour 2002). Moreover, in terms of explaining the outcomes we observe, the chapter offers fresh insights based on close 'ethnographic'-style observation of Vietnamese and international donor elites.

Neoliberalism unpacked

Neoliberalism is one of those terms which is frequently bandied about but rarely defined. In left-leaning academic circles, it often serves as catch-all for all the supposed ills of the World Bank and the IMF (i.e. neoliberalism as a term of abuse) (see, for example, Cammack 2001, 2004; Fine 2002, 2006b; Pincus and Winters 2002).[2] Here, neoliberalism in relation to ideas about development is associated with both the Washington and the Post-Washington Consensus so-called (Gore 2000). In particular, the focus is on the transition that occurred between the two consensuses as offering a particularly useful window onto one way in which we may conceptualize power in the world.

The heyday of the Washington Consensus, which occurred during the 1980s, was associated with a particularly radical emphasis on the market as the ultimate arbiter of how goods and services are allocated. This, therefore, was the era of fiscal discipline, floating exchange rates, trade liberalization, deregulation, and, of course, privatization (Williamson 1989). The state, by contrast, was required to take a back-seat role, ensuring the conditions for development by providing public goods and maintaining macroeconomic stability but not 'intervening in' or 'distorting' the market (Hoogvelt 2001).

In 1997, the World Bank published its flagship *World Development Report* with the title 'The State in a Changing World' (World Bank 1997). For an organization which had in recent years scarcely talked about the state, this marked a turning point since it seemed to signal that what the state did mattered to the Bank after all. The debate that emerged in the *Report*'s wake centred on the extent to which the so-called Post-Washington Consensus was really different from the early Washington Consensus (Fine 2006b). In this book, the Post-Washington Consensus is not seen as a retreat or a watered-down version of neoliberalism but rather as a more invasive form of neoliberalism made possible in part by the end of the Cold War (Clapham 1996). Thus, no longer concerned that developing states might 'go over' to the now collapsed Soviet Union, mainstream development agencies could now afford to push developing countries harder in terms of the attachment of stringent conditions to aid. Phrases such as 'local ownership' which emerged with the Post-Washington Consensus, or the end of contentious structural adjustment programmes (SAPs), did not mark the end of adjustment. Rather, adjustment remained but it was now dressed up in new language. Furthermore, renewed interest in the state on the part of leading development agencies was not simply a benign interest designed to make development happen but rather created the foundations for a more invasive form of intervention whereby domestic politics, or governance, which once had been beyond the remit of such agencies, was now clearly within their purview.

Kanishka Jayasuriya (2001) suggests that in the Post-Washington Consensus era a new kind of 'regulatory state' capable of protecting the market from the perceived 'corrosive influence' of politics has emerged:

> Governance projects suggest a deeply antithetical attitude to politics as conflict or rational deliberation, and instead substitute a

version of politics as the effective implementation of agreed technical procedures. (Jayasuriya 2001: 1)

According to this view of politics, special emphasis is placed on the
role of juridical processes in safeguarding and creating market order
(i.e. the emphasis on 'rule of law' in mainstream aid agency governance programmes). Moreover, in order to keep the political executive
out of the economy, the emphasis is on indirect rather than direct
regulation. It is in this context that we see the rise of 'independent'
central banks as the preferred policy received wisdom.

However, the point to make is that this is not a watered-down
form of neoliberalism. Instead, it represented an attempt to build a
state capable of shoring up, among other things, global capitalism
(McMichael 1996). That it represents a more invasive form of neoliberalism can be seen in developments which saw the World Bank,
and other agencies, become involved in a whole range of activities,
including anti-corruption programmes, under the umbrella of governance programmes (Marquette 2004).

It is in relation to this understanding of neoliberalism (i.e. Post-
Washington Consensus neoliberalism, seeking to uphold and advance
the original neoliberal project by manufacturing a particular kind of
state) that the chapter seeks to assess the changes which have occurred in Vietnam. It is to this we now turn, first making some comments about Vietnam's reform process and its relationship to these
wider ideas about development which have just been outlined.

Vietnam and 'reform'

Following the victory of the Communist-led North Vietnam over
the US-backed South Vietnam in April 1975 the country entered
a period of political and economic isolation from the West. While
partly a legacy of the war, Vietnam's isolation was compounded by
its invasion and occupation of Cambodia in December 1978 and its
moving closer to the Soviet Union, with which it signed a friendship

and cooperation agreement just prior to the invasion. In the late 1970s and in the first half of the 1980s, Vietnam's economic relations were almost entirely with the Soviet Union and its satellite states as the Vietnamese leadership presided over a distinctive version of central planning – distinctive in outcome if less so in design (Fforde and de Vylder 1996). In Vietnam, where state authority was relatively scattered, the plan was never implemented as robustly as in the Soviet Union and China, and in the context of much poverty and discontent, officials, farmers and workers soon started to take matters into their own hands, engaging in unsanctioned off-plan activities, and in some cases leaving the country in boats (the so-called boat people).

It was against this backdrop that moves were made to rescue matters in what later became known as *doi moi* (Fforde and de Vylder 1996). Also importantly, the leadership negotiated its way out of Cambodia, resulting in the withdrawal of Vietnamese troops in 1989 and a peace agreement in 1991 allowing for UN-supervised elections. The rise to power in the Soviet Union of Mikhail Gorbachev in 1985, culminating in the Soviet Union's collapse in 1991, turned the pressure on Vietnam to mend fences with the West into a necessity. Underlining that a thaw in Vietnam's relations with the West was occurring, the then French president, François Mitterrand, visited Vietnam in February 1993 – the first Western leader to do so since the end of the war. Shortly afterwards in December 1993, the Paris Club of creditor nations rescheduled Vietnam's hard-currency debts. Two months later, the US government lifted its trade embargo before establishing diplomatic relations with Vietnam in 1995.[3]

Having in effect missed out on the high tide of Washington Consensus-era international aid, Vietnam has seen, since the 1990s continuing until the present, the full complement of multilateral, bilateral and international non-governmental organizations associated with the international donor community set up offices in the country. Among multilateral and bilateral donors this has included the IMF, the World Bank, the UNDP, the UK's Department for

International Development, Australia's AusAid and the Swedish
International Development Agency (SIDA). While there are clearly
some differences of emphasis and outlook between the various aid
agencies operating in Vietnam, the dominance of Post-Washington
Consensus-era neoliberal policies is plain to see. Thus, in relation
to the governance field, all the mainstream agencies are operating in
a narrow range of areas which include public administration reform,
anti-corruption, legal reform, and civil society development. Beyond
this, the donors are also working in the areas of social inclusion,
public financial management, state-sector reform, and private-sector
development, all also reflecting Post-Washington Consensus-era
goals.

While the relationship between the Vietnamese state and the
international donor community is undoubtedly complex – and is
discussed in detail later in the chapter – there is no denying the
country's extensive exposure to Post-Washington Consensus neoliberal institutions, their ideas and practices. Since the mid-1990s,
aid pledges have regularly been in the region of $US3–4 billion
annually while Vietnam is currently the second largest borrower
after India from the World Bank's concessional lending arm, the
International Development Association (Rama 2008: 35). In turn,
billions of dollars have been disbursed and an army of international
consultants deployed.

The question is, what difference has this activity made and,
importantly, how do we explain the outcomes we observe? In particular, this question is important for this book in respect of the
impact engagement with the international donor community has had
on the Vietnamese state. This is addressed in the next section.

Conceptualizing change

The question that immediately comes to mind when thinking about
continuity and change is change in relation to what? There are
two possibilities: first, change in relation to a conceptualization of

how the state was prior to the reform years; and second, change in relation to neoliberalism, in particular Jayasuriya's writing on the regulatory state. That is, does the Vietnamese state today in any way show signs of resembling a regulatory state?

In trying to pin down the balance between change and continuity, this chapter pursues a combination of these two approaches. That is, it first paints a picture of the Vietnamese state on the eve of reform focusing on the state's self-image, its relations with its citizens, the role of patronage and money in political life, and the extent to which power was centralized. We then consider the extent to which any of this has changed over the last fifteen to twenty years. Second, the chapter looks at the key features of the regulatory state as described by Jayasuriya, asking whether the Vietnamese state today bears any resemblance to it.

The pre-'reform' Vietnamese state

In seeking to characterize the Vietnamese state in the period after 1975 but before the reforms kicked in, it is necessary to proceed quite carefully, in part because much of the writing from this period was conducted through the lens of a Cold War historiography which in retrospect can be seen to be distorting. Part of the problem was a tendency for scholars to interpret what they saw through a narrow 'state security' lens such that even policies which had an economic rationale were viewed solely as being about the social control or state repression. Bound up with such perspectives was also a post-war, anti-communist view whereby those on the 'losing side' did not miss an opportunity to show that they were right after all by highlighting the difficulties faced by the Vietnamese state. In addition, some of the pre-reform literature shows a tendency to overstate the extent of state control in Vietnam, possibly because of the influence of US Cold War perceptions of Soviet-type politics on scholarship on Vietnam, and we need to be mindful of this too.[4]

Such caveats aside, there are a number of points which can usefully be made in terms of characterizing the pre-reform state in Vietnam. Our first observation is simply that power was relatively concentrated in those days (even allowing for some overstating of this in the literature). This is not to say that in all situations it was concentrated, or that there was no institutional particularism, but it is simply to emphasize that in the post-war period the Communist Party was a relatively authoritative institution (for a review of some of the early positions, see Kerkvliet 1995). This can be seen with reference to the party's own critique of politics, which emerged at the Sixth Congress in 1986 when it spoke out against the tendency of party institutions to 'control the whole show' (Thayer 1992b). Implicit in this comment is the idea that the party did everything and that government institutions were relatively undeveloped. Moreover, while informal processes of consultation did occur in the wider state and society, decision-making was quite centralized and in the hands of a narrow political elite.[5] The National Assembly, meanwhile, was a rubber-stamp parliament (Thayer 1993).

The state's relationship with its citizens during the pre-reform period was formally managed via the party-controlled mass organizations, which sought to mediate the interests of various different social groups, such as farmers, women and youth. While it would be mistaken to suggest that no independent social organization occurred at this time (see, for example, Koh 2004), the establishment of social organizations outside of the mass organization structure was not permitted. More than this, the state played a key part in people's lives. In the 1970s and first half of the 1980s most people were employed by the state, either in collective agriculture, in the bureaucracy, or for state-owned enterprises. There was also food rationing. There was tight restriction on people's movement both within the country and outside. What media people were permitted to read or listen to was also tightly controlled, and generally the tentacles of the security apparatus were far-reaching (Canh 1985; Long and Kendall 1981).

Turning to the question of the state's self-understanding, this was at one level bound up with the war, and a belief that the party's legitimacy rested on having liberated the country from foreign occupation. However, elements of the state's self-understanding ran much deeper than this. For example, the state was strongly paternalistic, which manifested itself in a strong belief that 'the party knows best'. It also extended to the party's attitude to criticism, such that those who engaged in criticism or sought to organize outside the confines of party structures quickly put themselves beyond the pale, thereby surrendering any rights they might otherwise have had (as discussed in Chapter 1).

It is also possible to gain insights into the state's self-understanding in the pre-reform period by looking at its attitude to the economy. In the planning era, the state was heavily involved in the economy not only though the allocation of goods and services but also through the operating of state enterprises. However, more than this, that the state did these things was regarded as the morally right thing to do such that the notion that the economy might be in the hands of non-state forces was anathema. While much can be said about the origins of these ideas, they go a long way to explain the state's hostility to the private sector during this period.[6]

Finally, in respect of contemporary analyses of Vietnamese politics which tend to emphasis the growth of 'corruption' in the reform era, it is worth emphasizing that money, patronage and connections were an integral part of the operating of the Vietnamese state in the pre-reform period. The whole history of 'fence-breaking', whereby people started operating clandestinely outside of the central plan, engaging in markets as a precursor to 'reform', testifies to this (Fforde 1993). Moreover, recent writing has highlighted the way in which even in the so-called state subsidy period, as the pre-reform era is often referred to, there emerged a 'new class' from within the elite that has access to resources and materials that ordinary citizens did not.[7] Thus, any notion that Vietnamese society was entirely flat socially during this period is mistaken.

The question that arises in relation to the pre-reform state in Vietnam is, to what extent is the state still like this, or has it changed?

The post-'reform' Vietnamese state

In the post-reform Vietnamese state we see both continuity and change. In terms of the extent to which decision-making is concentrated in the hands of a narrow elite, power is more scattered, although it was never especially concentrated in the pre-reform period. Clearly, the Communist Party is still the ruling party and there are no legally tolerated opposition parties (for a discussion of recent challenges to one-party rule, see Thayer 2009a). However, there are now significant institutional interests associated with the government such that even though it is still the norm for people in the government to be party members, such institutional interests matter. In addition, the National Assembly has emerged as a centre of new institutional interests even if this is tempered somewhat by the fact that, as with the government, nearly all National Assembly deputies are party members (Salomon 2007).[8]

Beyond this, decision-makers in the post-reform era have had to be more attentive to a greater plurality of interests than previously, even if the way in which this occurs is generally not institutionalized. This is evident in at least two areas. First, the reform era has been associated with a significant expansion of the economy, which has led to the emergence of new business interests and, *de facto* if not always *de jure*, decentralization to the provinces (Gainsborough 2003a, 2004c; Malesky 2004a). Illustrating the rather fractured nature of the Vietnamese polity today and the way in which power has become scattered, these developments have at times occurred with reference to national politics (i.e. with the formal granting of new authority to the provinces by the political centre). However, very often, these new business and/or provincial interests operate with little regard to what the formal rules say, again pointing to a diffusion of power. Second, societal interests are more diverse and vocal than they were in the pre-reform era and this too is having an impact on decision-making. For example, the still formally state-controlled media today represent a far greater variety of perspectives than they did a decade and half ago, and they can at times be influential in pushing politicians to respond to a perceived public mood (Heng 1999, 2001; McKinley 2009).[9]

In terms of the state's relationship with its citizenry, there are signs of both continuity and change. The party-controlled mass organization structure still persists and the party continues to argue that it operates effectively both as a channel of communication between the state and the society and as a source of valued development activity. However, the mass organizations are creaking at the seams, primarily because they appear rather out of date in the context of the rapid social change that has accompanied the reform era. For example, Vietnam's population is not easily categorized as farmers, workers or intellectuals, which is the terminology referred to in the country's constitution (Constitution of Vietnam 1995: 155). Equally, it is doubtful that all youth, women and business people feel adequately represented by party-regulated groups such as the Youth Union, the Women's Union or the Vietnam Chamber of Commerce and Industry. The proliferation of a wide variety of non-governmental organizations – albeit under an uncertain legal framework – further suggests that there are an increasing number of individuals and groups which fall outside party-sanctioned organizational structures (Kerkvliet 2003).

Tight state control over Vietnam's citizenry, including invasive day-to-day surveillance by the security apparatus, is much less in evidence today. However, the state is still able and willing to clamp down on individuals or groups it deems a threat. Nevertheless, in contrast to the pre-reform era, the state is no longer the dominant employer. Moreover, media outlets, including the Internet, which has become a reality in Vietnam since 1997, are now so diverse that any state efforts to restrict access to information – for example, from foreign sources – are a drop in the ocean, apart from exceptional cases. The household registration system (*ho khau*), which seeks to limit internal population movement, is still in place but in practice – and in the context of strong demand for people in the country-side to move to the cities to work in factories – is poorly enforced. Furthermore, foreign travel is no longer subject to the restrictions it once was.

On the other hand, the notion that the reform years have seen a lessening of security-apparatus control across the board is mistaken. That is, while the state has been scaling back its activities in some areas, it has been expanding them in others. A good example is the government's involvement in tackling human trafficking, which, in tandem with global developments in this area and against the backdrop of significant international donor community support, has expanded massively in recent years. Moreover, while there is evidently a humanitarian dimension to anti-trafficking activities, operating in this area also provides scope for the state to police the population more generally.

In terms of the state's self-image, the state remains strongly pa-ternalistic despite two decades of engagement with international donors. The state's continued unwillingness to countenance oppo-sition parties is evidence of this, while the party's tolerance of non-governmental organizations remains grudging at best, such that whatever it might say the state continues to be uncertain about the merits of their contribution to the developmental process (Fforde 2004a). Evidence for this can be seen in relation to the tortuously slow advance, and then shelving, of legislation dealing with the regulation of civil society (i.e. the Law on Associations), which has been years in the making and remains highly sensitive (Thayer 2009b : 7).

In respect of the state's involvement in the economy, there has been some change in the reform era in terms of both practice and the ideas which underpin it. In large areas of the economy, for example, the state evidently has taken a step back, including presiding over a significant expansion of the private economy that two decades ago would have been unthinkable. Nevertheless, it would be mistaken to suggest that the state's view that it should play a pre-eminent role in the economy has disappeared completely. After dipping initially, the state share of economic output has remained relatively constant since 2002 at 37–40 per cent of GDP (IMF 2007). This is explained in large part by the fact that economic reform in Vietnam is not just to be associated with a retreat of the state. State actors or those with close connections to the state have led the way in terms of the expansion of Vietnam's business sector such that the state remains an important *direct* player in the economy (Cheshier and Penrose 2007; Fforde 2004b; Gainsborough 2003a; Painter 2003; UNDP 2006). Equally, increased cross-border trade during the reform era has seen not the retreat of the state but the emergence of new forms of state regulation and gatekeeping (Gainsborough 2009a).

In relation to the 'non-Weberian' features of the state – patronage, personal relations and the centrality of money in politics – there is scarcely any evidence of change in the reform era with such features as entrenched as ever. This is as true as it is for set-piece political events, such as the five-yearly party congresses when patronage in the form of public office is circulated (see Chapter 7), as it is for citizens' everyday dealings with the bureaucracy where connections and the ability to pay are crucial in order to get things done. Moreover, nepotism rather than meritocracy is the norm in appointments to the government and civil service, which are themselves governed by informal, discretionary rules rather than the 'rule of law' (Salomon 2008; Gainsborough et al. 2009). It is, of course, worth considering whether there are some subtle differences between such practices today and in the pre-reform period. Many would note that the sums of money involved in paying off office-holders are much larger today and that some practices which might have raised eyebrows a decade or more ago do not today (Gainsborough et al. 2009). However, we are dealing with questions of scale or extent here, and the basic practices are as they have always been.

We now turn to the question of whether the Vietnamese state bears any resemblance to the 'neoliberal' regulatory state.

Vietnam and the regulatory state

The notion that the market is free of the corrosive influence of politics, or that politics is understood as the implementation of agreed technical procedures, in Vietnam is anathema. Equally, while the Vietnamese state does talk at length about building a state ruled by law, the reality, as was highlighted above in respect of patronage, discretionary decision-making and nepotism, is very different. While decision-making involving the State Bank of Vietnam, the central bank, is far from transparent, it would be a mistake to suggest that the State Bank is independent of the executive. Rather, its decisions are heavily influenced by politicians. Furthermore, the state has been very reluctant to fully liberalize interest rates or the exchange rate, although there has been some movement in this direction in the period since the Asian financial crisis of 1997–98 (IMF 2008).

On the other hand, to suggest that the discourse of the regulatory state has had no impact whatsoever on the Vietnamese state's self-image and practice – even if it may be somewhat skin-deep – would probably be an exaggeration. A Post-Washington Consensus view of politics is certainly very noticeable in an influential publication about Vietnam's reforms produced by the World Bank's chief economist, Martin Rama, who offers a characterization of politics in Vietnam as being non-confrontational, faction free, and ultimately about the government simply 'collecting feedback on [citizens] issues and concerns' (Rama 2008). While the report is by a World Bank economist, and we might question whether such ideas have been internalized by Vietnam's elite, it is worth noting that Rama's account offers a portrait of the reform year which is very flattering to Vietnam's leadership, and in many ways tallies with their presentation of reform.

Beyond this, some scholars have drawn attention to ways in which neoliberalism may be having a more direct influence on the Vietnamese state. Thaveeporn Vasavakul, for instance, has highlighted the way in which the party appears to have been delegating certain functions that it once carried out itself to other institutions of the government (for example, to the former science and technology union, VUSTA, which has been developing an oversight role in relation to civil society) (Vasavakul 2003). While Vasavakul does not say this, it is striking how this bears some resemblance to the shift from direct to indirect rule highlighted in the governance literature (Pierre and Peters 2000). Others have noted how the introduction of 'user fees' and other reforms in Vietnam's health and education sectors bear at least some resemblance to neoliberal policy prescriptions even if actual practice is shot through with the more indigenous features which characterize the everyday working of the Vietnamese state (Painter 2006). Moreover, even if clearly observable practices mirroring the features of the regulatory state are hard to come by, it may be that change is occurring at a more subtle level. Following severe flooding in Hanoi in 2008, the secretary of the city party committee, Pham Quang Nghi, was quoted in the media as saying that 'the trouble with people today is that whenever there is a problem, they expect the state to fix it'. He suggested that citizens ought to be more ready to solve problems themselves.[10] The remarks proved controversial and he later apologized, but they clearly point to the way in which attitudes in the state may be changing.

So, what does this add up to in terms of an understanding of continuity and change in respect of the state in Vietnam?

To suggest that the state in Vietnam has been entirely unaffected by its encounters with neoliberal actors is an exaggeration. Reforms in health and education, for example, bear something of the imprint of the market-oriented received wisdom of the day, notably New Public Management.[11] Moreover, it is striking how the language and practice of indirect rule – delegating certain responsibilities – appears to have extended even to the Communist Party of

Vietnam, even if this may have occurred subliminally. Nevertheless, any suggestion that this represents 'neoliberalism incorporated', or an unmediated form of neoliberalism, would be mistaken. Much more likely is that we are witnessing the emergence of a hybrid state form not uninfluenced by neoliberal ideas and practices but where indigenous thinking and modes of operating remain dominant. It is in this context that we find that very little change has taken place in terms of the state's self-image, what it regards as the correct relationship between the state and its citizens, and in relation to the non-Weberian features of the state (money, connections, patronage, nepotism etc.).

Explaining outcomes

If neoliberalism is as powerful as some claim, then should we not expect to see institutions like the World Bank, and other like-minded donors, having greater impact in encouraging and cajoling the Vietnamese state in new directions? And yet we do not. So, how do we explain this?

The answer given in this chapter is that on the ground in 'developing' countries far away from Washington, London or Brussels, neoliberalism looks far less powerful than is often thought. The interesting question is why – which is what the remainder of the chapter sets out.

Many accounts of Vietnam's reform years emphasize the way in which Vietnam's political elite have adopted a selective approach to external engagement – that is, accepting those things they believe are helpful to it and rejecting or resisting those things they believe are not in their interests (Dixon and Kilgour 2002). In many respects, this kind of analysis is reasonable. It would, for instance, appear to make sense of Vietnam's relationship with the IMF, which was downgraded in 2004 when the Vietnamese government said it was not willing to provide the financial data that the IMF had made a condition of further lending (Hang 2007).

Yet it is not simply a picture of selective opening up. The Vietnamese state has also recognized that at times it is not possible to resist external pressure. On such occasions, it has proved adept at managing such pressure by appearing to sign up to things without then moving to implement them (a kind of 'take the money and run' approach). This comes across clearly in relation to donor activities in the field of anti-corruption. For a long period, corruption was a taboo subject in Vietnam such that it could scarcely be mentioned, especially by foreigners. However, in 2005, the National Assembly passed the country's first anti-corruption law following extensive donor engagement, notably by the Swedish development agency SIDA (Central Committee of Internal Affairs 2005). While a case can be made that there are aspects of the anti-corruption legislation which can be used to bolster sections of the Vietnamese state, it is also the case that important parts of the law, which follows a liberal approach to fighting corruption, sit uncomfortably with the state's self-image or outlook (see Davidson et al. 2008 for discussion of the anti-corruption law). In the context of whether to pass the law or not, this does not seem to have been of major concern, in part because pressure to implement the law is not especially strong, while in the context of Vietnamese politics there are clear benefits to be had for organizations such as the Government Inspectorate tasked with working with the donors in respect of corruption, since they are able to access donor money and enjoy the political cachet associated with doing so.

How it is possible for the Vietnamese government to operate in this way is particularly relevant to an understanding of the true nature of Vietnam's relations with the international donor community. In part the answer lies with the fact that the expatriate staff who work in the donor community are very often out of their depth in a political and cultural context they understand only poorly.[12] The fact that expatriate postings are only for a few years does not help in this respect since it means that just as people are beginning to make sense of the context in which they are working they leave, and

the learning process has to start again. For expatriates, confusion
is often greatest in respect of their understanding of the motives of
members of the Vietnamese elite for wishing to collaborate with
them. In particular, there seems to be little understanding of the
way elite–donor engagement plays in relation to domestic politics,
particularly the part aid plays in servicing domestic patronage networks (see Gainsborough et al. 2009).

That said, it is not simply that the donors have the wool pulled
over their eyes. Also relevant is the importance placed in the international donor community on the disbursement of aid money – the
so-called 'shifting budgets' – such that project quality or implementation is less important than hitting disbursement targets.[13] Also
important is the fact that Vietnam is viewed as a 'success story'
among the donor community (for an example, see Rama 2008). It
is therefore quite hard – and not necessarily good for one's career
– to look too closely or to highlight problems. Consequently, what
we see, then, is a marriage of convenience between Vietnamese and
external elites whereby their interests converge, albeit for very different reasons. However, poor implementation or insufficient attention
to project quality points further to the way in which neoliberalism's
influence is weakened.

Furthermore, the notion that the reforms being proposed by
the international donor community are all necessarily threatening
to Vietnam's elite and hence need to be resisted is also mistaken.
Rather, many of the donor-backed projects which the Vietnamese
government is involved in can be seen to be broadly supportive
of elite power, particularly but not exclusively at the central level.
For instance, the chapter earlier highlighted the potential gains
to institutions involved in anti-trafficking and in fighting corruption. Another example concerns the Ministry of Finance, which
has worked extensively with the World Bank in the area of public
financial management. While this may result in better financial
management, it also has the potential to strengthen the extractive
capacities of the Ministry of Finance in relation to both wider society

and other parts of the state, which is clearly something the Ministry of Finance would welcome.[14] That there is indeed a convergence of interests between the donors and Vietnam's elite can be seen in relation to what at times appears to be a very cosy relationship between the two sides (e.g. the annual Consultative Group meeting between the government and international donor agencies).[15] Against the backdrop of ever-growing elite Vietnamese embroilment in the global economy through trade, investment and other financial dealings that relations between the donors and Vietnam's elite might be moving closer together should not come as a surprise, although given Vietnam's history it is perhaps ironic (for analogous arguments, see Sklair 1995).

Conclusion

In this chapter it has been argued with reference to Vietnam that neoliberalism is not as powerful a force in world politics as is sometimes implied in some Western scholarship. Moreover, it has been suggested that this is the case even in relation to a more invasive form of 'Post-Washington Consensus' neoliberalism which has seen multilateral and bilateral donors become more involved in the domestic politics of recipient states through the governance agenda. The argument has been substantiated by an analysis of the Vietnamese state, highlighting a significant degree of continuity in its ideas and practices despite nearly two decades of neoliberal-inspired donor engagement. A more tricky issue concerns the extent to which change is occurring at the margins in respect of the Vietnamese state and its encounter with neoliberalism. Here, it has been argued that it is not a case of no change at all, but rather change that it is still quite subtle and embryonic.

Over the last two decades, elite interests in Vietnam *have* moved closer to those of external elites, such as those working within the international donor community. This makes sense in relation to Vietnam's growing integration into the global economy, a process where Vietnamese elites have led the way both as regulators of the market economy and as direct players. It is not the case that elite interests in Vietnam are now the same as those of external actors. Nevertheless, there has been some convergence such that elite Vietnamese and donor actors are able to work together while pursuing very different agendas (i.e. a marriage of convenience).

By highlighting the way in which elite interests both inside and outside Vietnam converge, we are able to go some way towards transcending some of the binaries which typically govern the way we talk about power (inside/outside; national/international; global/local etc.), even if in some ways the very language we use fails us. Viewed in this way, it is possible to conceive of neoliberalism as *both* weakened as a force in global politics (i.e. elites with interests which converge but are not the same, turning a blind eye to what the other is doing) *and* strengthened as the interests of elites in Vietnam genuinely become bound up with that of global capitalism such that there is a real convergence of interests with external elites. Seen like this, it is not beyond the bounds of possibility that Vietnamese elites might one day genuinely internalize aspects of the regulatory state discourse as serving a kind of a market order they could support.

In the final analysis, we are dealing with a moving target here. The mixing of 'external' or 'indigenous' ideas and practices will continue to occur with both buffeting and influencing the other – as they have always done. What we can be certain of, however, is that external forces will never completely swamp internal ones. Instead, we will continue to see further gradual evolution of the state in Vietnam drawing on diverse inputs.

CONCLUSION

At the start of this book, a method for studying the state was proposed which entailed – paradoxically perhaps – not focusing our attention directly on the state, arguing that to do so risked defining the object of our study in advance. Instead, it was suggested that what we needed to do was to try to surrender any preconceptions as to what the state is, trusting that a more authentic picture of the state would eventually come back into view in light of our empirical work. Central to this approach was a commitment to looking at 'actors' – whether formally of the state or not – considering what Béatrice Hibou has referred to as their 'games, their strategies and their historical practices' (Hibou 2004: 21), and seeing what this tells us about the nature of the political, and ultimately the state. To talk like this is really to ask how people act politically. The conclusion to the book, therefore, offers some final thoughts on how people act politically in Vietnam, before asking what it tells us about the state. The conclusion also incorporates the outlining of a new research agenda born of the empirical work presented in this book, combined with a preliminary reading of parts of the state theory literature.

How do people act politically in Vietnam?

The question of how people act politically in Vietnam – or elsewhere – is a deceptively complex one. However, to pose it is to ask how people think about the environment in which they operate, how they get things done, and how they head off potential threats. To the outsider, the stakes appear much higher in Vietnam, compared with the United Kingdom or the United States, for those who have aspirations to move and act politically. Of course, this could be debated, and may be a partial perspective influenced by our own closeness to power. However, to fall politically, or really come unstuck, in Vietnam seems to have consequences which go beyond just losing one's job: it affects your family, your livelihood, your standing, and it makes you vulnerable to a loss of opportunities or to further bad things happening.

Against this backdrop, we can say that politics in Vietnam is dominated by whom you know, what position you hold, and how much you can pay. Political umbrellas, whereby people higher up in the hierarchy look out for you and protect you, are a recognized part of the political landscape in Vietnam. This is a form of network politics, with the word 'network' simply used to point to the existence of a loose agglomeration of personalities. How do these networks form? As has been emphasized throughout this book, it is fundamentally about personal relationships – blood or marital ties, shared home town, time served together, past obligations and past debts.

In Vietnam, the norm is that everyone owes their position to someone, which puts people in a hierarchical relationship, which in turn comes with further debts and obligations. It is important to nurture one's relationship with one's patron by showing them appropriate deference or giving them gifts. This can include passing a portion of one's 'corrupt' takings upwards to the person to whom you owe your job, or who sits above you in the hierarchy. For instance, 'corporate' actors seeking to influence 'state' actors will go to great lengths to do so, including arranging overseas trips for them, indulging their wives, or perhaps contributing to their children's education.

With the holding of office also comes a place in the system, which offers access, opportunities to do business or to collect rents or fees, and protection. However, because of the nature of the system with its uniformly unclear rules, everyone is always sailing close to the wind, or in danger of falling foul of some authority. Consequently, people are always looking over their shoulder, trying not to attract unwarranted attention, trying not to get caught out, or taking care not to upset someone who is more powerful than they are.[1] To do anything in Vietnam, the ducks must line up, which in turns involves a constant process of wooing people, getting people onside, and neutralizing threats.

Everyone in Vietnam – from top to bottom – is involved in some kind of network, as described above. It is just that some networks are more heavyweight, or closer to the top, than others. No one in Vietnam – however elevated – ever has it all sewn up. There is always someone who may potentially stand in your way. Thus, while we see political continuity in Vietnam, the story of the reform years is not simply one of the persistence of old power structures, unchecked. As Hibou says, 'everywhere there are slip-ups' and 'spaces where freedom can slip in'. And, she continues, 'if there are none of these' it is always possible for 'astute actors' to 'invent ways of circumventing' (Hibou 2004: 17).

As old routes or opportunities for advancement are closed down, new ones need to be found. People's stars dim. Patrons grow old and die. Certain business interests survive, perhaps by diversifying into new areas. Others go to the wall. Of course, some people are better operators than others, and through a combination of luck or the fortune of their birth have more going for them. But success is never guaranteed. In the face of interventions – what are often referred to as 'reforms' – which seek to upset what people are doing, the system constantly reinvents itself to ensure that its underlying money-making and prestige-seeking functions are not upset. However, for the reasons just outlined, the system never entirely stays the same.

For most actors, debates about 'reform' or 'policy choices', or the consequences of World Trade Organization membership and such-like, are not their day-to-day concern. Instead, surviving, getting things done, using one's connections, and paying people off, all in a context where moneymaking and maintaining one's standing in the system are key, whether it be through doing business, exploiting a regulatory position, or milking the international donor community. This is the day-to-day stuff of politics.

With politics spoken of in these terms, the question remains, what is, or wherein lies, 'the state'?

Rethinking the state

In light of the preceding analysis, one could respond that to talk about politics we do not need to talk about the state at all. Indeed, to do so might be misleading. And yet such a response does not seem entirely satisfactory either. Many of the 'actors' we have been talking about in this book – though not all – hold public office. Public office, therefore, seems important, although how exactly, and what it tells us about the nature of entity we call the state, is less clear. There is, for instance, a very real danger at this juncture in the book that in trying to say something about how we understand 'the state' we will end up superimposing on the state the very things we were trying to avoid through our methodology of not looking directly at the state (i.e. things that are not actually warranted by the data). Nevertheless, it is important to try.

Perhaps the first thing to note about the state in Vietnam is the highly particularistic nature of the different institutions, offices and personnel which we commonly regard as comprising 'the state'. That is, what comprises 'the state' rarely moves in the same direction, rarely works together, and rarely sings from the same hymn sheet. Information is not shared between offices – in fact, it is often sold

– as different institutions and personnel vie for influence where, as we have seen, the right to regulate various parts of the economy and society, extract revenue from citizens, or to run a commercial operation affiliated to one's institutional base are among the key drivers of politics.

Second, what we notice about the state in Vietnam is a persistent blurring of the relationship between public and private, reflected in the use of public office for private gain, which is the norm, and a lack of clarity in relation to the business activities of government offices in terms of who benefits (principally but not exclusively financially) from what are ostensibly state companies.

In much writing on the state, including on Vietnam, a blurring between public and private is depicted as an aberration and not something which occurs in 'developed' Western states. In places where public and private are said to be blurred, it is also depicted as something which can be put right (through 'reform'). However, this is a distortion: public and private are blurred in all states by definition because, as state theorists tell us, the state is a conceptual abstraction (i.e. there is not a real boundary between state and society or between public and private). That it appears otherwise is testament to the state's unique character as a historically contingent form of rule, and indeed this blurring, and the policing of the boundary by those who inhabit the state, is central to how power is exercised.[2] This way of exercising power was evident in the book in a number of ways, but could be seen most clearly in our discussions of corruption.

Related to this is a third observation about the state, namely the importance of uncertainty as an instrument of rule. Keeping people in a state of uncertainty about what they can and cannot do is a sure way of exercising power over them. This dovetails nicely with the comments above about the policing of the state/society or public/ private boundary as the way in which rule occurs. Because the boundary is portrayed as a real one – an arbitrary line one must not cross – when in fact it only exists as a conceptual boundary, people are always in danger of crossing it, and thus are always vulnerable to being disciplined when it suits those capable of doing so.

In Vietnam, this comes across particularly vividly in relation to the labour market where regulations governing the right to strike are so confusing and Kafkaesque that it is said to be next to impossible to call a strike while keeping within the rules. While most of the time this is regarded as simply a fact of life, it provides those who inhabit the state with the means to discipline workers if they deem their activity is unusually threatening, or they wish to make an example of them. From the perspective of workers, this means they are never quite sure what the consequences of their actions will be, which tends to act as a constraint on their behaviour (i.e. uncertainty as an instrument of rule). As with the blurring of public and private, the use of uncertainty as an instrument of rule is depicted in much of the literature as the characteristic of a deviant state (Chabal and Daloz 1999; Duffield 2008). However, it is much more likely that the use of uncertainty is more universal, including extending into so-called 'developed' states.

To sum up, what we have, then, is a state which is little more than a disparate group of actors with a weak notion of 'the public good', using uncertainty, not impartial rules, as the basis of order. However, this is only part of the picture since the state also appears as greater than the sum of its parts – an institution which has 'self-preserving and self-aggrandizing impulses', to quote Benedict Anderson (1983), which takes people in and spits them out, and which re-creates itself in a way that cannot be reducible to the wit of any one individual. In Vietnam this comes across most clearly in terms of the way in which when this 'collectivity' of institutions and actors feel its core interests threatened, it is able to mobilize fairly robustly in order to clamp down on people or activities deemed to threaten the 'whole show'. In this book, we have seen this most vividly in respect of clampdowns on speculation in the foreign exchange and real-estate markets, which at various times appeared to threaten the stability of the banking system, or were simply troubling because they represented a flagrant ignoring of authority.

Understanding these 'self-preserving and self-aggrandizing impulses' expressed though the state's living members, but which 'cannot be reduced to their passing personal ambitions' (Anderson 1983), is particularly important for a holistic understanding of the state. On what basis – or for what reason – might the state harbour 'self-preserving and self-aggrandizing impulses', and how might they *not* be reducible to their personal ambitions of the state's members? One possible response would be to draw on post-structuralist ideas about the state, emphasizing the way in which 'the state' works at the level of the mind, entering social processes, working from within, and influencing what we see (Finlayson and Martin 2006; Mitchell 1991). Hence, we have a tendency to attribute coherence to what we call 'the state' when in fact it may not merit it.

Another, rather different, way to make sense of the state as greater than the sum of its parts might be to draw on Marxist ideas of the state as 'instrument', tending (but not guaranteed) to act in the general interests of capital (Barrow 2008; Hay et al. 2006: 59–78; Jessop 2008; Wetherly 2008). Thus, to refer back to the example cited above, when the state in Vietnam mobilized to clamp down on speculation in the forex and real-estate markets – acting against individual capitalists – it was doing so because its 'self-preserving and self-aggrandizing impulses' told it that not to do so risked the 'whole edifice' coming down. And here the 'whole edifice' is understood in terms of the emerging capitalist economy over which the state was presiding and in which, in the context of marketization and international economic integration, its interests were increasingly bound up.

To assert that the state in Vietnam is tending to act in the general interests of capital is a big claim. However, it makes sense with reference to a range of examples that we have seen throughout this book. This includes the difficulty the state appears to have representing organized labour, and the increased incidence of land conflicts which pit farmers against capital, where capital backed by the state is the frequent winner (in the name of 'development' or 'progress'). In addition, the Communist Party of Vietnam's decision in 2006 to amend its statutes to remove the clause which said that party members 'could not exploit' can also be seen as an attempt by the party to bring itself in line with the fact that many of its members do own and run private businesses, in turn further showing its alignment with capital.[3]

An argument which says that the state in Vietnam is today tending to act in the general interests of capital need *not* be premissed on the idea that there has necessarily been a sharp break between the pre-reform 'state socialist' state and the post-reform 'capitalist' state in terms of its relationship to capital – although mainstream writing on reform would tend to posit that this is what has occurred. The scepticism shown by some writers to the notion of collective ownership, 'belonging to the people', suggesting that in reality it means 'belonging to the party elite', combined also with the notion that the seeds of the reform era were laid via capital accumulation on the part of party elites in the pre-reform era, both point to a rather closer relationship to capital on the part of the state in the pre-reform era than is often thought (see Long and Kendall 1981; Cheshier 2009).

However we explain this paradoxical position of the state both as illusion and as something substantive (i.e. 'greater than the sum of its parts'), it seems clear that this is where a new research agenda should pick up. So what might this research agenda look like?

Towards a new research agenda

While this has been a book about Vietnam, it is evident that within it lie the seeds of a research agenda which go well beyond Vietnam. Underpinning this new research agenda is a quest for a universal theory of the state which can make sense of all states not just certain kinds of states. To talk in such terms is to move away from the tendency in much contemporary writing on the state to emphasize 'difference' between states (i.e. developed/developing; democratic/authoritarian states) – in turn suggesting that they are beyond comparison. This is problematic for a number of reasons, not least because it is a political position bound up with the way in which the West seeks to exercise power over the global South.

Two things are occurring here. First, in much contemporary writing on the state, Western states are held up as paradigms of virtue – i.e. how the state ought to be – which serves the purpose of putting them beyond reproach. Second, non-Western states, excluding to some extent those designated as 'success stories' *pour encourager les autres* (which is also a crucial part of how rule occurs), are depicted as deviant – that is, deviating from the Western ideal – which in turn provides the basis on which intervention can occur. This can take the form of outright invasion, or a seemingly 'softer' version of intervention via international donor aid. Either way, the result is very similar, with the goal being the promotion of a classic 'governance' agenda, and the creation of 'regulatory states' capable of safeguarding transnational capitalism (Jayasuriya 2001).

A number of important obeervations flow from the above analysis. First, that much of what is presented today as offering a robust analysis of the state is nothing of the sort, and in fact is a selective, politically motivated characterization of the state, serving consciously or unconsciously the political agenda mapped out above.[4] Second, that in order truly to gain a window onto the state as a distinctive, historically contingent form of rule it is necessary to break out of the straitjacket of states which cannot be compared, whether they are developed/developing, industrial/post-industrial/non-industrial, developmental/fragile/failing, or liberal democratic/illiberal/authoritarian, and ask what such states have in common simply by virtue of being states. Such a step serves two purposes: first, it will make for better theory (i.e. a theory of the general rather than the particular), and second, it will help unmask a key way in which rule occurs at the global level today.

What might a universal theory of the state look like?

From the outset, a universal theory of the state needs to begin with an awareness of one's own class position and how this might influence one's theorizing. One way to address this is to be open to the way in which the state is Janus-faced (i.e. it is experienced differently depending on your relationship to it). Thus, a universal theory of the state needs to be attentive to the way in which 'my experience of the state' is unlikely to capture the character of the state in its entirety. Put another way, a universal theory of the state needs to be able to make sense of the state's benevolent side as well as its predatory and abusive side. Recall here the comment made by the brother of Pol Pot that Pol Pot 'would not hurt a chicken', which in certain circumstances (e.g. among family members) was probably true. Or, in the UK, recall the comment of the former head of MI5, Stella Rimmington, who on trying to publish her memoirs following her retirement remarked that she had experienced for the first time what it was like 'to be on the wrong side of the state' (i.e. the same state, two different experiences).

Second, a universal theory of the state needs to get away from pluralist notions of the state as class-neutral, exploring in whose interests the state is acting. Here, while there is a strong sense that the state is likely to be aligned with capital, whether it is Vietnam or Indonesia, the USA or the UK, it cannot be guaranteed (see Jessop 2008 for a discussion). Hence there is always an empirical task to be carried out to establish whether this is the case, and indeed the precise relationship with which manifestation of 'capital'.

Third, a universal theory of the state needs to get away from neo-Weberian notions of the state as rational and bureaucratic and accept that the normal character of the state – all states – is one where public and private are blurred and where this, along with the use of uncertainty, is central to how rule occurs. In this regard, there is further work to be done to clarify what Weber actually said about the state because there is a tendency in much writing about the state to invoke Weber very selectively (see Dusza 1989; Greenfield 2001; Hibou 2004: 19; McVey 1992; Richards 2009 for some insights on this).

Fourth, a universal theory of the state needs to be able to make sense of the state both as illusion (i.e. why it appears more real than it actually is) and as an entity which has 'material effects', including trying to understand what the key motivators are for the state to unite to defend what it perceives to be its core interests. Once again, this may lead us back to the state's relations with capital but with a sense that while the state tends to align with capital it may not be reducible to it. That is to say, the state's 'self-preserving and self-aggrandizing impulses' may in large part be motivated by a desire to protect the general interests of capital. However, what motivates the state to defend its core interests – and indeed what those core interests are – may lie elsewhere too. In this respect, part of the state's core interests may lie in simply defending the public–private boundary from attack as an end in itself – and not one which is necessarily always shared by capital.

So, what we have here are a series of theoretical observations, most of which point to areas for regular and ongoing empirical investigation. The areas for empirical investigation are:

1. The (blurred) character of the public and private boundary and how this is used as an instrument of rule.
2. The use of uncertainty as an instrument of rule.
3. How the state is experienced differently depending on your relationship to it.
4. How a conceptual abstraction can appear to have real boundaries.
5. Where the state's core interests lie, including its relationship to capital, and the extent to which this is the principal motivator behind its self-preserving and self-aggrandizing impulses, or one of a number.

While there is much to recommend such an approach to thinking about the state, it leaves open, as we have seen, that what has been said needs to be verified by regular empirical investigation. At the same time, while this book is claiming through a discussion of Vietnam to be highlighting something universal in relation to the nature of the political, one should also expect to encounter variation within this. So, what kind of variation?

Variation within the universal

While expecting to find exploitation of the public–private boundary, and the use of uncertainty, both deployed as instruments of rule, and also anticipating that the collectivity of institutions and actors we call 'the state' will tend to act in the general interests of capital across a wide range of cases, we should nevertheless expect to encounter variation on this theme such that 'local colour' will be important in terms of how these mechanisms and tendencies play out.

One important area where we expect this to be the case concerns the extent to which violence forms a part of the state's everyday repertoire. Violence, or the threat of violence, is a feature of all states. However, what we need to make sense of is why it tends to be more pervasive in certain states than others, even while the underlying 'universal' features of the state described above remain in play.

Invoking the Lukesian adage that the 'supreme exercise of power' is to 'get another or others to have the desires you want them to have – that is to, to secure their compliance by controlling their thoughts and desires' (Lukes cited in Hindess 1996: 68), we can say that states which invoke violence less, or where it is the exception rather than the rule, represent a stronger form of power. A good example is contemporary Singapore, where citizens by and large behave how the state wishes them to behave (Barr 2003; Rodan 1992; Tremewan 1994). Certainly the state in Singapore deploys a battery of legal and other means to undermine or wrongfoot its critics, but it rarely kills people. That said, it would be erroneous to suggest that uncertainty is not used as an instrument of rule in Singapore. Nor is it the case that there is a clear separation of public and private in Singapore even though state discourse powerfully seeks to suggest there is: witness the close links between the family of Lee Kwan Yew and business in Singapore or the fact that the older Lee's son is prime minister as examples of a greater blurring of public and private than is often implied (Gainsborough 2009b; Hamilton-Hart 2000). Nevertheless, we could say that in Singapore the state's ideological effects are particularly strong and that it is this – rather than any objective differences in terms of how power is exercised – which distinguishes the state in Singapore from some other states.[5]

An example of a weaker state, where the use of uncertainty and exploitation of the public–private boundary are still key instruments of rule – just like in Singapore – is Burma/Myanmar. Here the use of violence is much more part of the normal fabric of the state, and in contrast to the Lukesean view of power represents a weaker application of power for it. An important feature of states where violence is commonplace, and where the state's ideological effects are much weaker, is that state rule has to be constantly backed up by performative practices, such as hastily convened 'mass rallies' where public-sector workers are wheeled out to chant their support for the regime irrespective of what they really think (Duffield 2008: 23–4). As with the use of violence, it is not the case that performance plays no function in states where the ideological effects are stronger but the need to resort to such performances to reinforce a fragile, or fading, legitimacy is perhaps less.

There may well be other areas where we are likely to encounter (local) variation in terms of the character of the state, notwithstanding the existence of the state's more 'universal' features which have been highlighted in this book. This may, for instance, apply to the nature of the state's relationship to capital, particularly if one extends the analysis to the sub-national level. Is, for example, the relationship of the state to capital in say sub-national Indonesia likely to be the same as metropolitan Singapore, or Washington and Westminster for that matter? A further area where we might expect to encounter local variation has to do with the extent to which other forces – distinct from capital – may seek to inhabit the state and utilize it as an instrument. Nevertheless, more work is required in both these areas before the analysis can be extended further.

NOTES

CHAPTER 1

1. This is not a relativist position (i.e. it makes no claim that all political systems can be equally justified on ethical grounds simply because of differences in philosophical and cultural traditions).

2. Annual average GDP growth rate averaged 7.2 per cent in the period 1997–2007 and 7.7 per cent in the period 1987–97. Per capita income was estimated at $US890 in 2008 compared with 390 in 2000. See World Bank 2008.

3. The closure of the independent think-tank the Institute of Development Studies (IDS), in Hanoi in 2009 points to just such dissatisfaction in the business community. IDS, which had impeccable elite credentials and was also close to business, announced its decision to close saying that changes in government regulations affecting its operation made it impossible to operate.

4. See Kerkvliet 1995 for a summary.

5. Ibid.

6. This juxtaposition between a state with both weak and strong attributes is also captured in writing on China. Yia-hing Liu (1992) writes of a 'sporadic totalitarian state' with strong despotic power but weak infrastructural power. Lieberthal and Oksenberg (1988) talk of a 'fragmented authoritarian regime'.

7. For background on the composition of the Politburo since 1976, see Thayer 1988, 1997. The military and security representation of the

Politburo declined at the Ninth National Communist Party Congress in 2001, compared with the Eighth Congress in 1996. At the Tenth Congress in 2006 military and security representation plateaued.

8. Soon after becoming Communist Party general secretary in 2001, Nong Duc Manh said that Vietnam would never permit opposition parties; interview with *Time* magazine (Vietnam News Agency, 29 January 2002).

CHAPTER 2

1. Ho Chi Minh City's official population was estimated at 6.6 million in 2008, or 7.7 per cent of the total population. The city contributes around 18 per cent to nationwide GDP, 21 per cent to nationwide industrial output, and 35 per cent to the country's exports. Average annual per capita GDP in the city is estimated to be around five times the national average of US$790. Between 1988 and 2008, Ho Chi Minh City received approximately 20 per cent of the country's total approved foreign direct investment. See General Statistics Office 2009.

2. Ho Chi Minh City has generally averaged double-digit GDP growth since the 1990s compared to the more usual 7–8 per cent for the country as a whole. See General Statistics Office 2009.

3. See, for example, the statement of Vo Van Kiet in October 1985, when he was party secretary in Ho Chi Minh City, in which he called for 'stern punishment' to be meted out to 'party cadres and members who engage in under-the-counter deals, work hand in glove with speculators and smugglers, and who lend a hand to economic sabateurs'. This seems distinctly mainstream, if not anti-market. See BBC Summary of World Broadcasts, FE/8078/B/5–6, 10 October 1985. For further discussion of Kiet's posture, see also Vasavakul 1997a: 101–8.

4. See, for example, the sections in Thrift and Forbes 1986 that deal with Ho Chi Minh City after 1975.

5. In terms of services, manufacturing and construction, annual growth rates were always in double digits during the 1990s, and often in the 15–20 per cent range. See General Statistics Office 2009.

6. During the 1990s Saigon Tourist had two directors. Both had served as People's Committee chairman in District 1. For a time, one held the posts of People's Committee chairman and Saigon Tourist director concurrently.

7. For a clear statement of this position, although it is not her position, see Duckett 1998.

8. See, for example, *Thoi Bao Kinh te Sai Gon*, 18 March 1999. The article

described the closure of the Cereals Department (*So Luong thuc*) in Ho Chi Minh City and the merger of four smaller departments to create the Agriculture Department.

9. *Sai Gon Giai Phong*, 16 May 1998.

10. The decree (Decree 18/CP) sought to do this by putting a stop to borrowing capital from banks using land use rights as collateral, a practice that was widespread at the time.

11. The chairman of Satra's management board, Le Minh Chau, was a former director of the Trade Department. Satra's general director, Do Hoang Hai, was the former director of numerous Trade Department companies, many of which were brought under Satra's umbrella when it was founded in 1995.

12. For literature that is helpful in this regard, see Dacy 1986; Scigliano and Snyder 1960; Taylor 1961; Trued 1960; Taylor 2001.

13. Reflecting the policy of de-urbanization and resettling people in the New Economic Zones, Ho Chi Minh City's population fell sharply in 1976 and continued falling until 1984.

14. Le Van Kiem of Huy Hoang, profiled earlier in the chapter, described the beginnings of his business in this way.

15. See *Nguoi Lao Dong*, 8 April 1998. Rather tellingly, the title is 'Create the conditions for Cho Lon to Return to Business Buoyancy'. There are far fewer Chinese banks in Ho Chi Minh City compared to neighbouring Cambodia, even taking into account the fact that some banks in Ho Chi Minh City have covert Chinese shareholders.

16. The late Nguyen Huu Dinh, referred to earlier in the chapter in connection with Saigon Jewellery Company, was described in this way although his pre-1975 experience appears only to have been a degree in economics received in the 1970s.

17. Some 600,000 people moved from north to south from 1976 to 1980 (Thrift and Forbes 1986: 132).

18. Vo Viet Thanh lost his seat on the Central Committee in 1991 after serving just one term. The loss of his seat was widely thought to have put a ceiling on his subsequent advancement.

CHAPTER 3

1. Other big corruption cases have included Minh Phung-Epco, Tan Truong Sanh and PMU 18. PMU 18 is discussed in Chapter 7.

2. The primary source was the BBC Summary of World Broadcasts, Far East section.

3. Interview 5 July 1999.

4. *Thoi Bao Kinh te Sai Gon*, 20–26 August 1992; 22–28 April 1993; 27 June–3 July 1996 and 27 August–3 September 1997.

5. This makes sense given the amount of time a member of the Politburo is required to spend in Hanoi and their constant exposure to party strategy at the centre.

6. Interview 18 February 1998.

7. Interview 20 February 1998; *Nguoi Lao Dong*, 10 April 1998.

8. *Thanh Nien*, 30 March 1995.

9. This was mainly the General Department of Land, which is a central institution. See *Tuoi Tre*, 13 March 1995.

10. *Thoi Bao Kinh te Saigon*, 10–16 October 1991; 18–24 June 1992; 4–10 February 1993.

11. *Thoi Bao Kinh te Saigon*, 26 May–1 June 1994.

12. *Thoi Bao Kinh te Saigon*, 6–12 October 1994.

13. In the end total losses in the Tamexco case were estimated at just under 500 billion dong. See *Thoi Bao Kinh te Saigon*, 12–18 August 1999.

14. *Tuoi Tre*, 26 October 1996. The twelve others not mentioned by name here were charged with corruption, exploiting their public position, or gambling. They included people who had held positions within Tamexco or other limited liability companies, or had held public office in Ba Ria-Vung Tau. Some of them were relatives of Pham Huy Phuoc. For full details, see *Tuoi Tre*, 1 February 1997.

15. *Sai Gon Giai Phong*, 27 May 1996 and *Thoi Bao Kinh te Saigon*, 19–25 June 1997.

16. *Vietnam Investment Review*, 5–11 August 1996; *Thoi Bao Kinh te Saigon*, 19–25 June 1997. When the case came to court, Phuoc said that he had given Van US$11,000 US to fund foreign trips, although Van denied this. There was also a dispute over two Nissan cars which Phuoc reportedly gave to Van's family. Here, the issue was not about whether the transaction had taken place but whether both cars had been paid for. Van insisted they had.

17. *Tuoi Tre*, 29 October 1996.

18. *Tuoi Tre*, 28 January 1997.

19. Ibid.

20. One informant suggested that it was the then party secretary in Ho Chi Minh City, Vo Tran Chi, who had signed. Interview 4 February 1998.

21. In fact, eight months after the trial Truong My Hoa was promoted, being appointed vice president of the National Assembly. See BBC SWB FE/3035 B/1–2 27 September 1997.

22. Announcing the change in Le Minh Hai's sentence, Justice Pham Hung

said, 'Hai's father's deeds were the crucial factor in saving him. Hai himself had done no good for the Party and the State of Vietnam and he is very lucky that he has a hero as a father.' See *Vietnam Investment Review*, 22–28 September 1997.

23. *Reuters*, 24 January 1997.
24. *Reuters*, 23 January 1997.
25. Interviews 8 March and 15 June 1999.
26. Interview 28 March 1998.
27. Interview 23 June 1999.
28. *Tuoi Tre*, 1 February 1997.
29. Interview 23 June 1999. There was a rumour that as Phuoc was led away to be executed he requested to make a statement but was not permitted to. However, this was impossible to verify.
30. Interview 28 March 1998.
31. Ibid.
32. Such a distinction has also been made with reference to China. See Yufan Hao 1999: 416.

CHAPTER 4

1. This interpretation is premissed on the assumption that state enterprises operate rather more like private businesses than is commonly thought: see Fforde 2000; Gainsborough 2003a; Nolan and Wang Xiaqiang 1999.
2. *Saigon Times Daily*, 17 September 2001.
3. For discussion of the State Enterprise Law passed in 1995 and the establishment of the general corporations, see Freeman 1996: 218–20; Jerneck 1997; Cheshier and Penrose 2007. Freeman has spoken in terms of enterprise reform representing an attempt to bring off-balance-sheet activity 'back on' (email communication 14 May 2002).
4. *Bao Hai Phong*, 4 June 2002.
5. *Bao Can Tho*, 31 May 2002.
6. *Bao Can Tho*, 5 February 2002.
7. *Bao Hai Phong*, 31 May 2002; *Bao Tay Ninh*, 22 June 2002.
8. See, however, UNDP 2006 and Cheshier and Penrose 2007 for insights into how the government's position later shifted with regard to equitizing general corporation member companies.
9. Jean Oi's comment with reference to China that there is no inherent reason why property rights are effective incentives only if they are assigned to non-government entities is helpful in explaining the growth of new state business interests in Vietnam from the late 1980s and early 1990s: see Oi 1999: 10.

10. The effective marginalization of workers comes across clearly in the literature on Russian privatization too: see Clarke and Kabalina 1995: 146.
11. See, however, Chapter 5 for further insights here.
12. Confidential correspondence with people connected to the project.
13. Email communication with Nick Freeman, 14 May 2002.

CHAPTER 5

1. Ministry of Finance data cited in VietNam Net, 29 December 2008. For an earlier source, which put the figure at 10 per cent, see Kokko 2004.
2. The provinces were chosen to have a mixture of urban and rural provinces in northern and southern Vietnam. The companies were chosen at random from a list compiled from a reading of the provincial press. All equitized companies contacted agreed to be interviewed.
3. More recently considerable attention has been paid to the consequences for politics in Russia of the rise of the oligarchs following privatization in the early 1990s. See, for example, Aslund 2007; Goldman 2004; Guriev and Rachinsky 2005.
4. See, for example, *Tai Chinh*, 2 November 2005. The article, which had the title 'Do Equitized State Assets End Up in Private Pockets?', describes how the director of an equitized company allegedly told his shareholders that he could not find any business. The director then leased the company offices to a private company of which, unbeknown to them, he happened to be the owner. The director then re-leased the company offices at a substantial premium, in the process pocketing the difference. As the article said, the state, through its shareholding in the company, lost a lot of money. It is thus worth emphasizing that it would be wrong to see equitized companies simply as victims, even if private indirect government implies a measure of state control over them.
5. In the case of the centrally managed company, the ministry seemed quite distant and by the time the company equitized it appeared to all intents and purposes to be a locally managed company.
6. All directors spoken to were universally agreed that they – and sometimes the management board – would be held responsible if things went wrong and that the regulations were clear on this.
7. By outsiders, Mr Nam meant that they were not employees of the company. Nevertheless, it was evident that the 'outsiders' were closely connected to the company since Mr Nam said that they had bought shares because they 'understood' clearly about the company.
8. See also Cheshier 2010 who uses the language of the 'new class'.

9. More recent figures suggest there are 948 companies in line for equitiza-tion in the 2008–10 period. See Ministry of Planning and Investment 2005: 113; Vietnam News Agency, 3 September 2008, www.vnagency. com.vn/Home/EN/tabid/119/itemid/265823/Default.aspx, accessed 22 January 2009.

CHAPTER 6

1. The Greater Mekong Subregion (GMS) encompasses countries contig-uous to the Mekong river, namely Cambodia, Laos, Burma, Thailand, Vietnam, and China's Yunnan province. It is the label of choice for this area of the multilateral institutions, such as the Asian Development Bank and the World Bank. For background, see Oehlers 2006 and the ADB website www.adb.org/GMS/program.asp accessed 11 October 2009.

2. The difference can largely be explained by reference to the existence of a large mining sector in Lao Cai province.

3. Company interviews in Lao Cai and Tay Ninh, August and November 2003.

4. Tay Ninh is one of the more sensitive provinces in Vietnam to con-duct research. This is because of the presence of the Cao Dai religious sect in the province. The Cao Dai religion has it headquarters in the province and historically has had poor relations with the Communist government.

5. High levels of smuggling and weaknesses in data collection mean that official figures are likely to underestimate the true extent of trade.

6. This likely reflects a range of factors, from the high risks associated with start-up businesses, an inhospitable business climate for pri-vate-sector companies, and the impact of the Asian financial crisis in 1997–98 (Webster and Taussig 1999).

7. Based on figures for cumulative approved foreign investment from 1988 to mid-2003, Tay Ninh and Lao Cai ranked seventeenth and thirty-sixth out of Vietnam's sixty-four provinces and municipalities.

8. See *Bao Lao Cai*, 17 May 2002 and 31 May 2002; *Bao Tay Ninh*, 16 April 2002 and 11 June 2002; *Vientiane Times*, 26–28 November 2002.

9. There has been a proliferation of Internet cafés in the provincial capital and key tourist spots in Lao Cai and Tay Ninh in recent years, but else-where provision is low. However, few people enter or leave the province by air.

10. Standard & Poor's, Fitch and Moody's issue regular reports about Vietnam.

11. For an equivalent discussion of the elite in Ho Chi Minh City, see Gainsborough 2004b.

12. Interviews with foreign companies in Vietnam, August and November 2003 and January 2005.

13. Interviews in Vietnam with the IMF, the World Bank, the Department for International Development, Oxfam UK, January 2005.

CHAPTER 7

1. While there was an element of voyeurism about the public interest in PMU 18, there were also genuine expressions of anger that certain officials exposed by PMU 18 as allegedly corrupt were so close to being appointed to the Central Committee, or that the party had gone to the dogs. Such views were expressed respectively by members of the professional middle class and retired party members. Interviews, Hanoi, April 2006.

2. Le Kha Phieu, quoted in *Tuoi Tre*, 17 April 2006. Le Kha Phieu also called for *doi moi* in the area of democracy 'in the same way that Vietnam launched reform in the economic sphere twenty years previously'.

3. Vu Khoan, quoted in *Tuoi Tre*, 19 April 2006; *Thanh Nien*, 24 April 2006.

4. *Thoi Bao Kinh Te Sai Gon*, 16 March 2006; *Tuoi Tre*, 18 April 2006. The *Thoi Bao Kinh Te Sai Gon* article answered its own question by concluding that what Vietnam needed was creative people – party members or not – who were committed to bettering themselves and society and were not constantly worrying about whether they have contravened some petty rule.

5. *Tuoi Tre*, 2 March 2006. This was a coded way of drawing attention to the fact that this is what was already happening.

6. Ibid.

7. Brantley Womack, for example, wrote on the Eighth Congress, 'Indeed the conservative mood at the ... Congress was stronger than it had been at the Seventh in 1991' (Womack 1997: 84).

8. Other scholars have also argued for a process of recentralization in the 1990s, albeit drawing on qualitative sources. See Vasavakul 2002; Fforde and de Vylder 1996; and Chapter 3 in this volume.

9. Over the years, the percentage of new entrants to the Central Committee has fluctuated. In the 1976–2001 period, new entrants to the Central Committee accounted for 37.7 per cent of the total. At the Ninth Congress in 2001, the figure was 42 per cent. See Thayer 1988, 1997; IISS 2001. At the Tenth Congress the figure was just over 51 per cent.

10. PMU 18 precipitated some of the first public discussion in Vietnam of the fact that official positions are sometimes bought.

11. Interviews with public-sector employees in Hanoi, April 2006.

12. Interviews with public-sector employees and journalists in Hanoi, April 2006.

13. This was stated in the official Ministry of Foreign Affairs statement at the time, but it is also repeated in Womack 1997: 84.

14. Interestingly, Douglas Pike does not mention Tran Xuan Bach's fall in his assessment of the Seventh Congress written soon after the event. See Pike 1992.

15. Conversations and correspondence with Adam Fforde. See also Fforde 2004b, 2004c.

CHAPTER 8

1. On the point about change, the argument is that at the level of *discourse* the emphasis is on reform as change. This is not to say that scholars do not offer caveats to the change discourse – they do – but the default position is always that Vietnam is undergoing a process of change. This 'default' discourse, which is evident in nearly all scholarship on Vietnam, is ultimately distorting of the record.

2. John Williamson, the man credited with coining the phrase 'the Washington Consensus', commented that some people cannot mention it 'without foaming at the mouth' (Williamson 1989).

3. Informal contacts between the Vietnamese government and the international financial institutions, notably the IMF, got under way from the late 1980s. See Kolko 1997; Rama 2008.

4. For examples of literature that falls into this category, see Duiker 1989; Pike 1978.

5. There was a time in the early 1990s when even for a relatively lowly citizen in Ho Chi Minh City to go abroad required a signature from high up in the city Party Committee.

6. In terms of the origins of these ideas, the debate concerns the extent to which Marxist ideas about the economy struck a chord with much earlier Confucian thinking on the subject.

7. Strikingly, this came across in an exhibition organized by the Museum of Ethnology in Hanoi on the state subsidy period, where it was evident that access to superior foodstuffs, goods and services for members of the elite was officially sanctioned. See also Cheshier 2010 for discussions of the 'new class'.

8. Note, it is important to remember that the party is no more monolithic than the government.
9. Heng's point is that even under the auspices of state control, media outlets in Vietnam can be highly critical of the state.
10. Deutsche Press Agency, 6 November 2008.
11. Note, however, it is unclear whether this is correlation or causation.
12. Personal observations while working as a senior technical adviser for UNDP (2005–06) and later as a UNDP consultant (2008–09).
13. Personal observations.
14. This is based on interviews conducted in 2005 on intergovernmental fiscal relations in Hanoi and four provinces at the central provincial and district levels. Informal conversations also occurred with staff at the IMF's Hanoi office and international consultants working in this area.
15. Personal observations.

CONCLUSION

1. Note, we are talking here about people operating from *within* the system, not those operating *outside* the system (e.g. dissidents). For the latter, the looking over their shoulder may entail a different degree of fear and potential conflict. People manoeuvring within the system are generally at ease with doing so.
2. It is this which lies behind Timothy Mitchell's observation that we should not – as many social scientists do – seek to locate the boundary between the state and society (or public and private) as a matter of conceptual precision, but rather we should examine it as a clue to how rule occurs (Mitchell 2006: 170).
3. The amendment of party statutes was discussed in *Vietnam News*, 25 April 2006.
4. Note that the state is rarely theorized in the state-building, governance and failed/fragile state literature. However, this belies an implicit, normative, understanding of the state. For some insights into this, see Gainsborough 2009b.
5. A similar argument could be made in respect of the state in the UK or the USA compared with some other states.

REFERENCES

Abrami, R., E. Malesky and Yu Zheng (2008) 'Accountability and Inequality in Single-Party Regimes: A Comparative Analysis of Vietnam and China', Harvard Business School Working Paper.

Abrams, P. (1988) 'Notes on the Difficulty of Studying the State', in A. Sharma and A. Gupta (eds), *The Anthropology of the State: A Reader*, Blackwell, Oxford.

Abuza, Z. (2001) *Renovating Politics in Contemporary Vietnam*, Lynne Rienner, Boulder CO and London.

Amer, R. (1999) 'Sino-Vietnamese Relations: Past, Present and Future', in C.A. Thayer and R. Amer (eds), *Vietnamese Foreign Policy in Transition*, Institute of Southeast Asian Studies, Singapore.

Anderson, B. (1983) 'Old State, New Society: Indonesia's New Order in Comparative Historical Perspective', *Journal of Asian Studies*, vol. 42, no. 3.

Anderson, B. (1988a) 'Cacique Democracy in the Philippines: Origins and Dreams', *New Left Review*, vol. 169, no. 1, May/June.

Anderson, B. (1988b) 'From Miracle to Crash', *London Review of Books*, vol. 20, no. 8, April.

Anderson, B. (1990) *Language and Power: Exploring Political Cultures in Indonesia*, Cornell University Press, Ithaca NY.

Anti-Corruption Resource Centre (2008) 'Corruption in Fast-Growing Markets: Lessons from Russia and Vietnam', 29 April.

Aslund, A. (2007) *Russia's Capitalist Revolution: Why Market Reform Succeeded and Democracy Failed*, Peterson Institute for International Economics, Washington DC.

Barnett, C. (2004) 'The Consolations of Neo-liberalism', *Geoforum*, vol. 36, no. 1.

Barnett, M., and R. Duvall (eds) (2007) *Power in Global Governance*, Cambridge University Press, Cambridge.

Barr, M.D. (2003) 'Perpetual Revisionism in Singapore: The Limits of Change', *Pacific Review*, vol. 16, no. 1.

Barrow, C.W. (2008) 'Ralph Miliband and the Instrumentalist Theory of the State: The (Mis)construction of an Analytic Concept', in P. Wetherly, C.W. Barrow and P. Burnham (eds), *Class, Power and the State in Capitalist Society: Essays on Ralph Miliband*, Palgrave Macmillan, Basingstoke and New York.

Beeson, M. (2000) 'Mahathir and the Markets: Globalisation and the Pursuit of Economic Autonomy in Malaysia', *Pacific Affairs*, vol. 73, no. 3.

Beeson, M. (2003) 'Sovereignty under Siege: Globalisation and the State in Southeast Asia', *Third World Quarterly*, vol. 24, no. 2.

Bell, D.A., D. Brown, K. Jayasuryia and D.M. Jones (1995) *Towards Illiberal Democracy in Pacific Asia*, St. Martin's Press, New York.

Beresford, M. (1989) *National Unification and Economic Development in Vietnam*, St. Martin's Press, New York.

Beresford, M. (1995) 'Interpretation of the Vietnamese Economic Reforms 1979–85', *Researching the Vietnamese Economic Reforms: 1979–86*, Australia–Vietnam Research Project, Monograph Series no. 1, School of Economic and Financial Studies, Macquarie University, Sydney, January.

Beresford, M. (2008) 'Doi Moi in Review: The Challenges of Building Market Socialism in Vietnam', *Journal of Contemporary Asia*, vol. 38, no. 2.

Beresford, M., and B. McFarlane (1995) 'Regional Inequality and Regionalism in Vietnam and China', *Journal of Contemporary Asia*, vol. 25, no. 1.

Berger, M.T. (1997) 'Old State and New Empire in Indonesia: Debating the Rise and the Decline of Suharto's New Order', *Third World Quarterly*, vol. 18, no. 2.

Booth, A. (2001) 'The Causes of Southeast Asia's Economic Crisis: A Sceptical Review of the Debate', *Asia-Pacific Business Review*, vol. 8, no. 2.

Boycko, M., A. Shleifer and R.W. Vishny (1996) 'A Theory of Privatization', *Economic Journal*, vol. 106, no. 435.

Bratsis, P. (2006) *Everyday Life and the State*, Great Barrington Books, Boulder CO.

BTVTU (1996) *Thanh Pho Ho Chi Minh Hai Muoi Nam (1975–1995)* [Ho Chi Minh City: Twenty Years (1975–1995)], Ban Thuong Vu Thanh Uy Dang Cong San Viet Nam Thanh Pho Ho Chi Minh [Standing committee of the Ho Chi Minh City Communist Party], Ho Chi Minh City Publishing House, Ho Chi Minh City.

Cameron, A., and R. Palan (2004) *The Imagined Economies of Globalization*, Sage, London.

Cammack, P. (2001) 'Making the Poor Work for Globalization', *New Political Economy*, vol. 6, no. 3.

Cammack, P. (2004) 'What the World Bank Means by Poverty Reduction and Why It Matters' *New Political Economy*, vol. 9, no, 2.

Canh, Nguyen Van (1985) *Vietnam under Communism, 1975–1982*, Hoover Institution Press, Stanford CA.

CDNDNTD (1997) *Chan Dung Nhung Doanh Nghiep Thanh Dat* [A Portrait of Business on the March], Ho Chi Minh City Publishing House, Ho Chi Minh City.

Central Committee of Internal Affairs (2005) *Report on the Findings of the Diagnostic Study on Corruption*, Communist Party of Vietnam supported by the Swedish government, Hanoi.

Cerny, P. (1990) *The Changing Architecture of Politics: Structure, Agency and the Future of the State*, Sage, London.

Cerny, P. (2000) 'Restructuring the Political Arena: Globalization and the Paradoxes of the Competition State', in R. Germain (ed.), *Globalization and Its Critics*, Macmillan, London.

Chabal, P., and J. Daloz (1999) *Africa Works: Disorder as Political Instrument*, James Currey and Indiana University Press, Oxford and Indianapolis.

Chan, A., and I. Norland (1999) 'Vietnamese and Chinese Labour Regimes: On the Road to Divergence', in A. Chan, B.J. Kerkvliet and Jonathan Unger (eds), *Transforming Asian Socialism*, Rowman & Littlefield, Lanham MD.

Chau, T.H. (2000) 'Trade Activities of the Hoa along the Sino-Vietnamese Border', in G. Evans, C. Hutton and K. Eng (eds), *Where China Meets Southeast Asia: Social and Cultural Change in the Border Regions*, Institute of Southeast Asian Studies, Singapore.

Cheshier, S. (2009) 'State Corporations, Financial Instability and Industrialization in Viet Nam', UNDP Viet Nam Policy Dialogue Paper no. 1, February, Hanoi.

Cheshier, S. (2010) 'The New Class in Vietnam', Ph.D. thesis, University of London.

Cheshier, S., and J. Penrose (2007) *Top 200: Industrial Strategies of Vietnam's Largest Firms*, UNDP, Hanoi, www.un.org.vn/index.php?option=com_docman&task=doc_details&gid=27&Itemid=210.

Chibnall, S., and P. Saunders (1977) 'Worlds Apart: Notes on the Social Relativity of Corruption', *British Journal of Sociology* 28.

Clapham, C. (1996) *Africa and the International System: The Politics of State Survival*, Cambridge University Press, Cambridge.

Clarke, G. (2004) 'The Social Challenges of Reform: Restructuring State-owned Enterprises in Vietnam', in D. McCargo (ed.), *Rethinking Vietnam*, RoutledgeCurzon, London.

Clarke, S. (2006) 'The Changing Character of Strikes in Vietnam', *Post-Communist Economies*, vol. 18, no. 3.

Clarke, S., and V. Kabalina (1995) 'Privatisation and the Struggle for Control of the Enterprise', in D. Lane (ed.), *Russia in Transition: Politics, Privatisation and Inequality*, Longman, London and New York.

Constitution of Vietnam (1995) *Constitution of Vietnam: 1946–1959–1980–1992*, Gioi Publishers, Hanoi.

Cudworth, E., and J. McGovern (2007) 'The State and the Power Elite', in E. Cudworth, T. Hall and J. McGovern (eds), *The Modern State: Theories and Ideologies*, Edinburgh University Press, Edinburgh.

Dacy, D.C. (1986) *Foreign Aid, War and Economic Development: South Vietnam 1955–75*, Cambridge University Press, Cambridge.

Dahm, D., and V.J.H. Houben (eds) (1999) *Vietnamese Villages in Transition: Background and Consequences of Reform Policies in Rural Vietnam*, Department of Southeast Asian Studies, Passau University.

Dau, Nguyen Dinh (1998) *From Saigon to Ho Chi Minh City: 300 Year History*, Land Service, Science and Technics Publishing House, Ho Chi Minh City.

Davidson, S., Nguyen Viet Ha, Hoang Ngoc Giao, T. Vasavakul and M.A. Garrido (2008) 'Implementation Assessment of the Anti-Corruption Law: How Far Has Vietnam Come?', consultancy report, Hanoi.

de Mauny, A., and Vu Thu Hong (1998) 'Landlessness in the Mekong Delta: The Situation in Duyen Hai District, Tra Vinh Province, Vietnam', report prepared for Oxfam Great Britain, June–July.

Dicken, P., and A. Malmberg (2001) 'Firms in Territories: A Relational Perspective', *Economic Geography*, vol. 77, no. 4.

Dinh, Dang Ngoc (2008a) 'Land Use Conflict Resolution in the Urbanisation Process in Vietnam', unpublished manuscript, Hanoi.

Dinh, Dang Ngoc (2008b) 'Corruption in Viet Nam: Nature, Causes and Recommendations', unpublished manuscript, Hanoi.

Dinh, Dang Ngoc (2008c) 'Anti-Corruption in Viet Nam: The Situation after Two Years of Implementation of the Law', research report, Formin, Finland and Cecodes, Vietnam, November.

Dittmer, L., Haruhiro Fukai, and P.N.S. Lee (eds) (2000) *Informal Politics in East Asia*, Cambridge University Press, Cambridge.

Dixon, C., and A. Kilgour (2002) 'State, Capital and Resistance to Globalisation in the Vietnamese Transitional Economy', *Environment and Planning A 34*.

Dosch, J. (2006) 'Vietnam's ASEAN Membership Revisited: Golden Opportunity or Golden Cage', *Contemporary Southeast Asia*, vol. 28, no. 2.

Duckett, J. (1998) *The Entrepreneurial State in China*, Routledge, London and New York.

Duffield, M. (2008) 'On the Edge of "No Man's Land": Chronic Emergency in Myanmar', independent report commissioned by the Office of the UN RC/HC, Yangon and UNOCHA, New York.

Duiker, W. (1989) *Vietnam Since the Fall of Saigon*, Southeast Asia Series, Ohio University Center for International Studies, Athens OH.

Dusza, K. (1989) 'Max Weber's Conception of the State', *International Journal of Politics, Culture, and Society*, vol. 3, no. 1, Autumn.

Emmers, R. (2003) 'ASEAN and the Securitization of Transnational Crime in Southeast Asia', *Pacific Review*, vol. 16, no. 3.

Esterline, J. (1987) 'Vietnam in 1986: An Uncertain Tiger', Asian Survey, vol. 27, no. 1.

Evans, G. (1988) The *Politics of Ritual and Remembrance: Laos since 1975*, Silkworm, Chiang Mai.

Evans, G., C. Hutton and K. Eng (eds) (2000) *Where China Meets Southeast Asia: Social and Cultural Change in the Border Regions*, Institute of Southeast Asian Studies, Singapore.

Evans, M. (2006) 'Elitism', in C. Hay, M. Lister and D. Marsh (eds), *The State: Theories and Issues*, Palgrave Macmillan, Basingstoke.

Fforde, A. (1993) 'The Political Economy of "Reform" in Vietnam: Some Reflections', in B. Ljunggren (ed.), *The Challenge of Reform in Indochina*, Harvard Institute for International Development, Cambridge MA.

Fforde, A. (1996) 'Vietnam: Economic Commentary and Analysis', research report no. 8, Aduki, Canberra.

Fforde, A. (1997) 'Public Administration Reform in Ho Chi Minh City: A Report on the "Vietnamese Process" with Suggestions for How to Support It', unpublished manuscript prepared for the Government Committee on Organization and Personnel and UNDP, Hanoi.

Fforde, A. (2000) 'Vietnamese State-Owned Enterprises: Real Property, Commercial Performance and Political Economy', report for CIDA, Aduki, Canberra.

Fforde, A. (2004a) 'Vietnam in 2003: The Road to Ungovernability?' *Asian Survey*, vol. 44, no. 1.

Fforde, A. (2004b) 'Vietnamese State-owned Enterprises: "Real Property", Commercial Performance and Political Economy', Working Paper Series 69, City University of Hong Kong, August.

Fforde, A. (2004c) 'State-Owned Enterprises, Law and a Decade of Market-

Oriented Socialist Development in Vietnam', Working Paper Series 70, City University of Hong Kong, September.

Fforde, A., and S. Seneque (1995) 'The Economy and the Countryside: The Relevance of Rural Development Policies', in B.J. Kerkvliet and D.J. Porter (eds), *Vietnam's Rural Transformation*, Westview Press, Boulder CO.

Fforde, A., and S. de Vylder (1996) *From Plan to Market: The Economic Transition in Vietnam*, Westview Press, Boulder CO.

Fine, B. (2002) 'Economics, Imperialism and the New Development Economics as Kuhnian Paradigm Shift?', *World Development*, vol. 30, no. 12.

Fine, B. (2006a) 'Introduction: The Economics of Development and the Development of Economics', in Jomo K.S. and B. Fine (eds), *The New Development Economics: After the Washington Consensus*, Zed Books, London.

Fine, B. (2006b) 'The New Development Economics', in Jomo K.S. and B. Fine (eds), *The New Development Economics: After the Washington Consensus*, Zed Books, London.

Finlayson, A., and J. Martin (2006) 'Poststructuralism', in C. Hay, M. Lister and D. Marsh (ed.) (2006) *The State: Theories and Issues*, Palgrave Macmillan, Basingstoke.

Forbes, D., and N. Thrift (eds) (1987) *The Socialist Third World: Urban Development and Territorial Planning*, Basil Blackwell, Oxford.

Freeman, N. (1996) 'The Role of Equitisation in Vietnam's Reform of State-Owned Enterprises', *Communist Economies and Economic Transformation*, vol. 8, no. 2.

Fritzen, S. (2005) 'The "Misery" of Implementation: Governance, Institutions and Anti-corruption in Vietnam', in N. Tarling (ed.), *Corruption and Good Governance in Asia*, Routledge, New York.

Gainsborough, M. (2002) 'Understanding Communist Transition: Property Rights in Ho Chi Minh City in the late 1990s', *Post-Communist Economies*, vol. 14, no. 2, June.

Gainsborough, M. (2003a) *Changing Political Economy of Vietnam: The Case of Ho Chi Minh City*, Routledge, London and New York.

Gainsborough, M. (2003b) 'The Politics of the Greenback: The Interaction between the Formal and Black Markets in Ho Chi Minh City', in L. Drummond and M. Thomas (eds), *Consuming Urban Culture in Contemporary Vietnam*, RoutledgeCurzon, London.

Gainsborough, M. (2004a) 'Key Issues in the Political Economy of Post-Doi Moi Vietnam, in D. McCargo (ed.), *Rethinking Vietnam*, RoutledgeCurzon, London.

Gainsborough, M. (2004b) 'Ho Chi Minh City's Post-1975 Political Elite: Continuity and Change in Background and Belief', in B. Kerkvliet and

D. Marr (eds), *Beyond Hanoi: Local Government in Vietnam*, Institute of Southeast Asian Studies, Singapore.

Gainsborough, M. (2004c) 'Rethinking the Centralisation/Decentralisation Debate in Vietnam Studies – An Introduction', *European Journal of East Asian Studies*, vol. 3, no. 2.

Gainsborough, M. (2005) 'Party Control: Electoral Campaigning in Vietnam in the Run-up to the May 2002 National Assembly Elections', *Pacific Affairs*, vol. 78, no.1.

Gainsborough, M. (2009a) *On the Borders of State Power: Frontiers in the Greater Mekong Sub-region*, Routledge, London and New York.

Gainsborough, M. (2009b) 'The (Neglected) Statist Bias and the Developmental State: The Case of Singapore and Vietnam', *Third World Quarterly*, vol. 30, no. 7.

Gainsborough, M., Dang Ngoc Dinh and Tran Thanh Phuong (2009) 'Corruption, Public Administration and Development: Challenges and Opportunities', in *Public Administration Reform and Anti-Corruption: A Series of Policy Discussion Papers*, UNDP, Vietnam.

General Statistics Office (2001) *Socio-Economic Statistical Data of 61 Provinces and Cities in Vietnam*, Statistical Publishing House, Hanoi.

General Statistics Office (2009), General Statistics Office of Vietnam, www.gso.gov.vn/default_en.aspx?tabid=491, accessed 1 October 2009.

Gibson, J., and P. Hanson (eds) (1996) *Transformation from Below: Local Power and the Political Economy of Post-Communist Transitions*, Edward Elgar, Cheltenham.

Gillespie, J. (2001) 'Self Interest and Ideology: Evaluating Different Explanations for Bureaucratic Corruption in Vietnam', *Australian Journal of Law*, vol. 3, no. 1.

Goldman, M.I. (2004) 'Putin and the Oligarchs', *Foreign Affairs*, vol. 83, no. 6.

Gong, Ting (1997) 'Forms and Characteristics of China's Corruption in the 1990s: Change with Continuity', *Communist and Post-Communist Studies*, vol. 30. no. 3.

Gore, C. (2000) 'The Rise and Fall of the Washington Consensus as a Paradigm for Developing Countries', *World Development*, vol. 28, no. 5.

Gorta, A., and S. Forell (1995) 'Layers of Decision: Linking Social Definitions of Corruption and Willingness to Take Action', *Crime, Law and Social Change* 23.

Government of Vietnam (2008) 'National Strategy for Preventing and Combating Corruption Towards 2020', draft document, 7 September, Hanoi.

Greenfield, L. (2001) *The Spirit of Capitalism: Nationalism and Economic Growth*, Harvard University Press, Cambridge MA and London.

Guriev, S., and Rachinsky, A. (2005) 'The Role of Oligarchs in Russian Capitalism', *Journal of Economic Perspectives*, vol. 19, no. 1.

Hadiz, V.R. (2004) 'Decentralization and Democracy in Indonesia: A Critique of Neo-Institutionalist Perspectives', *Development and Change*, vol. 35, no. 4.

Hadiz, V.R., and R. Robison (2005) 'Neo-Liberal Reforms and Illiberal Consolidations: The Indonesian Paradox', *Journal of Development Studies*, vol. 41, no. 2.

Hamilton, C. (1989) 'The Irrelevance of Economic Liberalization in the Third World', *World Development*, vol. 17, no. 10.

Hamilton-Hart, N. (2000) 'The Singapore State Revisited', *Pacific Review*, vol. 13, no. 2.

Hang, Nguyen Thi Thu (2007) 'Vietnam: Country Study', paper prepared for the project 'Southern Perspectives on the Reform of International Development Architecture', September.

Hanson, E. (2003) 'Authoritarian Governance and Labour: The VGCL and the Party-State in Economic Renovation', in B.J. Kerkvliet, R. Heng and D. Koh (eds), *Getting Organized in Vietnam: Moving in and around the Socialist State*, Institute of Southeast Asian Studies, Singapore.

Hanson, P., and M. Bradshaw (eds) (2000) *Regional Economic Change in Russia*, Edward Elgar, Cheltenham.

Hao Yufan (1999) 'From Rule of Man to Rule of Law: An Unintended Consequence of Corruption in China in the 1990s', *Journal of Contemporary China*, vol. 8, no. 22.

Harrigan, J. (1996) 'Review Article – The Bretton Woods Institutions in Developing Countries: Bêtes Noires or Toothless Tigers?' *World Economy*, vol. 19, no. 6.

Harrison, G. (2004) *The World Bank and Africa: The Construction of Governance States*, Routledge, London and New York.

Haughton, J. (1998) 'Room to Move', *Vietnam Business Journal*, vol. 6, no. 5, October.

Hay, C., M. Lister and D. Marsh (2006) *The State: Theories and Issues*, Palgrave Macmillan, Basingstoke.

Hayton, B. (2010) *Vietnam: Rising Dragon*, Yale University Press, New Haven and London.

He Zengke (2000) 'Corruption and Anti-corruption in Reform China', *Communist and Post-Communist Studies* 33.

Held, D., A. McGrew, D. Goldblatt and J. Perraton (eds) (2000) *Global Transformations: Politics, Economics and Culture*, Polity Press, Cambridge.

Heng, G., and Janadas Devan (1992) 'State Fatherhood: The Politics of Nationalism, Sexuality and Race in Singapore', in A. Parker, M. Russo,

D. Sommer and P. Yaeger (eds), *Nationalisms and Sexualities*, London: Routledge.

Heng, R. (1999) 'Of the State, for the State, yet against the State: The Struggle Paradigm in Vietnam's Media Politics', Ph.D. thesis, Australian National University, Canberra.

Heng, R. (2001) 'Media Negotiating the State: In the Name of the Law in Anticipation', *Sojourn*, vol. 16, no. 2.

Hibou, B. (ed.) (2004) *Privatising the State*, trans. Jonathan Derrick, C. Hurst, London.

Hiebert, M. (1996) *Chasing the Tigers: A Portrait of the New Vietnam*, Kodansha International, New York.

Hindess, B. (1996) *Discourses of Power: From Hobbes to Foucault*, Blackwell, Oxford.

Hirsch, A., and A. Gillan (2008) 'Ask Parliament, Not Courts, Whether Your Husband Can Help End Your Life', *Guardian*, 30 October.

Holm, H., and G. Sorensen (eds) (1995) *Whose World Order? Uneven Globalization and the End of the Cold War*, Westview Press, Boulder CO.

Hoogvelt, A. (2001) *Globalization and the Postcolonial World: The New Political Economy of Development*, Palgrave Macmillan, Basingstoke.

Huchet, J. (2000) 'The Hidden Aspect of Public Sector Reform in China: State and Collective SMEs in Urban Areas', *China Perspectives* 32, November–December.

Hughes, C. (2001) 'Conceptualizing the Globalization–Security Nexus in the Asia-Pacific', *Security Dialogue*, vol. 32, no. 4.

Hutchcroft, P.D. (1991) 'Oligarchs and Cronies in the Philippine State: The Politics of Patrimonial Plunder', *World Politics*, vol. 43, no. 3, April.

IISS (International Institute of Strategic Studies) (2001) 'Vietnam's Ninth Party Congress: Reform Reaches a Crossroads', *Strategic Comments* vol. 7, no. 2.

IMF (1996) *Vietnam: Recent Economic Developments*, IMF Staff Country Report no. 96/145.

IMF (2007) *Vietnam: Statistical Appendix*, IMF Country Report No. 07/386.

IMF (2008) 'Vietnam's New Challenges Amid Signs of Overheating', www.imf.org/external/pubs/ft/survey/so/2008/CAR03708A.htm, accessed 19 October 2009.

Jayasuriya, K. (2001) 'Governance, Post-Washington Consensus and the New Anti-politics', Southeast Asia Research Centre, Working Paper Series, No. 2, April, City University of Hong Kong.

Jeffrey, C., and J. Lerche (2000) 'Stating the Difference: State, Discourse and Class Reproduction in Uttar Pradesh, India', *Development and Change* 31.

Jerneck, A. (1997) 'The Role of the State in a Newly Transitionary Economy: The Case of Vietnam's General Corporations', report prepared as part of a collaboration between SIDA, Stockholm, the Department of Economic History, Lund University, and the Embassy of Sweden in Hanoi, Vietnam, September.

Jessop, B. (2008) 'Dialogue of the Deaf: Some Reflections on the Poulantzas–Miliband Debate', in P. Wetherly, C.W. Barrow and P. Burnham (eds), *Class, Power and the State in Capitalist Society: Essays on Ralph Miliband*, Palgrave Macmillan, Basingstoke.

Jomo K.S. and B. Fine (eds) (2006) *The New Development Economics: After the Washington Consensus*, Zed Books, London.

Jones, B.G. (2008) 'The Global Political Economy of Social Crisis: Towards a Critique of the "Failed State" Ideology', *Review of International Political Economy*, vol. 15, no. 2.

Kerkvliet, B.J. (1995) 'Village–State Relations in Vietnam: The Effect of Everyday Politics on Decollectivization', *Journal of Asian Studies*, vol. 54, no. 2.

Kerkvliet, B.J. (2003) 'Authorities and the People: An Analysis of State–Society Relations in Vietnam', in Hy V. Luong (ed.), *Postwar Vietnam: Dynamics of a Transforming Society*, Rowman & Littlefield, Oxford.

Kerkvliet, B.J. (2005) *The Power of Everyday Politics: How Vietnamese Peasants Transformed National Policy*, Cornell University Press, Ithaca NY.

Kerkvliet, B.J., and D.J. Porter (eds) (1995) *Vietnam's Rural Transformation*, Westview Press, Boulder CO.

Kerkvliet, B.J., R. Heng, and D. Koh (eds) (2003) *Getting Organized in Vietnam: Moving in and around the Socialist State*, Institute of Southeast Asian Studies, Singapore.

Khanh, Tranh (1993) *The Ethnic Chinese and Economic Development in Vietnam*, Indochina Unit, Institute of Southeast Asian Studies, Singapore.

Kim, Jee Young (2005) 'Making Industrial Conflict Public: Patterns of Newspaper Coverage of Strikes in Vietnam', paper presented at Centre d'Études et de Récherches Internationales (CERI) and Institut d'Études Politiques de Paris (Science Po), 9–10 December.

Koh, D. (2000) 'Wards of Hanoi and State–Society Relations in the Socialist Republic of Vietnam', Ph.D. thesis, Australia National University.

Koh, D. (2001) 'Negotiating the Socialist State in Vietnam through Local Administrators: The Case of Karaoke Shops', *Sojourn*, vol. 16, no. 2.

Koh, D. (2004) 'Illegal Construction in Hanoi and Hanoi's Wards', *European Journal of East Asian Studies*, vol. 3, no. 2.

Kokko, A. (2004) 'Growth and Reform since the Eighth Party Congress', in D. McCargo (ed.), *Rethinking Vietnam*, RoutledgeCurzon, London.

Kolko, G. (1997) *Vietnam: Anatomy of a Peace*, Routledge, London and New York.

Kuah, K.E. (2000) 'Negotiating Central, Provincial, and County Policies: Border Trading in South China', in G. Evans, C. Hutton and K. Eng (eds), *Where China Meets Southeast Asia: Social and Cultural Change in the Border Regions*, Institute of Southeast Asian Studies, Singapore.

Levy, R. (1994) 'Corruption, Economic Crime and Social Transformation Since the Reforms: The Debate in China', *Australian Journal of Chinese Affairs* 33, January.

Lieberthal, K., and M. Oksenberg (1988) *Policy Making in China: Leaders, Structures, and Processes*, Princeton University Press, Princeton NJ.

Liu Yia-Ling (1992) 'Reform from Below: The Private Economy and Local Politics in Rural Industrialization', *China Quarterly* 130.

Long, N., and H.H. Kendall (1981) *After Saigon Fell: Daily Life under the Vietnamese Communists*, Institute of East Asian Studies, Berkeley CA.

Lu Xiaobo (2000a) 'Booty Socialism, Bureau-preneurs, and the State in Transition: Organizational Corruption in China', *Comparative Politics*, vol. 33, no. 2.

Lu Xiaobo (2000b) *Cadres and Corruption: The Organizational Involution of the Chinese Communist Party*, Stanford University Press, Stanford CA.

Ma, S.K. (1989) 'Reform Corruption: A Discussion on China's Current Development', *Pacific Affairs*, vol. 62, no. 1.

Malesky, E. (2004a) 'Levelled Mountains and Broken Fences: Measuring and Analysing De Facto Decentralisation in Vietnam', *European Journal of East Asian Studies*, vol. 3, no. 2.

Malesky, E. (2004b) 'Push, Pull, and Reinforcing: The Channels of FDI Influence on Provincial Governance in Vietnam', in B.J. Kerkvliet and D.G. Marr (eds), *Beyond Hanoi: Local Government in Vietnam*, ISEAS Publications, Singapore.

Malesky, E. (2006) 'Gerrymandering – Vietnamese Style: The Political Motivations behind the Creation of New Provinces in Vietnam', paper prepared for conference on Democracy, Governance, and Identity, University of Michigan, 5–6 May, version 4.

Malesky, E. (2008a) 'The Vietnam Provincial Competitiveness Index: Measuring Economic Governance for Private Sector Development. 2008 Final Report', *Vietnam Competitiveness Initiative Policy Paper* no. 13, Vietnam Chamber of Commerce and Industry and United States Agency for International Development's Vietnam Competitiveness Initiative, Hanoi.

Malesky, E. (2008b) 'Straight Ahead on Red: How Foreign Direct Investment Empowers Subnational Leaders', *Journal of Politics*, vol. 70, no. 1, January.

Malesky, E., and M. Taussig (2009a) 'Out of the Gray: The Impact on Provincial Institutions of Business Formalisation in Vietnam', *Journal of East Asian Studies*, vol. 9, no. 2, May–August.

Malesky, E., and M. Taussig (2009b) 'Where Is Credit Due? Legal Institutions, Connections, and the Efficiency of Bank Lending in Vietnam', *Journal of Law, Economics, and Organization*, vol. 25, no. 2, Fall.

Mann, M. (1984) 'The Autonomous Power of the State: Its Origins, Mechanisms and Results', *Archives of European Sociology* 25.

Marquette, H. (2004) 'The Creeping Politicisation of the World Bank: The Case of Corruption', *Political Studies*, vol. 52, no. 3, October.

Marr, D. (ed.) (1998) 'The Mass Media in Vietnam, Political and Social Change', Monograph 25, Department of Political and Social Change, Research School of Pacific and Asian Studies, Australian National University, Canberra.

McCargo, D. (2005) 'Network Monarchy and Legitimacy Crises in Thailand', *Pacific Review*, vol. 18, no. 4, December.

McCargo, D., and U. Pathmanand (2005) *The Thaksinization of Thailand*, University of Hawai'i Press, Honolulu.

McCormick, B.L. (1998) 'Political Change in China and Vietnam: Coping with the Consequences of Economic Reform', *China Journal* 40, July.

McKinley, C. (2009) *Media and Corruption: How has Vietnam's Print Media Covered Corruption and How Can Coverage Be Strengthened?* UNDP, Hanoi.

McMichael, P. (1996) 'Globalization: Myths and Realities', in J. Timmons Roberts and A. Hite (eds), *From Modernization to Globalization: Perspectives on Development and Social Change*, Blackwell, Oxford.

McNally, C.A. (2002) 'Strange Bedfellows: Communist Party Institutions and New Governance Mechanisms in Chinese State Holding Corporations', *Business and Politics*, vol. 4, no. 1, April.

McVey, R. (ed.) (1992) *Southeast Asian Capitalists*, Cornell Southeast Asia Program Publications, New York.

McVey, R. (ed.) (2000) *Money and Power in Provincial Thailand*, Institute of Southeast Asian Studies and Silkworm Books, Singapore.

Migdal, J.S. (1988) *Strong Societies and Weak States: State–Society Relations and State Capabilities in the Third World*, Princeton University Press, Princeton NJ.

Miliband, R. (1969) *The State in Capitalist Society: The Analysis of the Western System of Power*, Quartet Books, London.

Ministry of Planning and Investment (2005) 'The Five-Year Socio-Economic Development Plan 2006–2010', draft, September, Hanoi.

Mitchell, T. (1991) 'The Limits of the State: Beyond Statist Approaches and

Their Critics', The *American Political Science Review*, vol. 85, no. 1.

Mitchell, T. (2006), 'Society, Economy and the State Effect', in A. Sharma and A. Gupta (eds), *The Anthropology of the State: A Reader*, Blackwell, Oxford.

Moore, B.J. (1966) *Social Origins of Dictatorship and Democracy: Lord and Peasant in the Making of the Modern World*, Beacon Press, Boston MA.

Murray, M. (1980) *The Development of Capitalism in Colonial Indochina (1870–1940)*, University of California Press, Berkeley and Los Angeles.

Naughton, B (1995a) 'Cities in the Chinese Economic System: Changing Roles and Conditions for Autonomy', in D.S. Davis, R. Kraus, B. Naughton and E.J. Perry (eds), *Urban Spaces in Contemporary China: The Potential for Autonomy and Community in Post-Mao China*, Woodrow Wilson Center Press and Cambridge University Press, Cambridge and New York.

Naughton, B. (1995b) *Growing Out of the Plan: Chinese Economic Reform 1978–93*, Cambridge University Press, Cambridge.

Neilson Rankin, K. (2004) *The Cultural Politics of Markets: Economic Liberalization and Social Change in Nepal*, Pluto Press, London.

Nevitt, C.E. (1996) 'Private Business Associations in China: Evidence of Civil Society or Local State Power?', *China Journal* 36, July.

Nolan, P. (1995) *China's Rise, Russia's Fall: Politics, Economics and Planning in the Transition from Stalinism*, Macmillan, Basingstoke.

Nolan, P., and Wang Xiaoqiang (1999) 'Beyond Privatization: Institutional Innovation and Growth in China's Large State-Owned Enterprises', *World Development*, vol. 27, no. 1.

Nordholt, H., and G. van Klinken (eds) (2007) *Renegotiating Boundaries: Local Politics in post-Suharto Indonesia*, KITLV Press, Leiden.

Oehlers, A. (2006) 'A Critique of ADB Policies towards the Greater Mekong Sub-region', *Journal of Contemporary Asia*, vol. 36, no. 4.

Ohmae, K. (1995) *The End of the Nation State*, Free Press, New York.

Oi, J. (1989) 'Market Reforms and Corruption in Rural China', *Studies in Comparative Communism*, vol. 22, no. 2.

Oi, J. (1999) *Rural China Takes Off: Institutional Foundations of Economic Reform*, University of California Press, Berkeley CA.

OpenNet (2006) 'Internet Filtering in Vietnam in 2005–06: A Country Study', OpenNet Initiative www.opennetinitiative.net/studies/vietnam, accessed 16 October 2009.

Painter, M. (2003) 'Marketisation, Integration and State Restructuring in Vietnam: The Case of State-Owned Enterprise Reform', City University of Hong Kong, Working Paper Series 39, January.

Painter, M. (2006) 'Sequencing Civil Service Pay Reforms in Vietnam: Transition or Leapfrog?' *Governance*, vol. 19, no. 2.

Parker, D., and Kirkpatrick, C. (2005) 'Privatisation in Developing Countries: A Review of the Evidence and the Policy Lessons', *Journal of Development Studies*, vol. 41, no. 4.

Payne, A. (ed.) (2004) *The New Regional Politics of Development*, Palgrave Macmillan, Basingstoke and New York.

Pearson, M. (2005) 'The Business of Governing Business in China: Institutions and Norms of the Emerging Regulatory State', *World Politics* 57, January.

Peck, J., and A. Tickell (2002) 'Neoliberalizing Space', *Antipode*, vol. 34, no. 3.

Pei Xiaolin (2001) 'The Contribution of Collective Landownership to China's Rural Industrialization: A Resource Allocation Model', paper, Second International Convention of Asian Scholars, 9–12 August, Berlin.

Peou, S. (2001) 'Cambodia: After the Killing Fields', in J. Funston (ed.), *Government and Politics in Southeast Asia*, Institute of Southeast Asian Studies, Singapore.

Phillips, N. (1998) 'Globalisation and the "Paradox of State Power": Perspectives from Latin America', CSGR Working Paper 16/98: Centre for the Study of Globalisation and Regionalisation (CSGR), University of Warwick.

Phongpaichit, P., and C. Baker (2005) *Thaksin: The Business of Politics in Thailand*, Silkworm Books, Chiang Mai.

Pierre, J., and B.G. Peters (2000) *Governance, Politics and the State*, Palgrave Macmillian, Basingstoke.

Pike, D. (1978) 'Vietnam in 1977: More of the Same', *Asian Survey*, vol. 18, no. 1, January.

Pike, D. (1991) 'Vietnam in 1990: The Last Picture Show', *Asian Survey*, vol. 31, no. 1.

Pike, D. (1992) 'Vietnam in 1991: The Turning Point', *Asian Survey*, vol. 32, no. 1.

Pincus, J., and J. Sender (2007) 'Quantifying Poverty in Vietnam: Who Counts?', *Journal of Vietnamese Studies*, vol. 3, no. 1, Winter.

Pincus, J.R., and J.A. Winters (eds) (2002) *Reinventing the World Bank*, Cornell University Press, Ithaca and London.

Pirie, I. (2005) 'Better by Design: Korea's Neoliberal Economy', *Pacific Review*, vol. 18, no. 3, September.

Porter, G. (1990) 'The Politics of "Renovation" in Vietnam', *Problems of Communism*, vol. 39, no. 3, May–June.

Porter, G. (1993) *Vietnam: The Politics of Bureaucratic Socialism*, Cornell University Press, Ithaca NY.

Potter, D. (1992) 'Democratization in Asia', in D. Held (ed.), *Prospects for*

Democracy: North, South, East and West, Polity Press, Cambridge.

Qi Li, B. Taylor, and Stephen Frost (2003) 'Labour Relations and Regulation in Vietnam: Theory and Practice', City University of Hong Kong, Working Paper Series 53, September.

Rama, M. (2008) 'Making Difficult Choices: Vietnam in Transition', Commission on Growth and Development, Working Paper no. 40.

Rambo, T. (1972) 'A Comparison of Peasant Social Systems of Northern and Southern Viet-Nam: A Study of Ecological Adaption, Social Succession and Cultural Evolution', Ph.D. thesis, University of Hawaii.

Richards, R. (2009) 'Challenging the Ideal? Traditional Governance and the Modern State in Somaliland', Ph.D. thesis, University of Bristol.

Rivkin-Fish, M. (2005) 'Bribes, Gifts and Unofficial Payments: Rethinking Corruption in Post-Soviet Russian Health Care', in C. Shore and D. Haller (eds), *Corruption: Anthropological Perspectives*, Pluto Press, London.

Roberts, D. (2001) *Political Transition in Cambodia 1991–99: Power, Elitism and Democracy*, Curzon Press, Richmond.

Robison, R (1988) 'Authoritarian States, Capital-Owning Classes, and the Politics of Newly Industrializing Countries: The Case of Indonesia', *World Politics*, vol. 41, no. 1, October.

Robison, R., and V.R. Hadiz (2004) *Reorganising Power in Indonesia: The Politics of Oligarchy in an Age of Markets*, Routledge, London and New York.

Rodan, G. (1992) 'Singapore's Leadership Transition: Erosion or Refinement of Authoritarian Rule?' *Bulletin of Concerned Asian Scholars*, vol. 24, no. 1, January.

Rueschemeyer, D., E. Stephens and J. Stephens (1992) *Capitalist Development and Democracy*, Polity Press, Cambridge.

Rydin, Y. (1998) 'The Enabling Local State and Urban Development: Resources, Rhetoric and Planning in East London', *Urban Studies*, vol. 35, no. 2.

Salomon, M. (2007) 'Power and Representation at the Vietnamese National Assembly: The Scope and Limits of Political Doi Moi', in S. Balme and M. Sidel (eds), *Vietnam's New Order: International Perspectives on the State and Reform in Vietnam*, Palgrave Macmillian, Basingstoke.

Salomon, M. (2008) 'The Issue of Corruption in Recruitment, Appointment and Promotion of Civil Servants in Vietnam', Note for the 3rd Anti-Corruption Dialogue, June.

Sargeson, S., and J. Zhang (1999) 'Reassessing the Role of the Local State: A Case Study of Local Government Interventions in Property Rights Reform in a Hangzhou District', *China Journal* 42.

Scigliano, R., and W.W. Snyder (1960) 'The Budget Process in South Vietnam', *Pacific Affairs*, vol. 33, no. 3.

Sheppard, E. (2002) 'The Spaces and Times of Globalization: Place, Scale, Networks, and Positionality', *Economic Geography*, vol. 78, no. 3.

Shleifer, A., and Vishny, R.W. (1994) 'Politicians and Firms', *Quarterly Journal of Economics*, vol. 109, no. 4.

Sidel, J. (1996) 'Siam and Its Twin: Democratisation and Bossism in Contemporary Thailand and the Philippines', *Institute of Development Studies Bulletin*, vol. 27, no. 2, April.

Sidel, J. (1999) *Capital, Coercion and Crime: Bossism in the Philippines*, Stanford University Press, Stanford CA.

Sidel, J. (2001) 'Populism and Reformism in Contemporary Southeast Asia', *Southeast Asia Research*, vol. 9, no. 1, March.

Sidel, M. (1998) 'Vietnam in 1997: A Year of Challenges', *Asian Survey*, vol. 38, no. 1.

Sklair, L. (1995) 'Social Movements and Global Capitalism', in J. Timmons Roberts and A. Hite (eds), *From Modernization to Globalization: Perspectives on Development and Social Change*, Blackwell, Oxford.

Slater, D. (2004) 'Indonesia's Accountability Trap: Party Cartels and Presidential Power after Democratic Transition', *Indonesia* 78, October.

Smyth, R. (2000) 'Asset-Stripping in Chinese State-Owned Enterprises', *Journal of Contemporary Asia*, vol. 30, no. 1.

Solinger, D. (1992) 'Urban Entrepreneurs and the State: The Merger of State and Society', in A. Rosenbaum (ed.), *State and Society in China: The Consequences of Reform*, Westview Press, Boulder CO.

Stavrakis, P.J., J. Debardeleben and L. Black (eds) (1997) *Beyond the Monolith: The Emergence of Regionalism in Post Soviet Russia*, Woodrow Wilson Center Press, Washington DC.

Stern, L.M. (1985) 'The Overseas Chinese in the Socialist Republic of Vietnam, 1979–82', *Asian Survey*, vol. 25, no. 5.

Stromseth, J.R. (1998) 'Reform and Response in Vietnam: State–Society Relations and the Changing Political Economy', Ph.D. thesis, Columbia University.

Tan, Le, and Tran Thanh Phuong (1983) *Thanh Pho Ho Chi Minh City*, Ho Chi Minh City Publishing House: Ho Chi Minh City.

Taylor, M.C. (1961) 'South Vietnam: Lavish Aid, Limited Progress', *Pacific Affairs*, vol. 34, no. 3.

Taylor, P. (2001) *Fragments of the Present: Searching for Modernity in Vietnam's South*, Allen & Unwin and University of Hawaii Press, Crows Nest, NSW, and Honolulu.

Templer, R. (1998) *Shadows and Wind: A View of Modern Vietnam*, Little, Brown, London.

Thayer, C.A. (1988) 'The Regularization of Politics: Continuity and Change in the Party's Central Committee, 1951–86', in D.G. Marr and C.P. White (eds), *Postwar Vietnam: Dilemmas in Socialist Development*, Southeast Asian Program, Cornell University, Ithaca NY.

Thayer, C.A. (1992a) 'Comrade Plus Brother: The New Sino-Vietnamese Relations', *Pacific Review*, vol. 5, no. 4, November.

Thayer, C.A. (1992b) 'Political Reform in Vietnam: Doi Moi and the Emergence of Civil Society', in R.F. Miller (ed.), *The Developments of Civil Society in Communist Systems*, Allen & Unwin, St Leonards, NSW.

Thayer, C.A. (1993) 'Political Democratisation in Vietnam: Candidate Selection for the 9th National Assembly', paper presented to International Conference on the Development Prospects of East Asian Socialism, Contemporary China Centre, Australia National University, 13–15 January.

Thayer, C.A. (1997) 'The Regularization of Politics Revisited: Continuity and Change in the Party's Central Committee, 1976–96', paper presented to a panel on 'Vietnamese Politics in Transition: New Conceptions and Inter-Disciplinary Approaches, Part 2', 49th Annual Meeting of the Association for Asian Studies, Chicago.

Thayer, C.A. (2002) 'Vietnam in 2001: The Ninth Congress and After', *Asian Survey*, vol. 42, no. 1.

Thayer, C.A. (2008) 'The Structure of Vietnam–China Relations, 1991–2008', Paper for the 3rd International Conference on Vietnamese Studies, Hanoi, Vietnam, 4–7 December.

Thayer, C.A. (2009a) 'Challenges to the Political Legitimacy of Vietnam's One-Party State', paper, 'The Search for Legitimacy: Managing the Consequences of Asian Development', co-sponsored by Griffith University and National University of Singpore, Singapore, 27–28 July.

Thayer, C.A. (2009b) 'Vietnam and the Challenge of Political Civil Society', *Contemporary Southeast Asia*, vol. 31, no. 1.

Thirkell-White, B. (2007), 'The International Financial Architecture and the Limits of Neoliberal Hegemony', *New Political Economy*, vol. 12, no. 1.

Thomas, C., and P. Wilkin (2003) 'Still Waiting after All These Years: The "Third World" on the Periphery of International Relations', *British Journal of Politics and International Relations*, vol. 6, no. 2.

Thorsen, D.E., and A. Lie (2006) 'What is Neoliberalism?', http://folk.uio.no/daget/What%20is%20Neo-Liberalism%20FINAL.pdf, accessed 19 October 2009.

Thrift, N., and D. Forbes (1986) *The Price of War: Urbanization in Vietnam*, 1954–1985, Allen & Unwin, London.

Tickner, A. (2003) 'Seeing IR Differently: Notes from the Third World', *Millennium*, vol. 32, no. 2.

Tonkin, D. (1997) 'Vietnam: Market Reform and Ideology', lecture to the Royal Society for Asian Affairs, 22 January.

Transparency International (2006) *National Integrity Systems, Country Report, Vietnam*, www.transparency.org/news_room/latest_news/press_releases_nc/2006/2006_11_21_nis_vietnam, accessed 16 October 2009.

Tremewan, C. (1994) *The Political Economy of Social Control in Singapore*, St. Martin's Press, New York.

Trued, M.N. (1960) 'South Viet-Nam's Industrial Development Center', *Pacific Affairs*, vol. 33, no. 3.

Truong, H.C. (2004) 'Winter Crop and Spring Festival: The Contestations of Local Government in a Red River Delta Commune', in B. Kerkvliet and D. Marr (eds), *Beyond Hanoi: Local Government in Vietnam*, NIAS Press, Copenhagen.

Turley, W.S., and B. Womack (1998) 'Asian Socialism's Open Doors: Guangzhou and Ho Chi Minh City', *The China Journal* 40, July.

UNDP (2006), 'The State as Investor: Equitization, Privatization and the Transformation of SOEs in Viet Nam', UNDP Viet Nam Policy Dialogue Paper no. 3, October, Hanoi, www.undp.org.vn/undpLive/digital Assets/6/6155_HP_paper__E_.pdf, accessed 19 October 2009.

UNDP (2008) *Tackling Corruption, Transforming Lives: Accelerating Human Development in Asia and the Pacific*, Macmillan, Delhi.

Unger, E.S. (1987/88) 'The Struggle over the Chinese Community in Vietnam, 1946–84', *Pacific Affairs*, vol. 60, no. 4.

Vasavakul, T. (1996) 'Politics of the Reform of State Institutions in the Post-socialist Era', in S. Leung (ed.), *Vietnam Assessment: Creating a Sound Investment Climate*, Curzon Press, Richmond.

Vasavakul, T. (1997a) 'Sectoral Politics and Strategies for State and Party, Building from the VII to the VIII Congress of the Vietnam Communist Party (1991–96)', in A. Fforde (ed.), *Ten Years after the 1986 Party Congress*, Political and Social Change Monograph 24, Australian National University, Canberra.

Vasavakul, T. (1997b) 'Vietnam: The Third Wave of State Building', *Southeast Asian Affairs 1997*, Institute of Southeast Asian Affairs, Singapore.

Vasavakul, T. (2001) 'Vietnam: Doi Moi Difficulties', in J. Funston (ed.), *Government and Politics in Southeast Asia*, Institute of Southeast Asian Studies, Singapore.

Vasavakul, T. (2002) 'Rebuilding Authority Relations: Public Administration Reform in the Era of Doi Moi', study commissioned by the Asian Development Bank, www.aduki.com.au/PAR%20Report%20ADB%202002.pdf, accessed 16 October 2009.

Vasavakul, T. (2003) 'From Fence-Breaking to Networking: Interests, Popular

Organisations, and Policy Influences in Post-Socialist Vietnam', in B.J. Kerkvliet, R. Heng, and D. Koh (eds), *Getting Organized in Vietnam: Moving in and around the Socialist State*, Institute of Southeast Asian Studies, Singapore.

Vasavakul, T. (2008) 'Recrafting State Identity: Corruption and Anti-Corruption in Doi Moi Vietnam from a Comparative Perspective', paper presented to 'Rethinking the Vietnamese State: Implications for Vietnam and the Region', Vietnam Workshop, 21–22 August, City University of Hong Kong.

Vietnam Development Report (2004) 'Governance, Joint Donor Report to the Vietnam Consultative Group Meeting', Hanoi, 1–2 December 2003.

Vietnam Development Report (2007) 'Aiming High, Joint Donor Report to the Vietnam Consultative Group Meeting', Hanoi, 14–15 December 2006.

Vuving, A. (2006) 'Strategy and Evolution of Vietnam's China Policy: A Changing Mixture of Pathways', *Asian Survey*, vol. 26, no. 6.

Walker, A. (1999) *The Legend of the Golden Boat: Regulation, Trade and Traders in the Borderlands of Laos, Thailand, China and Burma*, Curzon Press, Richmond.

Webster, L., and M. R. Amin (1998) 'Equitization and State Enterprise Reform in Vietnam: Experience to Date', Mekong Project Development Facility, Private Sector Discussion Paper no. 3, Hanoi, March.

Webster, L., and M. Taussig (1999) 'Vietnam's Undersized Engine: A Survey of 95 Larger Private Manufacturers', Mekong Private Sector Development Facility, Private Sector Discussion Paper no. 8, Hanoi, June.

Weiss, L. (1997) 'Globalisation and the Myth of the Powerless State', *New Left Review*, vol. 1, no. 225.

Weiss, L. (1998) *The Myth of the Powerless State: Governing the Economy in a Global Era*, Polity Press, Cambridge.

Wells-Dang, A. (2010) 'Political Space in Vietnam: A View from the Rice Roots', *Pacific Review*.

Wetherly, P., C.W. Barrow and P. Burnham (eds) (2008) *Class, Power and the State in Capitalist Society: Essays on Ralph Miliband*, Palgrave Macmillan Basingstoke.

Wetherly, P. (2008) 'Can Capitalists Use the State to Serve Their General Interests', in P. Wetherly, C.W. Barrow and P. Burnham (eds), *Class, Power and the State in Capitalist Society: Essays on Ralph Miliband*, Palgrave Macmillan, Basingstoke.

White, G. (1996) 'Corruption and Market Reform in China', *IDS Bulletin*, vol. 23, no. 2.

Williamson, J. (1989) 'What Washington Means by Policy Reform', www.iie.com/staff/jwguide.cfm#topic3, accessed 19 October 2009.

Womack, B. (1997) 'Vietnam in 1996: Reform Immobilism', *Asian Survey*, vol. 37, no. 1.

Womack, B. (2006) *China and Vietnam: The Politics of Asymmetry*, Cambridge University Press, New York.

World Bank (1993) 'Vietnam: Transition to the Market', World Bank Country Operations Division, Country Department I, East Asia and Pacific Region, Bangkok, September.

World Bank (1997) *World Development Report 1997: The State in a Changing World*, http://econ.worldbank.org/external/default/main?pagePK=641652 59&theSitePK=469372&piPK=64165421&menuPK=64166093&entityID= 000009265_3980217141148, accessed 19 October 2009.

World Bank (1999) 'Vietnam: Preparing for Take-off? How Vietnam Can Participate Fully in the East Asian Recovery', Informal Economic Report of the World Bank Consultative Meeting for Vietnam, 14–15 December, Hanoi.

World Bank (2000) 'Vietnam's Economic Reforms: Progress, Next Steps and Donor Support: Background Note for Mid-term Review', 22–23 June, Dalat City, Vietnam.

World Bank (2001) 'Transforming the Rural Economy', in *Vietnam 2010: Entering the 21st Century*, Joint Report of the World Bank, Asian Development Bank and the United Nations Development Program, Consultative Group Meeting for Vietnam, 14–15 December.

World Bank (2002) *Transition: The First Ten Years: Analysis and Lessons For Eastern Europe and the Former Soviet Union*, World Bank, Washington DC.

World Bank (2006) *Vietnam Development Report 2007: Aiming High*, Joint Donor Report to the Vietnam Consultative Group Meeting, 14–15 December, Hanoi.

World Bank (2008) *Vietnam at a Glance*, http://devdata.worldbank.org/AAG/ vnm_aag.pdf, accessed 24 September 2009.

Yufan Hao (1999) 'From Rule of Man to Rule of Law: An Unintended Consequence of Corruption in China in the 1990s', *Journal of Contemporary China*, vol. 8, no. 22.

Zhu Ying and S. Fahey (2000) 'The Challenges and Opportunities for the Trade Union Movement in the Transition Era: Two Socialist Market Economies – China and Vietnam', *Asia–Pacific Business Review*, vol. 6, no. 3, Spring/Summer.

INDEX